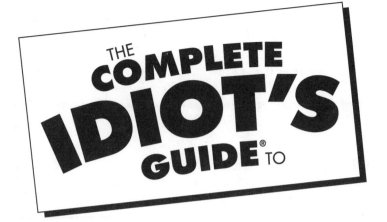

THE **COMPLETE** **IDIOT'S** **GUIDE®** TO

Home Repair and Maintenance

Illustrated

by David J. Tenenbaum

ALPHA

A member of Penguin Group (USA) Inc.

This book is dedicated to my father, Frank, who taught me that perseverance, ingenuity, and creative improvisation—combined with a certain dark humor—could overcome practically any home-repair nightmare. And to my mother, Frances, a writer who (usually) put up with the delays and the chaos.

THE COMPLETE IDIOT'S GUIDE TO and Design are registered trademarks of Penguin Group (USA) Inc.

International Standard Book Number: 1-59257-170-0
Library of Congress Catalog Card Number: 2003116927

04   8 7 6 5 4 3 2 1

Interpretation of the printing code: The rightmost number of the first series of numbers is the year of the book's printing; the rightmost number of the second series of numbers is the number of the book's printing. For example, a printing code of 04-1 shows that the first printing occurred in 2004.

Printed in the United States of America

Note: This publication contains the opinions and ideas of its author. It is intended to provide helpful and informative material on the subject matter covered. It is sold with the understanding that the author and publisher are not engaged in rendering professional services in the book. If the reader requires personal assistance or advice, a competent professional should be consulted.

The author and publisher specifically disclaim any responsibility for any liability, loss, or risk, personal or otherwise, which is incurred as a consequence, directly or indirectly, of the use and application of any of the contents of this book.

Most Alpha books are available at special quantity discounts for bulk purchases for sales promotions, premiums, fund-raising, or educational use. Special books, or book excerpts, can also be created to fit specific needs.

For details, write: Special Markets, Alpha Books, 375 Hudson Street, New York, NY 10014.

Publisher: *Marie Butler-Knight*
Product Manager: *Phil Kitchel*
Senior Managing Editor: *Jennifer Chisholm*
Senior Acquisitions Editor: *Mike Sanders*
Development Editor: *Lynn Northrup*
Copy Editor: *Drew Patty*
Illustrator: *Chris Eliopoulos*
Cover/Book Designer: *Trina Wurst*
Indexer: *Angie Bess*
Layout/Proofreading: *Becky Harmon, Donna Martin*
Graphics: *Tammy Graham, Laura Robbins, Dennis Sheehan*

Contents at a Glance

Contents

Appendixes

Foreword

In 35 years of working with houses as a carpenter, estimator, general contractor, amateur home-fixer, and professional real estate agent, I've learned three truths about home repair. First, what can go wrong, will go wrong. Second, what can't go wrong, will also go wrong, if you give it enough time. Third, the ideal home repair book will never be written.

The fact that you picked up this book shows that you appreciate the first two truths. But what's so hard about writing a great home repair book? It's the variables: Houses are built with different and ever-changing materials and techniques, and they must survive different climates. And then readers bring wildly varying levels of skill, ambition, experience, and tools to the job.

In the face of all the variables, I never figured one book could describe the world of home repair in a readable, comprehensible, compact, and accurate manner. But I was wrong. After working on hundreds of houses and examining hundreds more, my opinion is that *The Complete Idiot's Guide to Home Repair and Maintenance Illustrated* comes close to the ideal: It's a book that takes you from point A ("I think it needs repair, but what's it called, and where do I start?"), to point B ("Exactly what could be causing the problem? What are the possible solutions? Should I hire out the work?"), to point C ("These tools and materials will help me get the job done right"), and finally to point D ("Follow these steps to make an effective repair").

Through his lucid writing and excellent photos, David Tenenbaum proves that many repairs that seem intimidating are within the reach of a motivated homeowner. I'm particularly impressed by his treatment of patching drywall and plaster. His experience in the gritty world of plastering allows Tenenbaum to outline a comprehensive, practical approach to one of the knottiest problems in home repair—invisible patching of walls and ceilings. He describes so many patching techniques, in fact, that I almost began searching for nicks, cracks, and gouges in my home place!

Almost.

I see the same no-nonsense approach in chapters on painting, plumbing, the electrical system, even molding.

Don't get me wrong. Some repairs are too dangerous, laborious, or complex for an amateur. While I'd imagine that Tenenbaum would attempt most any type of repair, he doesn't suggest that you follow his lead. Instead, he'll help you identify tasks that call for a pro's combination of skills, strength, tools, and experience.

If I were new to home repair, I might buy this book solely for its sage advice on tool selection and purchase. Too many homeowners bungle their repair attempts because they either don't know which tool to use or they use an entry-level gadget that only superficially resembles a real tool. Yet while Tenenbaum respects good tools, he does not suggest that you buy out the entire store. Instead, he carefully distinguishes necessary tools from optional and frivolous ones. His excellent approach to buying, renting, or borrowing tools will save you money in the long run.

Even if Tenenbaum weren't a friend, I'd assure you that this is a book written by a home fixer for home fixers. It's a book that can save you aggravation—and the humiliation of phoning a pro to finish a too-tough-to-tackle project. It's a book that can introduce the satisfying sensation of learning to take care of the four walls around you without using the phone as your primary tool!

When I finished reading this book, I realized that the ideal person to write the ideal home repair book is someone like David Tenenbaum—someone with a lifetime of expertise. On every page, you can see that he has actually done this work.

Close enough may be good enough in horseshoes and hand grenades. In heart surgery and home repair, it helps to know what you are doing.

Tenenbaum knows what he's doing. That's why he has written an ideal treatment of the difficult topic of home repair.

Douglas Swayne
Madison, Wisconsin

Introduction

As I set out to write another book on home repair and maintenance, I again wonder what brings me back again to an endeavor that can be dirty and confusing, frustrating and expensive. The answer is simple. Home repair is satisfying, gratifying, and profitable:

◆ The satisfaction of making a new type of repair—who can forget, for example, that first victory over a plumbing problem?

◆ The gratification of solving a mystery. Today, for example, I started to remove a window sash that was squarely blocked by a loft bed. Admittedly, it took a half-hour of head-scratching before I figured out how to replace the glass—but at least I didn't have to take my poor son's room apart. That, after all, is *his* job …

◆ The fact that I save a bundle of money almost every time I pick up my tool bucket.

But home repair is more than just converting free time into money. It's a plain necessity in an era when fix-it help is so hard to find. Big repairs—if you can afford them—are one thing, but it's downright difficult to get someone to make small fixes. Imagine the economics of small-time home repair: First you make an appointment to examine the problem, then you drive over, analyze the situation, estimate time and materials, make an agreement with the homeowner, make another appointment, buy the materials, drive back, and *finally* start the repair. Between dealing with the homeowner's suspicions and returning to the store to get the junk you forgot, the hours add up fast. And when small things get expensive, homeowner paranoia skyrockets, making matters miserable for both sides.

The only way out of this conundrum—short of hiring a live-in mechanic—is to adopt the home-repair state of mind—a can-do attitude fortified with an eagerness to learn. By purchasing this book, you've shown that you have both essential attitudes.

I got my can-do attitude from my father, Frank, an electronic engineer possessed of the strange notion that he could do almost anything. Wiring? No problem. Television repair? All in a day's work for a guy who designed radar and computers. Carpentry? Well, anything was simpler than TV repair. A new phone line to the study? Sure—even if it wasn't quite legal at the time. A new darkroom in the basement? A great winter project (even if we drilled an awesome number of holes in concrete that was hard as … concrete).

Over time, I've apprenticed to a number of other teachers. Although some (who will remain nameless) had more loose screws than a '57 Chevy, they all had something to teach: that storing stuff logically is the only way to ease frustration and get things done fast; that the more you learn, the faster and better you work; that buying tools is not just fun, but a necessity.

I'm not sure exactly what's in your toolbox. But I know every toolbox needs a tool to make you confident, skilled, and ready for the confusing ailments that you, your home's new doctor, are bound to confront.

You're holding that tool—a home-repair book written, oddly enough, by someone who can actually fix houses! I firmly believe that, once you read the simple, realistic suggestions in *The Complete Idiot's Guide to Home Repair and Maintenance Illustrated*, you'll see home repair for what it is: satisfying, gratifying, and profitable.

Getting Oriented to This Book

This book is divided into four parts:

In **Part 1, "Lay of the Land,"** you take the first step in home repair: mentally positioning your-self as your own prime resource when something turns sour on the home front. I'll talk about fitting home repair in with the rest of your life, and distinguishing disasters that need immediate attention from semi-disasters that can wait. If the first rule of intelligent tinkering is to save all the parts, the second is to stay clear of the emergency room. Common sense requires you to make smart decisions about which projects require more skills, tools, or time than you can muster. Then I'll describe the basic hand and power tools for home repair, walk you through a hardware store, and talk about stor-ing all the junk you need to care for your house.

Part 2, "Looking Inside," describes a healing program for the gouges and flaws that impair the view from your easy chair—and the groans and grunts you cause as you walk through the house. Windows and doors are major sources of trouble, so I'll describe some easy fixes. I'll help you decide what to do when the floor squawks like a frightened hen, or when the drywall or plaster scream in silent agony. Fortunately, curing these woes is easier than you think—once you know some profes-sional tricks. Finally, we'll look at tile and molding, two key areas that novice home-fixers find unduly frightening.

Interested in outdoor recreation? **Part 3, "Looking Outside,"** deals with the foundation, siding, roofing, and masonry. Talk about important—these are your home's only protection against the ele-ments! We'll start easy, with painting, a chore that attracts even complete novices, and talk about your decaying deck. Then we'll get serious, and climb up on the roof to discuss safe, dry repairs. I'll give you the inside scoop on outside siding, and then devote a chapter to masonry and concrete, two ageless materials that should not be showing their age.

In **Part 4, "Mechanically Speaking,"** I've saved the best for last. If you think wires, pipes, and heating systems are complicated, you are on the right track. Still, the electrical system is a place where a determined homeowner can save plenty of bucks. We'll get our feet wet (but hopefully not cause a flood) in the plumbing department, where everything seems to leak, unless it's quit draining. We'll end up at the most intimidating area of all—the heating and cooling systems.

You'll also find two appendixes. The glossary answers your vital questions: Where does a soffit meet a rake edge? What is a light if it's not a kind of deflavorized beer? Why is glazing never galva-nized? Why does this guy keep asking stupid questions? Browsing through the glossary will reduce bafflement on your next trip to the building-supply house.

You'd expect the Internet to be an endless source of free advice on home repair. But in fact, it's only a supplement to the wealth of advice you are now holding. Still, you'll want to check the resources appendix to sample some of the most helpful help on the web and elsewhere.

Extras

The ability to use tools (and to read an instruction book) defines the human species. To help you make the most of this book of instructions, I've salted it with helpful signposts. Here's how they work:

Toolbox Tips

Have you ever watched a skilled worker do in 10 minutes what you couldn't do in an hour, and then realized that the faster job was also a much better job? With the hints in Toolbox Tips, you can even the score with the pros.

Fix-It Phrase

Knowing the "talk of the trade" will help you find what you need at the building-supply store. It will help you to talk with contractors. It will definitely impress your friends. Face it: It's way hip to know a joist from a joint, or a riser from a stringer.

All Thumbs

Here you'll find useful ideas for keeping your thumbs attached to your hands, your eyeballs in their sockets, your feet on the ladder, and your behind out of trouble.

Acknowledgments

Lots of people contributed to my handy-guy education. My old friend John Christenson offered a fine example through his patient, reverential use of tools. Orlando Kjosa, a talented carpenter and friend, paddled his last canoe entirely too young. I'm also grateful to the many friends, relatives, and neighbors who generously loaned me their ailing houses so I could fix them for the camera. Finally, or firstly, is my wife, Meg Wise, a ferocious beauty who always knew I could write books, but is everlastingly impressed to watch me patch drywall!

Special Thanks to the Technical Reviewers

The Complete Idiot's Guide to Home Repair and Maintenance Illustrated was reviewed by experts who checked the technical accuracy of what you'll learn here, to help us ensure that this book gives you everything you need to know to begin your transformation into a handy person. We extend special thanks to:

Doug Swayne, who spent many years in New Mexico as a carpenter and later a general contractor. Now retired from that rat-race, he's still involved in home repair, when he isn't distracted at a "day job," selling real estate.

Ken Schuster, a veteran roofer and builder, who insists on doing it right—the first time. More than most builders, Ken believes that the best fix stays fixed.

Fred Brown, a long-time electrical inspector and electrical apprentice instructor at Madison (Wisconsin) Area Technical College. He has taught electrical code, inspection, and installation at regional and national workshops.

Illustration Credits

Photography by David J. Tenenbaum, assisted by Alexander Tenenbaum, Joshua Tenenbaum, and Meg Wise.

Computer illustrations by David J. Tenenbaum and Scott Dougald.

Photo props courtesy of Robert Bosch Tool Corp., Dewalt Industrial Tool Co., Sears, Porter Cable, Delta Machinery, Rotozip Tool Corporation, Milwaukee Electric Tool Corp., Bucketboss (Fiskars Brands, Inc.).

The author wishes to thank the following for their kind permission to reprint artwork: W.H. Maze Company, National Manufacturing Company, M-D Building Products, Fluidmaster, Ken Schuster (Schuster Construction, Madison, Wisconsin), The Kohler Company, Moen Incorporated, Delta Faucet Co., Porta-Nails Inc., and Silver Line, Inc.

Trademarks

All terms mentioned in this book that are known to be or are suspected of being trademarks or service marks have been appropriately capitalized. Alpha Books and Penguin Group (USA) Inc. cannot attest to the accuracy of this information. Use of a term in this book should not be regarded as affecting the validity of any trademark or service mark.

In This Part

Part 1

Lay of the Land

What is it about home repair that makes intelligent people groan and reach for the ultimate home-repair tool—the telephone? Replacing electric outlets is nothing compared to writing software that actually works. Fixing wooden siding is not as tough as, say, writing novels. And while repairing masonry, like dentistry, involves removing and replacing rot, it's less exacting, and usually less painful as well. So why is it so few software engineers, fiction writers, and dentists know which end of the hammer hits the nail?

Well, some people give the excuse that home maintenance and repair can be complicated. That can be true, especially when a previous owner tested dumb repair ideas on your house, or you are trying to follow an outdated home-repair manual. But I think you'll be amazed at the logic that underlies most repairs, once you know, say, the difference between a shingle and a shake, or why an Allen (hexagonal) wrench is not a Phillips screwdriver. (*Hint:* It's not about "Al, pass Phil the screwdriver.")

In this part, I'll start taking a closer look at the home place. I'll tell you how to stay out of trouble while doing repairs, and discuss what you'll need in the way of tools, hardware, and a workshop. Before we finish, I hope to convince you that, when it comes to home repair, a telephone may be handy—but it's nothing compared to a good electric drill.

In This Chapter

- ◆ A realistic attitude toward home repairs
- ◆ Repair-savvy friends and pros as sources of help
- ◆ When to fix it, and when to leave it be
- ◆ Inspecting the roof, foundation, walls, and floors—the bones and sinews of your home
- ◆ Setting maintenance and repair priorities

Chapter 1

Is Your Home Looking Homely? Getting a Start in Home Repair

This chapter is about Murphy's law, carpenters' adages, perfectionism, and the "hero-or-wimp" conundrum. It's about why busy homeowners should happily accept some challenges—say caulking windows or replacing their panes—and duck others—like replacing a water heater or repairing a leak around a chimney on a steep roof. It's about the decisions you'll face as you ponder an upcoming home project, and about the satisfaction you'll get from tackling it. And it's about looking for trouble at your home place.

I'll begin by demystifying the professionals—simply realizing that even the pros can screw up is a huge morale booster. Then we'll work on the "who-when-how" decisions that must precede your first trip to the hardware store—or your call to a pro.

Dr. Murphy's Home-Repair Service

Carpenters have the best adages—easy to comprehend, steeped in dry humor, and freighted with the wisdom of the ages. My favorite is this absurdism: "I cut it off three times, and it's still too short." Much more helpful is, "Measure twice, cut once." But because houses can hide more horrors than a Stephen King novel, I'll expand on that: "Think thrice, measure twice, cut once."

You like this house. We like this house. But so do rot and decay. To keep it looking sharp, you'll need lots of money—or some tools and some skills.

If you think this adage does not apply to you, listen to a story about the late Orlando Kjosa, the classic "careful carpenter." For years, to save money on renovations or major repairs, and to get expert carpentry tutelage, I used to hire this skillful, experienced, and patient friend to work alongside me. One broiling August day, Orlando spent five hours nailing in roof rafters to support a new skylight. Then he marked the opening for the skylight, and sawed deliberately, precisely, and nonchalantly through those same new rafters. Had he stopped to think, of course, he would have realized that their job was to run alongside the skylight—in one piece.

Fix-It Phrase

This book focuses on home **repair** and **maintenance**. Generally, maintenance tasks—things like cleaning, painting, and caulking—keep the home in good condition, while repairs are designed to heal injuries. They work together like exercise and heart surgery: Ideally—but not always—the one prevents the other.

Orlando was unruffled—he'd been in the home repair business long enough to know that anything can go wrong, and on bad days, everything will. I learned that if you don't want to feel like a fool, you should never work on a home. But by liberating me from fear of foolishness, the experience also taught me to approach home repair with a healthy, if rather dark, humor. When you pick up your toolbag, things may go wrong. But in the last analysis, things will also get done.

A stone-and-tile hearth like such as this makes a nice focus for a room—as long as the room is in good condition!

Get Real: Can You, Should You, Try This Repair?

This is a home-repair and maintenance book—a book written by a realist for realists. Everybody who's tried home repair knows you can get in over your head. You may not have the skills, family support, finances, or the time for the project. You may run into problems with building codes. Let's address these make-or-break issues up front.

Keeping your basic tools in one toolbag is a real time-saver when you tackle a home-repair project.

Your Skills and Your Project

You cannot know whether you can handle a given repair until you understand the skills and tools it requires. If, after reading the relevant sections of this book, you need more information, either consult books about that specific topic or talk with knowledgeable friends.

Toolbox Tips

Many repairs are simply a matter of taking something apart, replacing some parts, then covering your tracks. These repairs are feasible for anyone who is observant and willing to buy some tools.

With a better notion of what the job requires, answers to these questions will help decide if it's for you:

◆ Are you good at solving problems in this field? If you're an ace roofer but a complete zero at plumbing, take this into account.

◆ Do you own—or can you borrow or rent—the necessary tools?

◆ Can you get professional advice— suggested for a major project?

Making invisible repairs on this nice cobblestone might challenge a seasoned mason. It would not be a great task for a novice.

◆ Can you do the work alone? If you'll need help, will it be available?

◆ How soon must the project be finished?

◆ Will bad weather hold you up?

◆ How much of your house will be out of commission because you had to shut off the electricity or water, or have floors covered with tools or drop cloths? Decommissioning a spare room is one thing, but it's not smart to put a bathroom or kitchen out of commission for long.

Your Family and Your Project

Think your project won't disrupt your family? After all, you're not ripping linoleum out of the kitchen, you're just replacing a light switch. But as you randomly shut off some circuits, you hear a shriek. Your switch-flippery cost your spouse three hours of unsaved computer work.

That problem could have been avoided if you'd heeded the home-repairer's first maxim: Communicate, communicate, communicate. At least make sure your family knows—and, if necessary, approves—your plans. It may be best to schedule your repair and maintenance projects when the house is empty—although if you hurt yourself, it's nice to have somebody around to help …

This is the attractive kitchen of an incorrigible home-fixer. Because he did his own work, he could choose unusual materials, making this pleasing result.

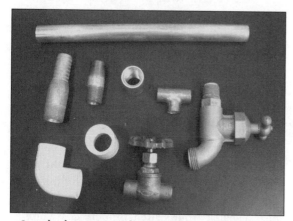

Somebody's going to have to make sense of these plumbing fixtures. If you tear out the bathroom or kitchen sink, that somebody is you.

All Thumbs

Electrical repairs are fearsome to many novice home-fixers. But done right, they are relatively simple in houses wired in the last 40 or 50 years. Be sure to follow the instructions in Chapter 16 to make sure circuits are *off* before you begin.

Your Money and Your Project

It's hard to know how much a given project will cost. With do-it-yourself home repair, you can end up wasting money—buying the wrong supplies or tools—or mangling innocent bystanders—like the drywall around an electric outlet you're replacing.

A good way to estimate cost is to price the major materials, estimate the incidentals, then multiply your total by at least two or three. You may be lucky and come in under budget. But in my experience, you are just as likely to spend double your estimate. And if you really need to estimate *time* on a job, think hard about how many hours it should require, then multiply that figure by two or three. (For better accuracy, throw dice. Estimates can be the toughest part of repair work.)

Toolbox Tips

Tools can cost more than materials, and you may always need another tool midway through a job. But buying tools when you need them should cut the cost of the next repair. Also consider renting a tool. You can save some major time by renting heavy-duty drills and saws. Just make sure the tool is sharp—rented tools have a way of leaving the shop with dull blades. (There's more on buying and renting tools in Chapter 3.)

Your Time and Your Project

The guy who wrote Murphy's law must have been a remodeler. "If anything can go wrong," the wise guy said, "it will go wrong, and at the worst possible moment." Yup. A memory lapse in the building-supply store will force you to return for a reducer to connect a ¾" elbow to a ½" pipe. And saws generally don't slip—until the last cut on a complicated, one-of-a-kind board.

Once upon a time, being a carpenter meant working with wood, not just installing stuff that comes in a box. If you're lucky enough to own this house, you may want to be a carpenter, too.

Building Codes and Your Project

It's tough to generalize about building codes, since there are at least three in the United States, not to mention codes covering natural gas, electricity, plumbing, heating, ventilating, air-conditioning and indoor kite-flying, for all I know.

Often, you need a building permit for a significant change, but not for a simple replacement. Thus you'd be okay just replacing a door, since you are just replacing an existing feature. But you might need a permit to cut in a new door. In some municipalities, you need a permit to re-roof, especially if you must strip off the old roof, or if the price of the project exceeds a certain value.

Your best bet for understanding your local codes is the building inspector. These folks seem like zealots wearing steel-rimmed spectacles who have memorized endless paragraphs on the size, safety, structure, materials, and use of a living space. But they can tell whether what you want to do is permissible, or whether a licensed contractor must do the work, as may be true of certain electrical and plumbing repairs.

Balance and harmony are what make these windows work together. When you make the repair, you can be sure to preserve these esthetic elements.

Why do building inspectors like to ask tough questions? I think part of their motivation is to learn about your skills, not just your plans. Once you convince them you can tell a soffit from a fascia board, they are usually more inclined to "sign off on" (approve) your project.

All Thumbs

Real trouble begins when an improvement triggers a requirement that the whole room, system, or building be "brought up to code." Your efforts to replace a storm window or realign a door should never trigger this awesome demand. If in doubt, ask the inspector, but don't go out of your way to make the job sound bigger than it is. Why beg for trouble?

Replacing a door is a job novices can do.

Friends and Pros—Vital Sources of Help and Information

Chances are some of your friends do home repair for fun. That may make the world a crazy place, but it also makes your friends good sources of information and help. I have a work-trading arrangement with my friend Doug Swayne, a recovering general contractor who now hawks real estate. When I needed help installing new kitchen counters, I was delighted to learn that he had actually done this before. (I knew I could bluff my way through, but his expertise made the job quicker and better.) I later repaid him by helping nail vinyl siding to a giant car-house that we immediately dubbed "the Taj m'Garage."

Working side by side is a great way to learn from the professionals you hire to fix your place, if you can wangle it. As an alternative, stick

around when you next hire a home-fixer. Which part of the job is done first? What tools are important enough to "live" in the toolbox? Your observations, let alone what you can learn from a talkative fixer, will come in handy down the line.

Toolbox Tips

When you hire a pro, consider that part of the fee goes to your education. Try to notice how this expert does things—the tools and steps involved in a project. What special power tools might you rent to do this job?

The Golden Mean: A Sensible Attitude Toward Home Repair

My attitude toward home repair was shaped by my father, Frank, who believed he could do just about anything—even fix televisions. My policy is to think about a repair for a while. Then, if my back starts to ache in advance, or I realize I don't have the time or skills, I call in the heavy artillery. In 16 years at my present address, I've yet to call an electrician. I did hire a drain cleaner to ream out a nasty clog in a sewer, which would have taken me far deeper than I wanted to go into that business.

I've also hired Carl Lorentz, a plumber friend. Once, after I wasted an hour trying to remove a pigheaded faucet, Carl wrestled with it for a sweaty half-hour. Then he muttered the dreaded phrase: "I need a special tool." (Special tools are fetish objects that separate mortals such as you and me from home-repair superheroes such as Carl.)

This gadget, a Sawzall, or reciprocating saw, is fiendishly useful for home repair. Every remodeler, plumber and electrician owns one for cutting into corners or, as shown, cutting nails to disassemble something (Note: That left hand would normally be holding the saw. I had Doug move it aside to show the saw a bit more clearly.) You may not want to spring for a "recip" saw, but you can rent them. They are real timesavers.

Home repair, you see, is a matter of degree. Particularly when you are getting started, the smartest course is to skim off the creamy jobs and hire out the gritty ones. I'll patch a roof that's not too steep, but when my entire roof gave out, I decided it was too much work, and hired a top-flight roofer to replace it.

The roof on this home may be a bit too steep for the novice repairer to handle.

But just as there's no shame in acknowledging your limits, there's no shame in going for what turns you on. If you develop into an eager-beaver roofer, or look forward to augering out drain pipes, I'll stand back and cheer. Likewise, if you're only interested in replacing the occasional light switch, I'm equally enthusiastic. In either case, you'll save some money, learn about your house, gather more tools, and gain confidence for the next repair.

All Thumbs

Even if you think the world is short on heroes, don't be a stupid hero. Don't hurt yourself making a repair that's beyond your capabilities (see Chapter 2 for a discussion of health, safety, and common sense). Even a complete idiot should know when to say when.

Is It Perfect Enough?

Does your blood congeal at the idea of finishing a job with a subtle flaw remaining? I'm sorry to hear that. Perfectionism may not be a diagnosable personality disorder, but it's a serious obstacle to learning home repair. Nitpickers can find problems with any repair, particularly ones they've done. My advice: Give yourself a break!

If you're not sure if I'm talking about you, repeat "it's good enough" aloud three times. If your teeth are gnashing, cut yourself some slack. You're just learning home repair, and you'll probably leave some jobs "perfect enough." Consider making a training run on something that isn't obvious—adjust a closet door before tackling the front door, for example. Then, as time passes, you'll learn what you're doing. You'll gather a better selection of tools and learn to distinguish possible projects from preposterous ones. When you're ready to play in the major leagues, be sure to say I knew you when you were just learning to hit.

Earning While Learning

For many people, the prime motivation for doing home repairs is saving money. Exactly how much you can save depends on your skill, needs, and local conditions. In my area, the cost of replacing a couple faucet washers (which sell for less than $1 apiece) starts at about $70—the plumbing contractor's hourly minimum.

It may look complicated, but with the right tools—and a decent source of architectural products—a motivated homeowner should be able to repair trim as complicated as this.

Fix-It Phrase _____

Home repairers charge either by **time and materials** or **by the job.** There are risks either way—the time needed may escalate, or the flat rate may be exorbitant.

Although you won't finish repairs as quickly as a pro, who may work three times as fast, you'll save money. That's particularly true when contractors charge a full hour for a quick repair, or "port to port" for travel to and from the shop.

There's another advantage: getting the job done at all. When the building business is busy, you may have a major problem finding a qualified person to accept a small job.

Beyond the economic imperative, many people experience a primitive gratification in, say, swinging a hammer. They get a sense of bizarre fulfillment while standing up, sweaty and grimy, and eyeing their first repair of splintered molding or a stuck window.

Home repair offers the most sublime form of education—being paid to learn. Whether I was farming, salvaging barn lumber, or working as a mason and plasterer, I've always believed in learning while earning. I bet your house has a boatload of opportunities to increase your portfolio of wealth and wisdom at the same time.

If It Ain't Broke ...

Have you ever stirred up a hornet's nest of home-repair trouble, then, while mulling over your options (all grim), been advised, "If it wasn't broken, why did you fix it?" This kind of brain-dead "wisdom" sounds reasonable enough, but it ignores the fact that most people don't deliberately stir up hornet's nests—they stumble into them.

Sometimes, you have no choice—you can't turn your cheek when a leaky pipe is irrigating your basement or the outlet behind your refrigerator is fusing into a glob of molten plastic.

Toolbox Tips _____

Home repair is a continual learning process. You learn how to use tools, how your house is built, and how to best accomplish specific tasks. It's not realistic to expect to learn everything at once.

When you are just getting started in home repair, this main water shut-off can be a friend indeed. Located near the foundation, it will keep you out of trouble in case a plumbing repair goes south. That big cable is used to ground the electrical system. It should be securely fastened at each end. Beyond that, do not mess with it!

And even if it "ain't broke," it may not be "factory-fresh." A faucet dripping ever so slowly may still stain the sink or drive you berserk. An electrical outlet that is not sparking may still have an ominous wobble. Should you fix these things? Often the answer is yes.

Looking into the Home-Inspection Biz

Have you taken a good look at the home place recently? Have you ever looked dispassionately at the roof, furnace, walls, doors, and windows of your dwelling? Have you crawled through the shrubbery to peer at the foundation or into that claustrophobic crawl space under the kitchen?

Maybe not. But while "out of sight, out of mind" may be a smart attitude toward some possessions, it's unsuited to something as weather-worn and expensive as a house. An inspection can save money if it reveals drafts or peeling paint caused by a buildup of moisture, but the greatest value may be on the roof. It's one thing to repair a few leaking shingles; it's quite another to replace roof boards, drywall, and rafters that were rotted by long-time leakage. Whether you inspect or not, you'll wind up making a repair. It's just a matter of how much you'll have to fix—and how much you'll have to pay.

Toolbox Tips

Here's one good use for cigarettes. Wait for a cold day, light one up, and hold it near a closed window or door. The smoke will pinpoint drafts.

Peeling paint like this, seen on a ceiling, is probably caused by a leaking roof or a moisture buildup. You could just scrape off the paint, repaint, and hope for the best, but unless you can heal the root cause, the peeling is likely to return.

Let's take a quick tour of the major parts of your house, and discuss which problems a home-repair novice can cure, and which might indicate a need for professional help.

A Worm's-Eye View: Foundation, Basement

The foundation—the walls that rest on the ground and support the structure—may look homely (it's usually concrete) but no part of your house is more important. From inside and outside, even if that means crawling into a *crawl space*, look for crumbling concrete or mortar, and loose blocks, bricks, or stones. A bit of *spalling* (usually the result of poorly formulated mortar or concrete) may be acceptable in older homes. Likewise, don't obsess about small cracks—they're usually harmless. But the gouges shown in the photo, together with the deep cracks visible in the old coat of plaster below, are both signs of major trouble.

This deteriorating foundation looks like a major problem, but it's often found only where the wall stays wet.

Fix-It Phrase

A **crawl space** is a mini-basement, with a ceiling generally less than 3' high. **Spalling** is surface deterioration on masonry or concrete, generally seen as soft or crumbling material.

Cracks that are moving or are wider than about ¼" can indicate serious settling. Examine the building above the crack: Are the windows and doors jammed or out-of-square? Will a marble start rolling across the floor? Do cracks on the interior walls indicate major movement? A moving crack may signal a structural problem that's beyond novice territory, but first see Chapter 15 for a discussion of foundation and basement repair.

Black discoloration   White discoloration

When a vent pipe leaked in this roof, it led to white and black discoloration—two forms of rot, caused by fungus. Fortunately, mold usually needs several years before it really softens the wood; this rot was stopped in time when roofers installed better flashing.

Both the black and white discoloration on the wood indicate that the flashing that supposedly sealed this plumbing vent pipe to the roof leaked at some time in the past. If the wood is dry, the leak may have been fixed already. To be sure, spray water on the roof. If the water seeps through to the underside, replace the leaking flashing.

Do you see evidence of carpenter ants (small holes and piles of sawdust) or termite damage (primarily tunnels from the soil to the wood)? If so, you may need to hire an exterminator. If you see the discoloration and softening that signals wood decay, particularly in damp areas, the first step is to dry things out, using suggestions from Chapter 15.

Shingle Talk

Although roof shingles are usually designed to last 25 to 40 years, you might want to check them occasionally. Maybe you are unlucky enough to have cut-rate shingles that are deteriorating ahead of schedule. Maybe the roofer flubbed the installation. From a ladder leaning against the roof, or through binoculars from the ground, search for torn, missing, or curled shingles. Inspect the sheet-metal flashing around skylights, vents, pipes, and chimneys. Is it tightly fastened and tarred as necessary, or is it rusty and loose? A mass of black tar or caulking on the flashing indicates that someone has repeatedly tried to close a leak, maybe without success. Chapter 13 has lots of information on roof repair.

When shingles lose their mineral surface and start to curl, it's time to replace them.

Examine the gutters for rust, plugging, and leaks. Gutters, also called eaves troughs, catch water from the roof and route it to the ground, protecting siding and windows from water. Through binoculars, you may be able to see that a buildup of leaves is plugging the gutter. You'll need a ladder to see if the gutters are full of mineral granules from the shingles; which signals that the roof is nearing retirement. Look inside the house or attic (particularly near the chimney) for discoloration that indicates leakage. Don't ignore leaks—no matter how many reasons you can invent for thinking they will go away, they'll just get worse.

Clearing out gutters is one of the best ways to prevent decay in your house. Getting rainwater away from the eaves and siding does wonders for the longevity of paint, siding, windows, and doors. And if you wear rubber or neoprene gloves, the task won't be too disgusting.

All Thumbs

Ladders are the fastest way to get in trouble during home repair. There are hundreds of rules covering ladder safety, as you can see in Chapter 2, but most of them come down to using common sense, using the right ladder, working slowly, and not leaning too far. Good home repairs should *never* involve a trip to the ER!

Siding, Windows, and Doors

Siding, windows, and doors can become big repair items if you let them go. Look for sections of peeling paint (indicating roof leakage or moisture migrating from the inside); fungus (a speckled discoloration that washes off in a dilute bleach solution); loose siding (see Chapter 14); delaminating plywood; and poor caulking between siding and windows, doors, trim, and vents (see Chapter 11).

Windows and doors can develop any number of problems. Look for clouding of double-thickness windows, or jamming of moving parts. Storm windows should be fairly tight and move easily. Doors may be tough to open and close, need new locks, or have nasty drafts. (Repairing windows and doors is covered in Chapter 6.)

With a dozen panes apiece, these double-hung windows practically scream for homeowner expertise in fixing windows.

Slide on Inside

When your inspection moves inside, you might start to obsess about surface defects—things like peeling wallpaper and butchered drywall. Far more important, however, are structural problems, which signal the need for major repairs. Look for cracks in walls and ceilings (particularly above doors or windows), which indicate weakening of posts, sagging of beams, or settling of the foundation. Stamp on the floor, feeling for the bounce that indicates weak spots. If you find these sorts of problems, see Chapter 7 for ideas on arresting and repairing damage.

This entryway looks great from the road. It would be a shame if you had to shoulder your way into the house because the door was coming loose from the hinges. Door repairs are often much easier than you think.

Other interior problems are unlikely to snowball, but they can still make a good house look dilapidated. Examine floors for stains, gouges, and degraded finish. Examine the drywall or plaster for cracks, decay, and discoloration (see Chapter 9). Check the condition of paint (see Chapter 11).

This floor needs sanding and refinishing. With rented tools and a bit of patience, it's a reasonable homeowner job.

Meet the Mechanicals

There is no disguising the fact that *mechanical* problems can be complicated and expensive. But it's often easy to check the operation of these systems and decide what action to take.

> **Fix-It Phrase**
>
> **Mechanicals** are the systems that use wires, ducts, or pipes—the plumbing, heating, air-conditioning, and wiring in your house. **HVAC** is shorthand for heating, ventilating, and air-conditioning.

Check that the heating and/or cooling system (the *HVAC*) responds to the thermostat. Examine the condition of ducts, vents, and registers. Are the furnace and air-conditioning units solid, with sound wiring, or is electrician's tape holding up dangling wires? These signs may mean nothing—or indicate that it's time for a checkup from the heating and cooling doctor (which is usually advisable every few years anyway). I'll discuss HVAC in Chapter 18.

Plumbing is more approachable than heating and cooling. Does your plumbing leak? Are the faucets too loose or too tight? Are they simply ugly and prime for replacement? Do the drains work fast enough to avoid a ring of scum on the sink or bathtub? All these problems are covered in Chapter 17.

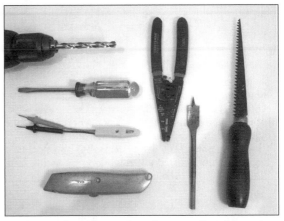

These simple tools are enough to install a new outlet or switch.

In general, electrical work is much more manageable than plumbing or HVAC work. Although electrical problems scare many people, they are usually rather simple in a house built within the last 40 or 50 years. For older homes, which tend to have bizarre wiring, it's best to leave the work to a professional.

Take a look at exposed parts of the electrical system (see Chapter 16), particularly in the basement. Is the wiring shipshape—or is it a spider's web of sagging cables and exposed wires? Do you see a rat's nest of boxes, switches, and cables around the fuse box or circuit-breaker box? Read the rating on the biggest fuse or the main circuit breaker: The overall electrical system should supply at least 100 amps. Any deficiencies you find may indicate an inadequate electrical system and perhaps a call for professional evaluation.

If you're the proud owner of this Colonial-era house, you already know that repairs lurk in every corner. The more recently the electrical service was installed, the luckier you are, since working on standardized, modern wiring is easier and safer than trying to patch up older systems. But it's smart to expect the unexpected when working on wiring in a house this old.

Many electrical problems are more manageable: Are the outlets the three-hole, grounded type required by many modern electrical gizmos? Use a circuit tester, or better yet, a receptacle tester, to check the operation and grounding of all outlets. Test all switches for correct operation.

Toolbox Tips _____

Want free help? Ask your utility company about a home energy audit. These evaluations will tell you how to save money on heating and cooling.

First Things First

After the gruesome inspection is done, sit back and assess your results, and plan how to tackle the problems you found. First, attack the major problems, like leaking roofs, structural weaknesses, drafty windows in cold climates, electrical hazards, and plumbing leaks. Other problems, like paint and wallpaper glitches, can be deferred.

For larger projects, it helps to organize your repairs by either the area of the house or type of task. Do the dining room first, then move to the living room. Or do all the electrical work, then move to the plumbing, and finally the drywall and painting.

Don't be tempted to ignore maintenance tasks, boring though they may seem, because they can keep you out of big trouble down the road. Is a railing getting rusty? Then you can paint it now or replace it later. Is the gutter clogged with leaves? Then you can either clean it in the fall (and think about putting on some screens to keep leaves out in the future), or have water pouring down your siding when the gutters plug up. That could force an even-more-disgusting cleanup in the spring—and maybe some siding repair, too, if you are as "lucky" as I've been.

Home repair, as I've indicated, is a rather logical affair. It's mainly a matter of balancing your needs with your skills, tools, and budget. Tackle the problems that can't be avoided first, and move to the more aesthetic ones later on. Be bold!

The Least You Need to Know

◆ The sooner you find and fix a problem, the cheaper it is likely to be.

◆ Problems in the foundation, roof, and structure can reverberate throughout a building and cause cascading disasters.

◆ Maintenance—the recurring problem of protecting your home from decay and the elements—may not be glamorous, but it will save you money in the long run.

◆ Size up your projects—some are easy and some are hard. Hire professionals for the ones that are plain impossible. Your morale and your home will both benefit.

◆ If it ain't broke, it may still need fixing.

In This Chapter

- ◆ Why most accidents are stupid accidents
- ◆ Keeping yourself safe from nasty chemicals
- ◆ All about ladders
- ◆ Protecting your home as you work

Chapter 2

Health, Safety, and Common Sense

Safety is high-class stuff these days: Those multiple warning labels make automatic doors sound more dangerous than a guillotine. And according to some paranoids, frying an egg would expose you to shock hazards from the electric stove, burning hazards from the pan, intestinal hazards from egg-borne bugs, and arteriosclerotic hazards from egg-borne fat. And that's not to mention the danger of slipping on the way to the table or goring yourself with the fork …

That's not my attitude. I'm more interested in the major safety hazards—the stuff you really need to watch. I'm also concerned with attitude problems—especially the stupidity factor—that makes accidents more likely. In this chapter, I'll talk about health hazards you might encounter in your home-repair battles, and discuss a reasonable, effective safety kit to protect you. I'll discuss safe use of ladders, which account for the lion's share of home-repair accidents. And I'll describe how to protect your house while you work.

The Stupidity Factor

A few years ago, trying to rig a hoist to lift my canoe, I confidently leaned my 14' ladder against a black locust tree and climbed up. Having written a book for painters, I knew this was folly, and when I reached the top, the ladder flipped and together, we squashed some shrubs.

Dazed but intact, I realized with embarrassment that I'd learned a simple lesson: Don't do stupid stuff. If you really must lean a ladder against a tree, find a football lineman to anchor the ladder. Or buy those straps made to secure ladders to trees. Best of all, forget the whole idea. Trees are round, and ladders are made to lean against walls, which are flat.

And the canoe hoist? It didn't work, either. Serves me right.

All Thumbs

If you're concerned about the toxicity of materials you are using, ask the store or manufacturer for a material safety data sheet (MSDS). The MSDS must, by law, be available to product users. Or go to the MSDS Search website (www.msdssearch.com), select the product's manufacturer, then

Because the stupidity factor explains so many accidents, I offer these suggestions for controlling the universal human urge to act like an absolute bozo:

- Don't try to do anything before you understand what needs to be done and how to do it.

- Don't work when you are exhausted, distracted, or angry. Under these conditions, you're likely to rush, ignore hazards, or act half-witted.

- Keep the place neat: Coil electric cords so you don't trip; stack lumber neatly, not strewn all over the place. Don't leave boards with nails sticking up, ready to impale you. Store and use sharp tools with caution, so they cut only what they're supposed to cut.

- Get help with big tasks—holding something while you fasten it, hauling heavy objects, or holding ladders that aren't perfectly stable.

- Work with adequate lighting, so you can spot and avoid hazards.

- Use appropriate health and safety equipment.

- See suggestions on electrical safety in Chapter 16.

The best antidote to the stupidity factor is to think ahead, work systematically, and avoid unreasonable deadlines.

The Best Protection Is Self-Protection

Many building products contain toxic chemicals. For example, the "treated wood" used so commonly often contains arsenic and chromium, which are deadly to wood fungus, and not so healthy for you, either. Naturally, you'll want to protect yourself while sawing or sanding treated lumber by using gloves and a dust mask.

Repair work can expose you to other forms of dust, grit, and toxic chemicals. But because you are not facing a day-after-day, industrial exposure, it's usually fairly easy to shield yourself with a combination of prevention, common sense, and protection.

To prevent toxic exposure, use products that don't contain toxic materials. For example, if you use latex or other water-based coatings, you will not need protection against the nasty ingredients in solvent-based paints (but check the label to be sure—some water-soluble paints may contain toxins). If I were building a new deck, I'd buy the new pressure-treated lumber that contains no copper chromated arsenic (CCA), which would reduce, if not entirely eliminate, the toxic exposure. Or I'd consider using the nontoxic plastic-impregnated lumber. It's expensive, but it supposedly lasts virtually forever without protection from the elements. Rot-resistant or "treated" lumber must be stained every year or two; otherwise, it will crack and deteriorate.

Toolbox Tips

One way to prevent exposure is to let someone else handle it. For example, instead of using a toxic paint stripper, take furniture to a business that strips finishes in a tank.

Common sense tells you to read the label and follow exposure precautions. Use toxic chemicals outside, or at least with the windows open. Common sense also says that since things will go wrong, you should anticipate problems and take steps to minimize their impact.

Finally, any serious home-fixer should keep these protective measures on hand:

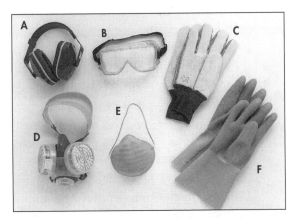

This health and safety equipment should protect you during almost any home repair in this book.

A. Ear protectors dampen the shriek of a circular saw or RotoZip tool. They are especially important indoors, where echoes amplify the noise. Ear plugs are a cheaper, less geeky, and equally effective alternative.

B. Goggles are helpful while nailing, hammering, sawing, demolishing, drilling, sanding, or any other home-repair sport that makes dust, chips, or other flying crud. For doing a lot of overhead work, the face shield in the next photo is mighty handy.

C. Leather work gloves are useful for handling rough lumber, working with masonry and concrete, and wrecking stuff.

D. A snug-fitting respirator will protect against various solvents and dusts (buy a cartridge to protect against the specific hazard you face, like dust or organic solvents).

E. A dust mask, even this cheap pollen mask, is useful for sanding, wrecking, sawing, and sweeping.

F. Neoprene gloves are excellent for painting, working with paint stripper, and other toxic tasks. They prevent solvents from passing through your skin. Bonus: When you take them off, your hands won't smell like turpentine or stain.

Full-face shields will protect you from massive amounts of flying debris. It's amazing how much you can see overhead when you're not squinting to avoid dust!

Toolbox Tips _____

Another good safety item is a pair of tough work boots. For real abuse, steel-toed boots have a steel liner to protect your toes from dropped tools.

Nervous About Leaded Paint?

If your home is more than 25 years old, chances are some of the paint contains lead. Lead is a good pigment, and it was used in many types of paint, particularly for trim, enamel, and exteriors. Lead is toxic to the nervous system, and children especially can be injured by even tiny amounts. A public-health or toxicology laboratory can test samples of painted surfaces for lead.

You can get leaded paint professionally removed, if you have the money (but check local regulations on lead removal first). A better option may be to keep the paint in good condition, and use caution any time you might raise dust by sawing or sanding, for example.

Ladder Safety and Use

Maybe your roof needs an inspection, or your gutters are plugged and leaking. So you burrow into the garage, drag out your old wooden ladder, and bet your life some kind of rot hasn't eaten its way through anything important. Then you slap it up against the wall and climb. Wrong! It may be a mite sexist to put it this way, but ladders can be real widow makers.

All Thumbs _____

Aluminum siding is easily dented. To prevent damage from a ladder, pull old gloves over the tops of the rails—and use caution.

Here's a better approach. You look at the job, clear away the obstacles, then go into your storage area and look over your ladders. You pick out the right ladder, inspect it for damage, and bring it to the job. You look overhead for electrical wires, and safely raise the ladder. Then you check that the ladder is soundly erected. Finally, you begin climbing.

Remember: One fall from a ladder is one too many. From the endless menu of ladder safety rules, these 10 are most important:

1. Look at your ladder first. Make sure it hasn't deteriorated since its last use.

2. Make sure the footing under the ladder is solid, so the ladder cannot slip away from the wall.

3. The foot of the ladder should be ¼ of the height away from the wall. This gives the best odds of staying upright without tipping over backward or having the ladder slip out from under you.

4. Wear dry, sturdy shoes (no sandals) so you don't slip on the rungs.

5. Climb with your hands on the rails (the side beams), not the rungs. Then, if you start to fall, your hands will always be in position to grab the ladder.

6. Don't climb above the third rung from the top, because you will be unstable and likely to fall.

7. Don't carry more than one hand's worth of stuff, or you won't be able to hold the ladder securely. If you need more tools or materials, get a tool apron (see Chapter 4), make another trip, or rig up a rope hoist.

8. As my father used to say, "One hand for yourself, and one for your work." In other words, hold on with one hand as you work. If you absolutely must work with both hands, slip one arm through the rungs, to hold yourself in case of a slip.

9. Keep your center of gravity inside the rails, so you don't tip the ladder sideways. Don't lean too far back, so you don't tip over backward.

10. Take the time to move the ladder so you can reach the work easily. Leaning sideways is asking for a fall.

For some short-and-sweet advice on ladder safety, go online at www.chess.cornell.edu/ Safety/Safety_Manual/portable_ladder_safety. htm. You'll also find links to many ladder-safety manuals at www.pp.okstate.edu/ehs/links/ ladder.htm.

Toolbox Tips

For siding repairs, tuckpointing (masonry-joint repair), and window replacement, a scaffold may be simpler, safer, and more convenient than a ladder. If you do rent a scaffold, consider also renting planks (the boards you walk on). Aluminum planks are lighter and easier to handle than wooden planks, and far safer to stand on than those old 2×10s stored near your compost heap.

A Ladder Made in Heaven

Ladders are an excellent place for neighbors to pool resources, since they're used infrequently. Or barter with a neighbor who's long on ladders. Ladders come in four basic types: stepladders, straight, extension, and folding. Because ladders lean while in use, and you cannot stand at the top, they will not take you quite as high as their length would indicate. For example, a 16' ladder will touch a wall at about 15' above ground. And since you will be standing three rungs below the top, your feet will be less than 12' above the ground. When you place a ladder against an eave (the lower edge of a roof), it should extend

about 3' above the eave. That gives you handholds to climb onto the roof.

Stepladders range in height from about 3'— which is ultra-handy for repairing and painting rooms—all the way past the 10' monster I use to replace light bulbs on a cathedral ceiling.

Notice how Jane keeps her weight centered inside the ladder. The stepladder is extended fully, and on a level surface.

A *straight ladder* is a self-explanatory name for an inexpensive ladder that's not very versatile.

An *extension ladder* joins two straight sections together, giving excellent adjustability in height. Since the sections must overlap when extended, an extension ladder made of two 10' sections extends to about 16'. You can use an extension ladder at its shortest setting—half the advertised length. Some extension ladders may be disassembled, so you can use the lower section as a straight ladder. (Don't use the upper section alone because one rung has been removed to allow room for the extension mechanism.)

A *folding ladder* can be used as a straight ladder, a stepladder, or a small scaffold. Folding ladders are convenient but expensive; you may be able to buy an extension ladder and a stepladder for the same price.

When it comes to working on gutters, windows, or ceilings, a folding ladder may be just the thing. Notice that the 2×8 plank extends only about a foot past the supports; if it's longer, you could overbalance it while stepping on the ends.

In fact, that's my advice: Get a stepladder and a short extension ladder. Depending on your house, 16' to 28' should be long enough.

Raising a Ladder

To raise a stepladder, simply stand it up, straighten the dividers between the sections, and position it so you can reach your work safely. Check the footing by rocking the ladder slightly—all four legs should be on the ground. Then climb, staying at least two steps below the top, and observe the usual don't-lean-too-far rules. A folded-up stepladder can be quite stable leaning against a wall when, for example, you need to clean or repair ground-floor windows.

I've seen too many people trying to wrestle straight and extension ladders into position while ignoring the laws of physics. Here's a much easier and safer technique for raising a ladder:

1. Place the base of your ladder against something solid, like your house or the foot of a willing slave. (Command your slave to push toward you, not down, on the bottom rung.)

Place the base of your ladder against something solid.

2. Lift the top of the ladder, and stand underneath it. Walk toward the base, lifting one rung at a time.

3. Ladders are easy to move once vertical. While moving a ladder, keep it near the building. If it starts to fall sideways, simply lean it against the building for stability. When the ladder is vertical and near the building, move its bottom into position, then lean it against the building.

Ladders are easy to move once vertical.

4. Check your work. Is the base about ¼ of the ladder's height from the building? Are both feet solidly planted? Are both rails firmly against the building? Give the ladder a slight shake: If it gyrates, something needs fixing. **Don't climb until both rails solidly touch the ground and the building.**

All Thumbs

Use common sense and caution while working on a ladder. Saws and other dangerous tools become all the more hazardous when you are on a ladder.

5. Once an extension ladder is standing, you can adjust the height with the el-cheapo rope-and-pulley system. Because the rope is much better for lowering the extension than raising it, I usually extend the ladder a bit more than necessary beforehand. Once the ladder is leaning against the wall, it's easy to lower into position.

6. Lower the ladder by reversing the above procedure.

All Thumbs

Fiberglass ladders are safest, because they don't conduct electricity, but they cost more than aluminum. Aluminum is cheap, light, and strong, but it conducts electricity. If you really *must* work near electric lines, be sure to use a fiberglass ladder. You can also ask your electric utility to install insulating sheaths over the wires. After all, utilities hate it when their customers are electrocuted—who's going to pay the bill?

Protecting the House While You Work

When I was in the masonry business, I measured my progress by how fast our crew messed up somebody's premises. Only after we had strewn a dismaying array of tools, scaffolds, ladders, and materials around the yard could we go to work. Fact is, messes are part of home repair. My natural inclination was to protect the premises until long after we'd started making the mess. If you do the protection beforehand, the cleanup will be much easier.

Need I mention that protecting the house—and the owner's roses—can avert a boatload of familial strife? Consider it mentioned.

Plastic tarps, used carpet (often found on the curb), duct tape, and plywood are key resources for protecting your house. Most home protection is common sense—combined with your recognition that many repairs make a phenomenal mess. If you're continually walking outside to fetch tools or materials, it's a good idea to catch dirt and grit on a carpet walkway leading to the work area.

Some types of work are predictably messy. These suggestions can help you contain the mess:

Job Type	Protection Suggestions
Dusty: Repairing drywall, plaster, tile, or masonry; or sanding. Any job using a power sander, grinder, or wire brush.	To contain dust, cover doorways and heat ducts with 4 mil plastic. (Don't skimp with those 1 mil dry-cleaner bags sold as "plastic drop cloths"—they are unworkable.) Fasten the plastic with duct tape, which holds much better than masking tape.
Filthy: Plumbing, masonry, and painting.	Use plastic or cloth drop cloths in the work area. Keep your hands clean to avoid spreading dirt, particularly with plumbing. Keep a broom and dustpan handy and occasionally sweep up. (For more on paint preparation, see "Preparing for an Inside Job" in Chapter 11.)
Dangerous to floor: Carpentry, masonry, and plumbing.	Protect floor with old carpet or scrap plywood.

The Least You Need to Know

- The stupidity factor is probably the biggest cause of accidents. It causes you to do idiotic things you would never do, idiotic things you didn't consider doing, and idiotic things you can't believe you did.

- Keep a small kit of safety equipment (goggles, work gloves, and so on) on hand to protect yourself against toxic chemicals, dust, and other hazards.

- Working safely on a ladder is a great way to improve your odds of surviving a home repair.

- For the sake of domestic sanity and to make cleaning up a lot easier, protect your home from your project.

In This Chapter

- ◆ Money-saving strategies for buying and using tools
- ◆ The fundamental hand and power tools for home repair
- ◆ Seven versatile tools—your secret weapons for fast, smooth home repairs
- ◆ Saws and sanders—handy when you need them
- ◆ Drills—first among equals in your electric toolkit
- ◆ Renting tools and tool-borrowing etiquette

Chapter 3

All Power to Your Tools

You can squander a bundle of money on tools—creative designers are inventing new ones by the bucketful. But since our goal is to minimize the time and financial cost of owning a home, and to give you a little satisfaction in the process, in this chapter I'll concentrate on the tools you really need. But an emphasis on basics will not prevent me from discussing some of the great innovations that are appearing in the tool aisle. Some of these labor-saving improvements actually make sense—they are innovations that would make a Swedish carpenter drool.

As I describe the basic tools for home repair, I'll help you decide if you really need it. I'll also suggest the best model and size, and offer tips for use. I'll talk about how much quality you need, and whether your power tools should be powered by a cord or a battery.

Selecting Tools: The Role of Price

How much can you spend for tools? Ferrari prices, if you buy from specialty woodworker's catalogs. But how much should you pay for tools? Probably more like Toyota truck prices. Remember, a good tool may make your job easier, and it will probably last longer, but it will not automatically improve your skill. That said, I must add that many cheap tools have little to recommend themselves except a bargain-basement price. The screwdrivers twist, the drills break, the files dull, and the saws don't even start sharp—this kind of economy can get expensive after a while!

Here are some suggestions for saving money on tools without buying garbage:

◆ Hunt around at rummage and estate sales.

◆ Make a detailed wish list for friends and family, in case they inquire before your birthday.

◆ Buy tools in sets—you'll pay about half what the individual tools would cost.

The Basic Hand Tools

Instead of buying everything at once, it's sensible to build up a toolkit over time. Eventually, your basic toolkit will contain many of the tools shown in the following photos. (Later chapters describe specialty tools for roofing, masonry, drywall and plaster, painting, electrical work, and plumbing. Chapter 4 has suggestions on smart toolbags and where to store all these tools once you acquire them.)

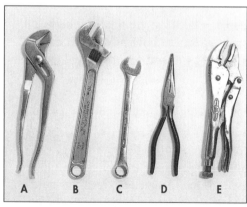

Pliers and wrenches.

A. The jaws of arc-joint (Channel Lock) pliers expand to 1½" or larger, useful for plumbing and mechanical work.

B. An adjustable (Crescent) wrench turns hexagonal and square nuts and bolts.

C. A combination wrench, with open-end and box ends, gets a better hold on nuts and bolts.

D. Long-nose (needle-nose) pliers are supremely useful, especially for connecting wires in electrical work.

E. Locking pliers (Vise Grips) can turn nuts, grab other tools, and pull nails. They also make an emergency vise, clamp, and handle.

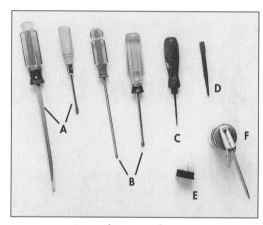

Screwdrivers and more.

A. You'll need several slotted screwdrivers for innumerable tasks.

B. Phillips screwdrivers are handy, although an electric drill also drives Phillips screws.

C. An awl marks wood and metal. It also punches holes to start small wood screws and makes dimples so a drill bit won't wander while starting.

D. A nail set punches finishing nails below the surface. A good, all-around size is ³⁄₃₂".

E. A magnetic stud finder locates nails in walls.

F. An oil can will lubricate tools, hinges, locks, and other metal mechanisms.

Toolbox Tips

Penetrating oil, like WD-40, is good for loosening rusted parts. To keep stuck parts moving, use motor oil, like SAE 10W30.

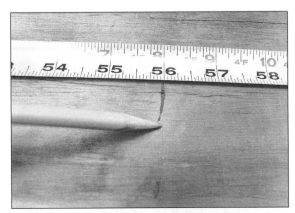

When you mark from a tape measure, does your line wander off toward Nebraska? Put your pencil at the tape and drag away, so the darkest part of the mark is also the most accurate. Or mark a V, with the vertex of the angle at the measurement.

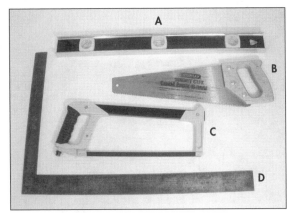

Level, saws, carpenter's square.

A. A 24" level helps to frame walls, lay out electrical boxes, install appliances and shelving, and fix doors.

B. This short, sharp hand saw has a new tooth design that's astonishingly effective at cutting wood.

C. A hacksaw cuts steel, copper, aluminum, or plastic. Minimize vibration by cutting within ¼" of a vise, locking pliers, or C-clamp.

D. A carpenter's square marks straight or square (90°) lines. Use it for layout work, picture framing, and door straightening. It also makes a good guide for sawing. (I often find the small square [either aluminum or plastic] shown in "Seven Cool Tools" to be much handier.)

Toolbox Tips

Are your steel tools—hand saws, hammers, and squares—rusting? Wipe on some boiled linseed oil, which will sink in and prevent rust, without gumming up the tool.

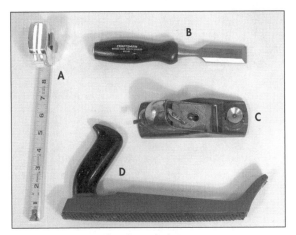

Chisels and planes.

A. A tape measure is essential for almost any repair. A good length is 12' or 16'.

B. A wood chisel (½" to 1" wide) removes wood to make mortises (cutouts) for locks and hinges. You'll also use it to trim wood to fit in countless repairs.

C. A hand plane smoothes the edges of doors, windows, and drawers, especially after sawing. Start with a shallow cut, and set the plane deeper if it cuts smoothly.

D. A Surform brand wood rasp will remove wood. It cuts both across and with the grain. The Surform leaves a rough finish but is handy for fitting doors, windows, and drawers, particularly on end grain. A Surform with a flat blade is perfect for trimming drywall.

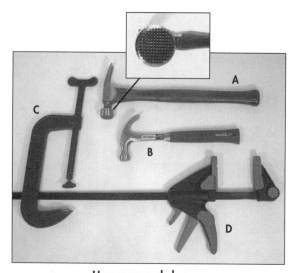

Hammers and clamps.

A. A framing hammer excels for pounding big nails. Long and heavy, it has a waffle pattern on the face to grip nails. Inset shows the waffle (checkered) pattern, used to grab nail heads. Warning: Don't use this baby where you will be able to see hammer dents!

B. A 16-ounce claw hammer is an all-around tool, best for smaller nails. Polish the hammer face with sandpaper so it won't slip off the nails. Because you'll be using it so often, it makes sense to pay for quality. This hammer has a straight claw, which is handy for prying and wrecking.

C. A C-clamp will hold wood for gluing or nailing and sometimes substitute for a vise.

D. A quick-release bar clamp adjusts easily. It's handy, but a C-clamp is stronger. This one also works as a spreader, to move things apart. Both types of clamp are excellent for holding wood while sawing or drilling.

A cat's paw (top) can take out nails, although it will definitely damage the wood. Hammer either end of the "paw" under the nailheads. Continue pounding as you pry. You can see how much damage a cat's paw will leave (bottom).

Seven Cool Tools You Must Meet

Every handy person has a set of favorite tools—the overlooked, underappreciated splendors of the toolbag. Meet mine.

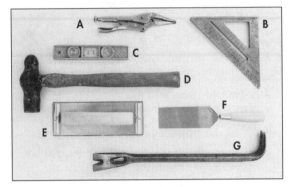

Seven cool tools.

A. Needle-nose locking pliers replace wire cutters, pliers, and needle-nose pliers.

B. A small aluminum or plastic square guides a circular saw for a perfect 90° cut, as shown later in this chapter. It's also handy for marking right angles and other angles.

C. A torpedo level can often substitute for a clumsy wood or aluminum level. Use it to level or plumb electric boxes, shelves, pictures, and cabinets.

D. A 3-pound hammer is the primordial blunt object, for cleaning masonry before repair, driving garden posts and stakes, and big-league metal chiseling.

E. A sanding block looks so moronic that many people (including your author) try substituting a hunk of scrap wood instead. This block grabs the sandpaper, which then lasts longer. With a lot less effort, you'll get a smoother surface.

F. A margin trowel is designed for patching masonry, but it's also perfect for working with drywall and plaster. I use mine to scrape paint, clean crud from old wood, glaze windows, mix mortar, and pry off molding.

G. This rigid, hexagonal wrecking bar disassembles stuff neatly because the flat tongue slips under the wood. Much better than big, clumsy bars.

Cutting Remarks on Slick Sawing Techniques

Cutting wood accurately sounds easy—until you try it. Then the saw binds in the board, strays from the line, or doesn't cut at all. That's when you realize you need a sharp saw and a savvy technique.

Saw horses are the traditional support for wood you're sawing, and they allow you to work at a comfortable height. Plastic milk crates, however, are cheap, easy to store, and helpful for supporting other stuff that may need fixing—from cabinets to lawn mowers. Whichever you use, arrange the supports so the cut-off piece can fall free. If you saw between the supports, the board will sag, the saw will bind viselike, and you'll get a crooked cut at best and an injury at worst.

Follow these steps for effective hand sawing:

1. Keep the cut within 4″ of the support, and hold the work securely. A clamp prevents vibration and improves accuracy.

2. Hold a square against the board to mark your cut.

3. Position the saw. Hold your thumb as shown in the following figure, well above the cut, so you can't gash yourself. Draw backward on the saw for a couple strokes to start, then stroke smoothly, following your line.

4. Finish with a hard push, to prevent splitting.

For circular sawing, see "Using a Circular Saw," later in this chapter.

Hand saw fundamentals.

Hammering for the Ham-Handed

When I was a kid, the county fair offered a prize to anybody who could whump a big nail into a knotty 2×4 with three whacks. I never came close to winning, but I did learn that while hammering may look Neolithic in its simplicity, it's a tricky knack. These suggestions can help:

◆ Use a natural swing, and flex your wrist.

◆ Try to hammer downward. Nailing overhead is tiring and clumsy; you may benefit by drilling a pilot (preparatory) hole first. Much better, fasten overhead with a power-driven screw.

A downward swing with this long, heavy framing hammer produces a lot of action on a big nail!

◆ Nail the thinner board to the thicker one—nail the siding to the stud, and the plywood to the floor framing.

◆ Use a nail set (see the photo earlier in this chapter) to prevent hammer dents in finish work. Nail sets also help you reach nails in tight spots.

◆ Get good support behind the work. If you must nail into something that springs back, use a screw, or hold the boards with a C-clamp. Or use my old friend John Christenson's trick: Hold a hammer behind the work so it can spring back when you strike the nail.

Nailing to a moving target.

Toolbox Tips ⎯⎯⎯⎯⎯

To quickly bring the tools you need to a repair site, store essential tools in one bag. I let screws and nails accumulate in the bottom of my tool-bag, and there's still room for special tools and hardware.

Toe nailing—nailing diagonally through one board into another—may be your only choice if you can't get behind a joint. Toe nailing is usually used for construction, not repairs, but it's handy to know. You may have to hold the upper piece in place with a clamp or a temporary block of wood. If you have trouble toe nailing, drill an angled hole and drive a Phillips screw into it. Or check out the truss plates shown in Chapter 5.

Hold the point in the dent you just made, but angle it steeply downward, then hammer it down. It may be easier to use a big nail set to hammer the nail home.

All Power to the Power Tools

Most homeowners need more than just hand tools. For many purposes, especially drilling and sawing, power tools are the logical choice. But if you've been in the tool aisle recently, you know that most small power tools are now sold in cordless models, which is a polite way of saying you'll have to mess with batteries instead of extension cords.

I used to think that battery-operated tools were toys, until I bought a cordless ⅜" reversible drill, and it quickly became my mainstay for screwdriving and drilling. The key advantage of cordless tools, shockingly enough, is that you won't have to bother with a cord or an extension cord. That translates into less to schlep, less to trip on, and one more outlet available for another tool.

But there are disadvantages. Batteries are heavy, especially if they have to be big enough for a tool that gets steady use. And batteries die. Translated, I wouldn't put much faith in batteries for a heavy-duty tool, like a circular saw. And not only do batteries go flat while you're using a tool, they also die while the tool is in storage. So if you suddenly need a drill,

To start toe nailing, punch a starting dent in the upper board, with the nail perpendicular to the wood.

unless you have a second battery on the charger, you may be stuck waiting for a recharge. Still, batteries are getting better all the time, and nothing beats a cordless drill for driving screws for a new bookshelf, drilling holes to fix roof flashing, or to mount a new garage door opener.

Toolbox Tips _____

How good a tool do you need? Those chosen for photos in this book are all high-quality tools, many marketed primarily to pros, not homeowners. Some people think homeowners should not waste money buying tools built for day-in, day-out work. Others think if you buy a great tool once, you'll never need to replace it. I shoot down the middle: I buy the best tools if I'll be using them often, and I try to save money on occasional-use tools.

Variable-Speed, Reversing Drill (Doubles as Power Screwdriver)

The drill has always been the first power tool to buy, simply for drilling holes in wood and metal, and wire-brushing paint and rust. A variable-speed, reversible drill will also drive screws, and for many home-repair artists, that is its primary use. A fiendishly handy improvement found on most drills is the "keyless" *chuck*, which tightens by hand instead of a chuck key. Many battery-driven drills also have a clutch that will slip at various loads; they are perfect for driving screws flush without overdriving them.

It doesn't take a genius to realize that a bigger battery brings more power and fewer trips to the charger. But this battery is seriously heavy too. Take weight into account when buying cordless tools.

Electric drills are sized by the maximum opening of the chuck. Power, weight, and price all increase along with chuck size. For home use, buy a ⅜" model. You should be able to drill holes up to about 1" in wood with this drill.

Fix-It Phrase _____

A **chuck** is the rotating thingy on a drill that holds a drill bit. A **pilot hole** is a preliminary hole drilled to guide a screw and prevent wood from splitting. For small wood screws in soft wood, you can "drill" a pilot hole with a finishing nail instead of a drill bit. If your bit is slightly too small to make a pilot hole for a wood screw, carefully wobble the drill while it's running.

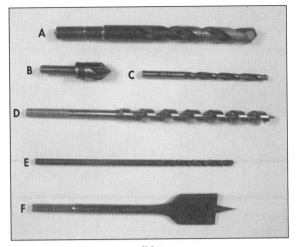

Drill bits.

A. Masonry bits drill masonry and concrete for an anchor. Buy only the size you need, as each anchor requires a specific drill size. For a big concrete-drilling job, rent a hammer drill for much faster cutting.

B. A countersink removes wood so a flat-head screw can rest flush with the surface.

C. Combination wood-or-metal drill bits make holes for rivets, sheet-metal screws, and bolts. These bits are the standard companion for an electric drill: Use them to drill small holes. Buy a ¹⁄₁₆″ to ¼″ kit, and also ³⁄₈″ and ½″ bits.

D. Self-feeding bits pull themselves into the wood, cut a cleaner hole, and require no pushing on your part. More expensive than spade bits, they are a real pleasure to use.

E. This extra-long bit is handy for reaching deep areas, or drilling pilot holes for long screws.

F. Spade bits are usually sold in sets, and used for drilling large holes in wood. These bits call for a lot of pushing, make a rough hole, and are wrecked if they hit a nail.

If You Gotta Drill Metal ...

Metal, particularly steel, hates being drilled. You'll need more force, more technique, and sharper bits. (Soft metals like brass, copper, and aluminum are far less challenging.) Follow these suggestions:

◆ Make a small dimple to prevent the bit from wandering as it starts. In soft metal, tapping a nail will make a good starting point. In iron and steel, use a center punch, a pointed tool that's shaped like a pencil.

◆ Use faster drill speed for smaller holes, and slower speed for big holes.

◆ To make holes ³⁄₁₆″ and larger in iron and steel, drill a pilot hole with a smaller bit, then enlarge the hole with a second bit.

◆ Cool the bit with motor oil to prevent damage from overheating.

◆ Keep bits sharp, or buy new ones.

The hardness of steel can vary greatly. A steel hacksaw can cut a steel bar because it's harder than the bar. Hardness explains why ordinary tools will not cut or drill steel locks, tools, and springs. Moral of the story: If you're getting nowhere while drilling steel, give up— it's probably hardened.

A variable-speed, reversible ³⁄₈″ drill is the most versatile electric tool for home repair. Can you get by without this tool? No. You can use a hand drill for a few small holes in wood, or a brace and bit for larger holes. But you need a power drill to drill metal, to drill many holes, or to wire-brush rust from metal (as shown in Chapter 11). And I haven't even mentioned those incredibly handy Phillips-head screws. 'Nuf said?

Toolbox Tips

Drywall screws. Construction screws. Deck screws. These are all variations on the same wonderful theme—strong, easy-to-drive screws that often don't need a pilot hole. There's no getting around it: Power-driven screws have revolutionized home repair and construction.

The Power of Screwdriving

Once upon a time, driving a screw meant drilling a pilot hole and wrestling with a screwdriver. No more. Power-driven screws work in places too tight to swing a hammer, and they're easy to remove if you (like me) tend to put things together bass-ackward. Unlike nails, screws won't crack plaster or drywall. Strong and non-violent, they would resemble a great son-in-law, especially since they are so easy to drive home …

The power-driven screws craze began with drywall screws. When carpenters began using them to secure framing and hardware, and to repair wood and fasten trim, manufacturers wised up and marketed a still-expanding line of specialty screws designed for power-driving, as shown in "Screwing Up Again?" in Chapter 5.

This square bit (left) gets a good hold on the screw, so you don't have to press as hard as with a Phillips bit. Most square screws use a #2 bit; a #1 bit is right for small screws. This straight-slot bit (center) is almost impossible to drive with a drill. If you have a choice, leave these in the tool museum. A Phillips bit (right) is the standard for power-driving screws.

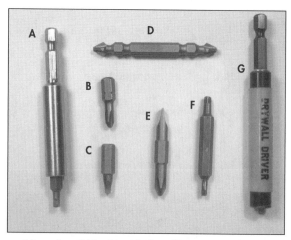

Virtually all bits intended to drive power-driven screws have the same hexagonal shank, so many fit the magnetized bit holder.

A. A magnetized screwdriver bit holder holds screws for easy driving and extends the reach of a screwdriver bit. For fastening hardware, this holder (shown holding square bit) is essential.

B. A Phillips bit, the power screwdriving gadget that revolutionized home repair.

C. A #2 square bit is needed for easy-to-drive square-slot screws.

D. A Phillips bit that also cuts a countersink for the screw. Sears sells these handy drivers.

E. This combination Phillips-straight bit fits directly in the drill chuck.

F. A bit that combines #1 (small) and #2 (regular) square bits.

G. This screwdriver-bit holder is designed for drywall; run it slowly, and it sets the screw to the right depth.

Here are some hints for using power-driven screws:

◆ Avoid slotted screws—the bit will slip. Use either Phillips or square drive. Phillips require more pressure on the drill—or a pilot hole. If you're doing a lot of screwing, square-drive screws will save wear-and-tear on your arms.

◆ For rough work, don't bother with a pilot hole if you're strong enough to press hard. Run the drill fast, with light pressure, until the screw starts to grab. Then increase the pressure.

◆ Use a pilot hole for finer work, split-prone wood, or big screws. The result will be more accurate, and your arms will sing your praises.

◆ When a screwdriver bit wears out, replace it. They're cheap.

◆ Keep your fingers away from the action end of a power screwdriver.

◆ To screw up a stack of drywall, rent or buy the drywall driver shown in Chapter 9. For heavy-duty screwdriving, it's much faster and more accurate than a drill.

All Thumbs

When driving screws, don't let the bit slip—it will ruin the screw head. If the bit starts slipping, (a) reverse the drill, pull the screw out a ways and try again; (b) drill a pilot hole; (c) use a square-slotted screw; or (d) put hand soap on the screw before you start.

The Kindest Cut: An Introduction to Power Saws

Drilling and screwing are critical to home repair, but you'll wind up cutting something sooner or later. Let's see how they saw these days.

Dancing the Jig—and Other Tricks with the Jig Saw

A jig or saber saw drives a small, straight blade back and forth, and is used to make straight or curved cuts. Push down while cutting to reduce vibration, and press forward lightly. When the saw is fully in the cut, press harder. Once considered a tool for amateurs, the jig saw is a real contender, largely due to the redesigned blades that cut frighteningly fast and with minimal splintering. To make a straight cut, glide the saw along a small square (see "Seven Cool Tools," earlier in the chapter).

With a sharp blade, a jig saw should cut pretty straight.

This saw may come with many features:

- **Variable speed.** Helpful for starting cuts, and for cutting plastic and ceiling tile.

- **Orbital-action.** Instead of running straight up and down, the blade digs in on the cutting stroke. The result is fearsomely fast sawing. That, at least, was the conclusion of two experienced carpenters who watched me use this jig saw.

- **Adjustable angle.** The blade can be angled to about 45° from the base. Use a square to reset the blade to 90°. A good saw, like the one shown, will reset accurately to the 90° position.

- **Pivoting blade.** A handle on top pivots the blade 360° so you can cut into a corner. You'll have a better view of the blade as you cut.

- **Quick-release clamp.** You install the blade without fussing with a screwdriver.

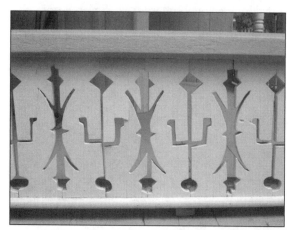

To repair this kind of trim, you need a good jig saw.

Can you get by without a jig saw? Yes. This tool is optional, handy for occasional cutting, intricate work like repair of "gingerbread" trim shown in the preceding photo, or installing electrical outlets in drywall or plaster.

Circular Saw

A circular saw, often called by the trade name Skil-saw, is a standard tool at construction sites. You can adjust the depth of the blade, and the cutting angle. Most circular saws have a 7¼" diameter blade, enough for most cutting. In general, adjust the blade so it reaches about ½" through the wood; a deeper setting will strain the motor and increase danger. To saw a 4×4, cut slightly more than halfway through, flip the wood, and complete the cut.

This saw shows the latest wrinkle in circular saws—the laser guide. By showing you the saw's alignment and angle, it gives a much straighter cut.

All Thumbs _____

A circular saw may be the most dangerous tool in a home workshop. Read and follow the instructions carefully, particularly about eye protection and setting up the cut. The blade guard should snap down to cover the blade when you finish a cut. Don't work in cluttered areas, in low light, or when tired. Guide the saw with two hands, and know what's under the board. Don't act stupid while holding a circular saw!

A circular saw needs just two blades. For cutting 1″ and 2″ lumber, get an 18-tooth, carbide-tipped blade. Carbide teeth stay sharp much longer than steel teeth, particularly after they hit a nail. The second blade is a fine-toothed plywood blade, also used to cut paneling and plywood board.

If your saw starts smoking, shrieking, and cutting crooked, the blade is dull. Dull blades can damage the motor, and draw enough current to blow a fuse. They are also unsafe because you have to push so hard. To avoid dull blades, you have to avoid nails, although normal cutting will eventually dull any blade. Good carbide blades can be professionally sharpened. Most people just replace cheap carbide blades.

Special circular-saw blades can cut some bricks and concrete blocks. It's a dusty, noisy job, totally devoid of recreational value. You can cut a few bricks or blocks by hand; see Chapter 15 for details.

Circular saws are used for *cross-cutting*, *rip sawing*, or cutting panels, especially of *OSB* or *plywood*.

Fix-It Phrase _____

Cross-cutting is cutting across the grain. **Rip-sawing** is cutting with (parallel to) the grain. Hand rip saws have coarser teeth, but for occasional use, either saw will work. For our purposes, an "all-purpose" or "combination" blade in a circular saw should do both just fine. **OSB,** or oriented strand board, is made of wood chips pressed and glued together. It is replacing **plywood,** made of glued-up layers of wood.

To make a straight cross-cut, take a hint from Doug: Guide your saw along a small square. Support the board on sawhorses, milk crates, or something equally solid. Watch the cord. Don't saw between the supports—your blade is bound to bind or get squeezed by a sagging board.

If you're cutting a long piece off a board, it may split as it falls. Have a helper hold the cut-off piece. Or rest it on a support the same height (not higher) as the other supports.

To accurately saw panels of plywood, paneling, or OSB, clamp a drywall square along the cut. Support the panel with long 2×4s placed parallel to the cut. Start the cut by guiding the saw along a small square, then shut off the saw and substitute the long square. Clamp the far end of the square to the panel. Then slide the saw along the square for a perfect cut. If you don't have a drywall square, hold a straight board in position with a pair of C-clamps.

When sawing a panel that you care about, place the good side down to prevent splintering. If both sides will be seen, slice the veneer on the top side at the cut line with a utility knife, guided along a square. (You'll see a utility knife in action in Chapters 6 and 9.)

Can you get by without a circular saw? Maybe. A hand saw will cross-cut a few 2×4s. But to cut many boards, rip saw a long plank, or cut plywood or OSB, get a circular saw. For accurate cross-cutting, a power miter box is mighty handy (covered next).

Power Miter Box

A power miter box (chop saw) is essentially a circular saw hinged to a small table. Once expensive, you can now pick one up for $175, making it suitable for serious do-it-yourselfers. When the saw is well adjusted, the advantage is simple: straight, true cross-cuts. Power miter

boxes are dynamite for cutting everything from 2×4s to molding. You can clamp a stop block to the fence and repeatedly cut short lengths to a single measurement.

All power miter boxes will cut miters (cuts at up to 45° to square) with the blade vertical. The more expensive "compound miter" saw, like the one shown in the photo, will also cut bevels: the blade pivots to the side and descends at an angle.

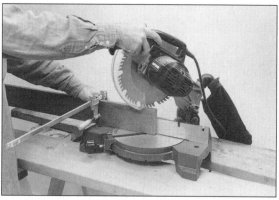

A power miter box makes accurate cross-cuts.

Can you get by without a power miter box? Probably. A small square and a circular saw give good cross-cuts for less than half the price. But a lot of formerly frustrated home repairers swear by power miter boxes, particularly for cutting molding. Get a basic or compound model, depending on whether you expect to cut crown molding—the molding along the ceiling that needs a compound miter.

All Thumbs

It doesn't take a genius to recognize that a power miter box can cause major damage to your anatomy. Read the manual carefully—and observe its cautions.

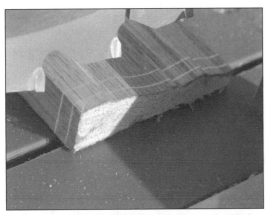

The latest in saw technology is a laser marker for the cuts. Instead of scrunching down to see where the blade will cut, you just eyeball the marks. It's awesome cool—and the laser is bright enough to be seen in sunlight. This is another innovation that's been getting ovations from carpenters.

Rotary-Cutting Tool

The RotoZip, or rotary cutting tool, is one of the newest and handiest gadgets in the tool aisle. The Zip was invented by a guy just down the road from me who re-engineered a drill bit to cut on the side. Originally designed to cut drywall, the RotoZip now cuts tile, insulation, metal, wood, and even stone. All you have to do is guide the little thing along, and cut to the line. But you will want earplugs—it's a whiner.

Unlike a circular saw, the RotoZip is happy cutting curves, as it's doing here in this piece of parquet floor. You won't find a handier tool for cutting wall tile for a pipe, countertops for a sink cutout, or drywall for switch holes.

Playing in the Sander Box

Sanding is nobody's idea of a good time. Don't take my word for it—just notice how many sanders have been invented in recent years. Here, I'll discuss the two most common power sanders (for information on floor sanders, see Chapter 7).

Belt Sander

Belt sanders drive a sanding belt the way a bulldozer drives its tracks. They are great for removing a lot of material during heavy-duty refinishing. They can smooth the edge of a door, or flatten wood patching compound, as seen in Chapter 6. But a belt sander can cause a lot of damage really quickly, if you lose control, let the sander stand still, or sand across the grain rather than with it. If you ever need to flatten some gouged wood or straighten the edge of a door, consider getting a belt sander. (However, a power planer, shown in action in Chapter 6, is the ideal tool for trimming door edges.)

A belt sander is the tool for making really flat surfaces.

A sander with a 3×24" belt, like the one shown, is plenty big for home work. If you're more interested in finishing work, check out the orbital sander, described in the next section.

Orbital Sander

Orbital sanders rotate a disk of sandpaper—about 5" in diameter at about 25,000 revolutions per minute. Orbital sanders (also called "random orbital sanders") are great for refinishing. They won't flatten a surface as nicely as a belt sander because they remove less wood, but orbitals are perfect for dressing up furniture, especially after stripping paint.

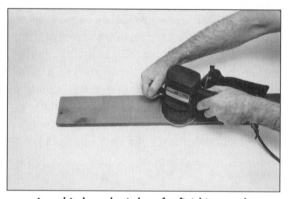

An orbital sander is best for finishing work.

Using Belt and Orbital Sanders

Follow these hints when using a belt or orbital sander for the first time:

◆ Wear safety goggles.

◆ Practice on scrap wood.

◆ Hold the sander with both hands and allow it to reach full speed. Moving parallel to the wood grain, slowly bring the sandpaper into contact. Don't stop your forward movement while the tool is operating.

◆ Holding the sander at an angle may cause skipping and gouging. The whole belt or disk should touch the wood.

◆ To cut damaged spots deeper, move the sander back and forth.

◆ Don't press too hard, or the sander will slow down and cut less effectively.

◆ Coarse sandpaper is needed for rough, gouged surfaces. But if the surface is in fair shape, start with medium or fine paper. Don't skip grades as you move toward fine or extra-fine sandpaper.

So can you get by without a power sander? You bet. A hand sanding block will take care of minor sanding. Don't buy a power sander for drywall repair; it will cut too deep and cause a dust storm. To flatten rough wood, a belt sander is faster than an orbital sander. But an orbital sander is handy for refinishing furniture—and for the flat sections of moldings and doors. If you do much furniture refinishing, the orbital sander is both cheap and handy.

Renting or Borrowing Tools

Howard Tate, an unjustly forgotten rhythm 'n' blues singer, sang this plaintive line: "Got to find me a part-time love." That's how I see renting tools—as an opportunity for part-time love, with a monster tool that I don't have to maintain, repair, or store (not to mention buy in the first place).

Toolbox Tips

If you rent a tool on Saturday, a one-day fee may take you through to the rental yard's opening time on Monday—so you'll get almost two days for the price of one.

Even though I have a good collection of tools, I've rented floor sanders, chain saws, wood splitters, post-hole diggers, concrete mixers, and an electric jackhammer over the years. Tool rental yards have an amazing number of goodies. Many of the tools are designed for large jobs, but that's the point—this is where you get pro equipment. Even if you don't push these tools to their limit, you will still lighten your load. Tool rental outfits also rent ladders, scaffolding, and extension cords. Or check if there are any tool-lending libraries in your area.

Rental outfits are not the only source of tools—friends can be equally valuable, and much more affordable. But before you ask to borrow your neighbor's pipe cutter, consider the parable of David and Roger. Roger used to borrow drills, hacksaws, even the occasional sledgehammer. I didn't mind—after all, there was no point in him wasting money on something he'd only need once in his lifetime. But that's how long it seemed to take for Roger to return my tools—a lifetime. I've quit offering, and he's quit asking.

At the other extreme, when my friend Doug Swayne borrows my reciprocating saw, he does it in style: He asks ahead of time, so I can make plans. Then he borrows it for the minimum time, and when he does return the saw, I find a couple new blades in the case.

More tool-borrowing etiquette:

◆ Don't ask to borrow a tool you can't control. For example, I'm happy to lend out an electric drill, but not my chain saw.

◆ Return the tool—quickly, and in good condition.

◆ Offer to repay the favor by helping out your benefactor.

◆ As you amass your own set of tools, lend them in return.

The Least You Need to Know

◆ Many tools are more versatile than most people realize, giving you one more reason to buy them.

◆ Your most frequently used tools should be your best-quality tools.

◆ Save time and frustration by keeping your basic tools in one place, ready to go to work.

◆ When it comes to power tools, buy the most versatile ones first. A variable-speed, reversible ⅜" drill is the first electric tool for any homeowner.

◆ Don't assume you need a cordless tool. A corded model will be cheaper, lighter, and more reliable.

◆ Just because you'll need a tool once in a while does not mean you should buy it. Try borrowing from a friend or renting.

In This Chapter

- ◆ The essential home workshop: storage, lighting, and workspace

- ◆ How to store more stuff in less space

- ◆ The all-important workbench

- ◆ Lighting and outlet considerations

- ◆ Time-saving hints for putting tools away—so you can find them quickly

 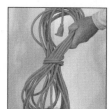    

Chapter 4

A Workable Workshop

To some people, "workshop" conjures up a gaggle of elves patiently painting dollhouses in a quaint sweatshop near the North Pole. To me, a workshop is not a candle-lit cavern but rather an essential tool for fast, painless home repair. Your workshop can be plain or picturesque— so long as it satisfies three basic functions. It's got to store the junk you need so it's accessible when you need it. It's got to give you a place to do things fast. And it's got to have good light and plenty of electrical outlets.

Storage, a work surface, and lighting and electricity are the holy trinity of the home workshop. Fancy is fine if you have the time and money, but only if your workshop also satisfies these essentials.

A Working Shop

Key question: where to put the workshop? A basement—if you have one—is warm and accessible. But it's got too little air circulation for dusty work or working with toxic chemicals, and you probably can't haul in large projects. The garage may be hot in summer, cold in winter, and liable to usurpation by motor vehicles. Still, it's a better place than the basement for painting, sanding, noisy work, and large projects. My compromise is to have a primitive workshop in the garage, and a more complete one in the basement.

All Thumbs

Lights and outlets are not just a convenience in the workshop—they are a necessity. Poor lighting causes frustration, mistakes, and accidents. Tripping over extension cords is an annoyance, and lousy electrical hookups can cause electrical fires.

But location is not so important as convenience. Most home repairs, after all, don't occur in the workshop but rather at the site of the problem. So the need for fast-in, fast-out access dictates the iron rule of organization—everything gets a place.

Storage Solutions

The main reason to fuss about good storage is because nobody likes searching for stuff. In the interest of saving money, I've suggested some low-rent storage solutions. But whatever you use, make it logical, make it handy, and make it accessible.

For less than $5, you can buy an excellent organizer like this one. Get one that's designed to prevent nails and screws from falling out when you carry it. With a dozen fasteners at your side, you may actually have the one you need. That saves effort.

Toolbox Tips

Inexpensive plastic milk crates make rough-and-ready sawhorses that won't damage your saw blade if you accidentally cut into them. They make a decent rack for tools and hardware. And they make temporary props for all sorts of projects.

Could you use these kinds of storage?

Item	Storage Suggestion
Power tools	Cases, open shelves, hooks (for tools with handles), or plastic milk crates.
Hand tools	Pegboard (see the following section), tool bag (coming up), drawers, nails or hooks for squares, levels, etc.
Clamps	Hanging on pegboard, beefy nails, or lag screws.
Health and safety equipment	A closed box. Store masks and respirators in plastic bags to keep them clean.
Extension cords	Nails or hooks. Coil the cord, wrap the last 3' around the hank, and tuck it through the loops, as I'm doing in the following photo.
Fasteners	Cans, original packaging, or plastic containers. The 4" high by 4" deep shelves shown in the photo later in this chapter can store many fasteners, with the label facing out for fast action.
Wood	Place on rack, or stand almost vertical. Keep bottoms dry by resting on scrap wood.

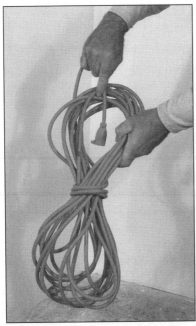

Wrapping an extension cord this way will keep it from snagging your other tools.

Get Organized with Pegboard

Follow these suggestions for using *pegboard*:

◆ Screw pegboard to ¾×1½" wood "furring strips" fastened to the wall. Pegboard hangers must stick through the pegboard, so they need a bit of clearance.

◆ Store similar tools together, but don't waste space by being compulsive about it.

◆ Use labels or trace the outline of larger tools on the board.

◆ Reserve pegboard for commonly used tools.

Fix-It Phrase

Pegboard is a pressed-wood material with holes spaced 1" apart. It's sold in 4×4' or 4×8' sheets, in two thicknesses—I'd buy the thicker, stronger ¼". You'll also need an assortment of hangers to use with pegboard.

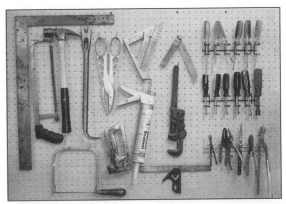

Pegboard takes away every excuse for disorganization.

It's in the Bag

Pegboard is for important tools, but crucial tools live in the toolbag or toolbox. (I use a toolbag, so that's what I'll call this essential item. For more information on home-repair tools, see Chapter 3.)

Ideally, the tools in this bag will allow you to complete a repair without fetchit trips for more tools. This bucket-style toolbag does not collapse, so the tools it holds are always ready to work. And it has a holster for a cordless drill.

These tools live in my toolbag:

- 16 oz. claw hammer
- ⅜" reversible, variable-speed, cordless drill
- Assortment of drill bits and screwdriver bits, in small bag
- Assorted screwdrivers
- Locking and needle-nose pliers
- Nail set
- Pencils and scriber (divider)
- Torpedo level
- Utility knife
- Hand plane
- Wood chisel
- Margin trowel
- Magnetic stud finder
- Tape measure
- Small square
- A few screws and nails
- Wire stripper, twist-on wire connectors, and electrical staples
- Circuit tester

Toolbox Tips

You can buy a number of all-in-one wheeled tool carriers that claim to have enough space to carry power tools as well as hand tools. Some of these are mighty appealing, and surprisingly cheap. But if you store all your common tools in one of these, you might end up shlepping a ton of tools to every job. What's best is your call—but I'd suggest aiming for convenience and speed.

The Workbench

While the workshop is not the scene of most home repairs, it does serve as a receiving area for tools and supplies when you're caught up in a project. Ideally, you'll stow this detritus *WIG* (*where it goes*).

Fix-It Phrase

WIG, or **where-it-goes,** is shorthand I developed to guide my kids into putting a small percentage of their stuff where it belongs. But the idea applies equally well to the workshop ...

The workbench should have a surface at least 2' deep, and about 8' wide. There's no good reason to *buy* a workbench—they're easy to build from 2×4s and ¾" plywood. If you're feeling really cheap and lazy, scrounge an old kitchen cabinet from the curb and screw some plywood or an old door to the top. Prevent sway with diagonal bracing or by fastening the workbench to the wall.

A workbench must have a decent vise, firmly attached and instantly available. The vise (shown in Chapter 6) will hold tools for sharpening, and other objects during drilling, sawing, or filing. When sawing, keep wood (and particularly metal) as close as possible to the vise. No way around it: In the workshop, a good vise is nice.

Lighting and Outlets

You simply can't have too much lighting in your workshop. Fortunately, fluorescent lights are cheap, and offer a no-shadow illumination that can't be beat. To save time, wire several lights to one switch.

Just as important is good access to electric outlets. In too many basements, the wiring ranges from lamentable to downright dangerous. It pays—in safety and convenience—to upgrade this kind of junk, using the suggestions in Chapter 16. Place an outlet every 4' along the wall behind the workbench. Cover the outlets with protective steel plate, and double-check the grounding system.

Sawhorses are fiendishly handy—for supporting tool stands or work tables—and even for sawing. Sawhorses made with plastic brackets are collapsible but still sturdy—a vast improvement over those using folding metal brackets. Loosen the nut to remove the legs.

Tips for Saving Time

One thing's for sure in home repair: You want to save time. I'll admit my suggestions may sound pedestrian, and you are free to ignore any or all. I suggest that you set up systems in your spare time; in the midst of a repair, who wants to label the nails or organize the wrenches?

- ◆ Store tools intelligently. Use the kind of ready-to-go toolbag described earlier in this chapter. Keep other tools in their places, so you can get to work instead of searching for tools.
- ◆ Use labels. I keep a stack of adhesive mailing labels and a marker in the workshop, along with a bunch of empty containers.
- ◆ Store containers with the label facing out.

These narrow shelves are excellent storage for fasteners.

- ◆ To avoid extra trips to the hardware or building supply store, keep a supply of extra, half-broken, and didn't-fit parts. Buy extra hardware—it's usually cheaper than making another trip to the store.
- ◆ Don't lose stuff. As conservationist Aldo Leopold said, "The first rule of intelligent tinkering is to save all the parts." (Leopold was talking about species extinction, but his advice is also valid for home repair.) Put small parts in small containers so they don't run away while you are working.
- ◆ Know what you're doing—by reading this and other books, and by talking with people who have been in your shoes.

Toolbox Tips

When you buy a new tool, don't just throw the manual on the workbench and let it collect sawdust. A central file, or just a folder, can keep the manuals in good condition—and in a place where you can find them.

◆ Always bring the carcass of whatever you're replacing to the store (unless it's a refrigerator!). You may be amazed at how many sizes, features, threads, and materials the store stocks for any particular part. By referring to the old one you can be sure you're buying the right one.

◆ Bring a list to the store so you don't forget anything.

◆ Don't start an optional plumbing or electrical project just before your in-laws arrive for the weekend. Pick a moment when you won't feel pressed for time.

◆ Do stuff in logical sequence: all the demolition, all the framing, all the electrical, all the drywall, and all the painting. This reduces the need to haul tools and helps you concentrate on the task.

It may make you feel self-conscious, but a simple tool belt will speed up many repairs, especially carpentry and electrical work. It's worth its weight just to prevent stooping.

The Least You Need to Know

◆ A home workshop should be built for speed. Plenty of lights, lots of storage, and handy electric outlets help you work efficiently.

◆ Don't trust your memory: Use labels promiscuously. Trace tool outlines on pegboard.

◆ A rough-and-ready workbench is fine, since you'll be doing most repairs on-site, not in the shop.

◆ Keeping essential tools together in a tool-bag is a real timesaver in home repair.

In This Chapter

◆ How to select and use nails, screws, and anchors

◆ Identifying and choosing hardware for repair projects

◆ Time-saving hints for using fasteners

◆ Getting the most from glue

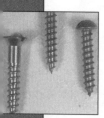   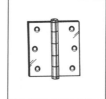  

Chapter 5

Fast Guide to Fasteners

Fasteners—the generic term for nails, screws, and anchors—are like the joints in your body. They aren't exactly the structure, but there is no structure without them. Almost every home repair project—replacing a bookshelf, patching a roof, or hanging a lamp—calls for fasteners. So you've gotta know what the hardware mavens are selling.

Nails have come a long way since manufacturers realized that their main job is not splitting wood. But screws are now the fastener of choice for many purposes, since they are strong, accurate, and nondestructive. Following the lead of the nail- and screw-makers, other hardware manufacturers have redesigned their products to make them stronger, easier to use, and a bit easier on the eye.

A Nail for What Ails You

Except for bark and vines, nails are the oldest wood fastener. A glut of new nail varieties has reached the market in recent years. These nails are less likely to split the lumber and more likely to grab it. Some are almost as strong as screws—but faster to drive.

When it comes to hardware, David Masse, proprietor of Masse Hardware in Cambridge, Massachusetts, has seen it all. The store has been in the family for more than a century.

Fix-It Phrase

Nails are sized by the archaic **penny** system. A 4d (4 penny) nail is 1½" long, while a 16d nail is 3½' long. Nail packages list the length in inches, fortunately.

While pro carpenters rely more on power-driven nails, that's beyond idiot territory. These are the typical nails you'll need for home repair:

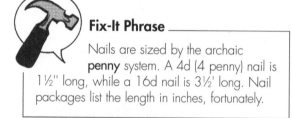

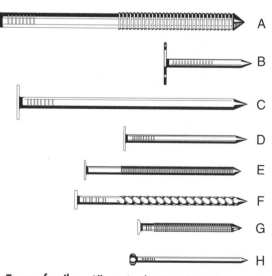

Types of nails. *(Illustration by W. H. Maze Company)*

A. **Pole barn:** Tough and springy, up to 6" long, for fastening framing lumber; rings prevent pulling out, so *never* put one in the wrong place!

B. **Roofing:** A galvanized, big-headed nail for asphalt shingles. Sold up to 3" long; at least ½" must enter roof sheathing.

C. **Sinker ("coated"):** A thinner version of the common nail, it causes less splitting; cement coating eases driving and improves grip. For 2" lumber.

D. **Box:** A light-duty nail for thin or brittle wood, it's almost split-proof.

E. **Siding:** A galvanized (rust-resistant) version of the box nail, up to 3½" long, for wood siding.

F. **Spiral:** This heavy flooring nail gets a screw grip that resists pull-out and reduces squeaking; buy the galvanized version for outdoor use.

G. **Paneling:** A skinny, hard nail for wood paneling and trim; buy a color to match the wood.

H. **Finishing:** A thin, inconspicuous nail for window, door or baseboard trim. 4d, 6d, and 8d are handy sizes. A panel nail of matching color may be a better choice, if it allows you to avoid filling the nailhead.

Screwing Up Again?

When it comes to fastening, screws have four advantages: they're strong, they're gentle, they're secure, and they're removable. Old-style screws require a pilot hole, but many people drive in self-tapping screws (drywall, construction, and trim screws in the photo below) without pre-drilling. These power-driven screws have a Phillips or square drive, and no taper, so they drive easily with a variable-speed drill.

The thread of wood, drywall, and sheet metal screws is tailored to the particular material. Wood and sheet-metal screws are made with straight (slotted), square-drive or Phillips heads. For a price, you can buy solid brass screws, which are attractive but soft. If you're having trouble driving them, drive in a steel screw to cut the threads. After you remove the steel screw, the brass screw should ease right in.

Toolbox Tips _____

For screwdriving, remember this rule: Righty-tighty, lefty-loosy. Tighten a screw by turning the top of the screwdriver handle to the right; to loosen, turn it to the left.

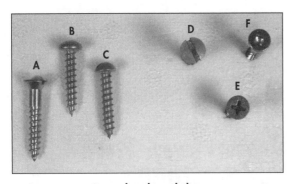

Screw heads and slots.

A. **Flat-head:** The top of the head sits flush to the surface—ideal for mounting hinges.

B. **Pan-head:** A decorative version of the round head.

C. **Round-head:** Attaching hardware to wood.

D. **Slotted:** Old and okay for hand screwdriving. Don't try to drive with a drill.

E. **Square drive:** Designed for power driving, this head requires less pressure on the drill than a Phillips head.

F. **Phillips:** The most common slot for power screwdriving.

Screws for Wood, Drywall, and Sheet Metal

Not too long ago, drywall was fastened with nails. These days, it's attached with power-driven screws. In fact, you can buy power-driven screws for many other purposes, too. Try them!

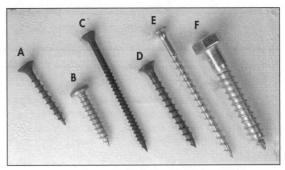

Wood, drywall, and sheet-metal screws.

A. Drywall screws have Phillips or square drive heads (length: ⅞" to 3").

B. Sheet metal screws hold sheet metal but also work in wood (⅜" to 2" or so).

C. Trim screws hold railings, moldings, and other indoor wood. They are strong, but have a small shank and head (1⅝", 2¼", and 3").

D. Construction screws are beefier (1¼" to 3" or more).

E. Deck screws hold deck planking, railings, and other outdoor wood. Available in rust-resistant galvanized, ceramic-coated, or stainless steel (1¼' to 3").

F. Lag screws are for heavy-duty fastening; they have a square or a hexagonal head (1" to about 6" long, in various diameters).

This wood screw rack shows a small part of the huge assortment of screws available at your hardware store. Read the previous suggestions for ideas on which screw you really need.

Toolbox Tips

Wrestling Phillips-drive screws into the wall can exact a toll on the hands. Square-drive screws are much easier to drive, and you can change over for $1—the price of a square-drive bit (see Chapter 3).

Machine Screws

Machine screws and machine bolts mate with a nut with the same *thread*. Compared to wood screws, machine screws and bolts are stronger (because they fasten all the way through the joint) and less likely to pull out, but more homely.

Fix-It Phrase

To have the same **thread**, a machine screw or bolt must be the same diameter *and* have the same number of threads per inch. Coarse threads (with fewer threads per inch than fine threads), are okay for most purposes.

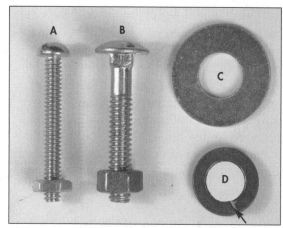

Machine screws and washers.

A. Machine screw and nut.

B. A carriage bolt and nut is a heavy-duty version of the machine screw, designed to grab in wood. Other machine bolts have a hexagonal head.

C. Flat washers strengthen a joint, reduce friction, work as shims, and let you use a small bolt in a large hole.

D. Lock washers have a split (arrow) to prevent vibration from loosening machine nuts.

Anchors Away—Plaster and Drywall

So you're trying to hang that gilt-framed, 70-pound, black-velvet Elvis portrait on plaster or drywall, and you can't find the studs, even after you read "Seven Ways to Find a Stud" coming up in Chapter 9. Nailing or screwing into studs is the strongest way to fasten to the wall, but there's not always a stud where you need it. Fortunately, many types of anchors will hold towel racks, light mirrors, photographs, and posters. The general routine for anchors is to drill a hole, insert the anchor, drive the screw into the anchor, and tighten.

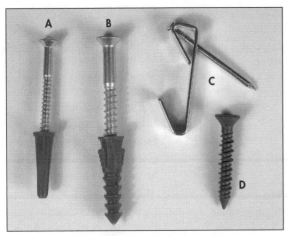

Small anchors for drywall, plaster, and concrete.

A. A light plastic anchor is quick and cheap, for light duty.

B. A ribbed plastic anchor is somewhat heavier-duty.

C. A picture hook is much stronger than a nail because it pulls evenly.

D. A hardened Tapcon screw cuts a thread in concrete, concrete block, mortar, and some bricks. One advantage over lag shields: You can drill a smaller hole in the concrete. Buy a special drill for Tapcons.

All Thumbs

Spring toggles are easy to use—but impossible to re-use. Make sure you have the hole in the right spot before you insert the toggle. If you remove the bolt, the toggle will fall inside the wall.

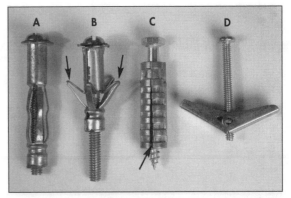

Large anchors for drywall, plaster, hollow doors, and concrete.

A. A Molly-screw (expansion) anchor is cumbersome, but it makes a strong fastening to drywall or plaster. Drill a hole, insert the anchor, and tighten the screw to expand it. Then remove the screw (the anchor will stay in the wall), stick the screw through whatever you are mounting, and screw it back into the anchor. Drive screws with a drill to save time.

B. A Molly screw as it would appear, expanded, in the wall. The arrows point to the "wings" that form to grab the plaster or drywall.

C. A lag shield makes a strong anchor in concrete. Drill a hole in concrete with a special masonry bit, insert the anchor, slip a lag screw through the hardware and into the anchor, and tighten. The two-piece shield expands (see arrow). I tend to prefer Tapcon screws because you don't have to drill such a big hole in the concrete.

D. To use a spring toggle, drill a hole, insert the screw through your hardware or whatever you are fastening, thread it into the anchor, slip the anchor into the hole, and tighten. The wings automatically expand to grab the wall.

Good hardware stores (not those cut-rate chain stores) carry much more than nails and nuts. They have drawers filled with washers and other fasteners in every conceivable size, shape, and material. They may also cut glass, repair screens, cut and thread steel pipe, and sharpen knives, scissors, and saws.

More Hardware

Besides screws and anchors, you may need hinges and various types of reinforcers. The following illustrations show a bit of the variety you'll see at a good building-material supplier.

Doors are a major user of hardware, as you can see from this sampling.

Door Hardware

Item	Uses
	Butt hinge: For standard doors, sized up to 4" long; must be screwed in a recess ("mortise").
	Strap hinge: For doors and gates in yard, basement, and garage. Use where the door and trim are flush with each other.
	Tee hinge: Similar uses as strap hinge.

Item	Uses
	Semi-concealed hinge: Mainly for kitchen cabinets; the hinge is screwed to the back of the door. You'll also see fully concealed hinges.
	Doorstops: Prevent a door from damaging walls; may be screwed to baseboard or slipped over the hinge pin.
	Door straightener: Prevents sag in a wooden screen door (see the photo in Chapter 6).
	Storm door closer: Closes door slowly without slamming (also shown in Chapter 6).
	Hook and eye: A quick, light-duty latch.
	Barrel bolt: For quick, easy locking of door.

(Drawings courtesy of National Manufacturing Company)

When things start to fall apart, there's help in the hardware bin.

Other Hardware

Item	Uses
	Corner iron: Reinforcing furniture or installing shelves.
	Joiner (strap, L, and tee): Reinforcing furniture and shelving.
	Shelf bracket: Installing shelves.

Item	Uses
	Continuous (piano) hinge: Strong attachment for folding shelves or box lids.
	Pull: Replacing or updating drawers and cabinet doors.
	Chair and corner brace: Strengthening leg attachment on chairs and tables.

(Drawings courtesy of National Manufacturing Company)

These galvanized connectors can play a major role in replacing rotten or damaged wood. Use special heavy-duty, 1½" nails sold for truss plates for fastening, or drive in construction screws. Many of these fixtures can be bent to suit in the vise, and they are all *much stronger* than toe nailing—and easier to use. They are cheap; about the only drawback is homeliness: Make sure to hide these connectors!

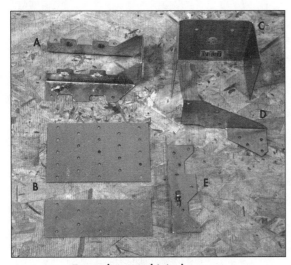

Truss plates and joist hangers.

A. **Joist hanger:** Attaches 2" lumber (1½" actual thickness) to a flat surface.

B. **Truss plate:** Restores strength to damaged areas, joins flat wood together. Two of many sizes are shown.

C. **Post cap:** Holds something to the top of a post.

D. **Hurricane tie (clip):** Secures rafters to top of walls. Vastly strengthens roof attachment for resistance to storms; usage is shown in the next photo.

E. **Angle:** Use to reinforce connections.

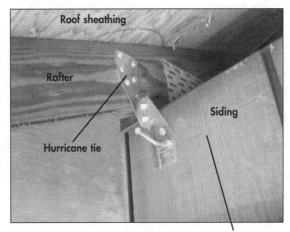

Hurricane ties being installed.

The Glue Doctor Will See You Now

When used right, wood glue makes a strong and invisible repair. A bottle of yellow carpenter's glue should be in any toolkit, for fixing split wood, building or repairing furniture, and so on. The joint must fit well and be nailed, screwed, weighted, or (preferably) clamped for 30 minutes while the glue sets. Yellow glue cleans up with water, has no odor, and is as strong as the wood itself—so long as the joint fits well and stays dry. For damp areas, buy the water-resistant variety of wood glue.

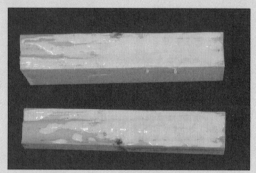

This looks like a lot of glue, but always err on the side of excess when applying wood glue.

Don't botch a wood-gluing job—a second repair will likely fail, because the parts fit poorly. If you must try again, buy the polyethylene glue made for caulking guns—this stuff will fill any gaps and is incredibly strong.

Good gluing calls for good clamps to hold the parts while the glue sets. The bar clamps shown in the following photo cost $10 to $15 apiece. They are easy to adjust, strong and versatile, and best used in pairs. Sometimes you can hold the wood together with locking pliers, heavy weights, rope, or wire.

Here are more tips for great gluing:

◆ Before gluing, clean off old glue or splinters so the parts can mate.

◆ If wood starts to split, ease some glue into the crack with a finishing nail or a piece of paper (or blow it in with a can of compressed air). Then clamp securely.

◆ Gluing back chips from moldings and furniture makes an invisible repair.

◆ Glue the entire mating surface. Glue must ooze out as you clamp.

◆ Work quickly. Don't glue a complicated joint unless you can finish within the glue's setting, or "working," time (for carpenter's glue, 10 to 15 minutes).

◆ End grain makes a weak joint. If you must glue it, use extra glue, and if possible, screw a wood block beside the joint as a reinforcement.

◆ Mop up spills with a wet rag before the glue sets. Remove beads of dried glue with a sharp chisel or knife.

◆ Clamp thoroughly. If you have extra clamps, use more than you think you need.

Plenty of glue is squeezing from the joint—that's good. Wipe this stuff off with scraps of cardboard and then a wet rag. Note the scraps of plywood, used to prevent the clamps from marking the wood.

A word of caution: Most yellow carpenter's glue is water-based and nontoxic. Some glues, however, have a nasty stench, and should be used with plenty of ventilation. Contact cement, and some glues sold for the caulking gun, call for these protective measures.

The Least You Need to Know

◆ Fasteners are available in a bewildering variety of types, sizes, and finishes.

◆ Buy extra fasteners for your project; eventually your collection will save you trips to the store.

◆ Instead of nailing, look into power-driven screws. You'll save time and the project will be much stronger.

◆ Glue can make invisible repairs if you save the broken part and work quickly.

In This Part

Part 2

Looking Inside

In the bank robbery biz, an "inside job" is one that takes advantage of an employee's generous assistance. In home repair, an inside job is one that fixes windows, doors, floors, and walls. When they scream "Fix me!" your have no more options than a bank teller facing a 9mm pistol. The teller forks over the swag. You grab your tool bucket and loudly threaten to "fix" something.

Still, there are advantages to working on the interior. You should not be bothered by rain, unless you happen to be doing plumbing … And aside from the odd cathedral ceiling, you won't be dealing with high-altitude repairs. And most important, you should be able to admire your handiwork from the comfort of your very own Barcalounger.

So if your floors are squeaking, your plaster is rotting, your paint is peeling, or your molding is positively moldy, turn the page and start saving money on an inside job. I think you'll agree that, with good advice, most inside jobs are easier than stealing money from the bank— and they're legal.

In This Chapter

- ◆ How to keep your windows sliding

- ◆ Removing and replacing glass, step by step

- ◆ Screen repair and replacement

- ◆ Sticks, squeaks, and sags—the enemies of a blissful entry

- ◆ How to install a deadbolt lock

- ◆ The easy way to replace a door

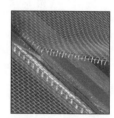

Chapter 6

A Transparent Guide to Windows and Doors

If you want some air, light, or a view, a window beats a solid wall, but when it comes to staying out of trouble, I'd bet on the wall any day. Windows leak. They break. Even double-pane windows, which are great for keeping cold weather out, eventually get cloudy.

You may also be noticing your doors more than you wish. Some won't open without a full-back shove or only lock after you give a King Kong crank on the key. Maybe they squawk like a sixth-grader learning tenor sax, or a pound of weather strip doesn't seal the gaps. In this chapter, I'll share some cures for ailing windows and doors.

Window Lingo

Windows come in many styles and shapes—they slide up and down, they slide side to side, and they swing from the top or side edge. The double-hung window is still one of the most common, so let's use it to learn window lingo.

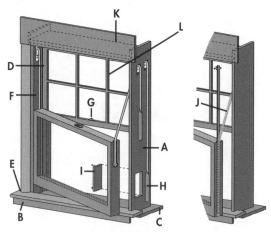

Parts of a double-hung window.

A. Side jamb

B. Apron

C. Sill

D. Inside stop (parting stop)

E. Stool

F. Outer stop

G. Meeting rail

H. Counterweight (in some windows)

I. Pocket and cover (in some windows with counterweights)

J. Counterweight spring (may replace counterweights)

K. Head jamb

L. Muntins

Unsticking Stuck Wood Windows

Why is a wood window like a jazz quartet? Because it loves to jam. Yuk yuk. But seriously, windows do get stuck. The problem is most serious when due to a shifting foundation. If that's your problem, it's worth trying to stop the movement, which can also crack plaster and jam doors (see Chapter 15 for more on foundation repair). Here, we'll discuss cures for stuck windows that are painted shut or have poor counterweights.

Painted Shut

Amazing but true, people actually freeze windows shut by slobbering paint into the cracks between the *sash* and the *jambs* and *stops*. To free a stuck window, you'll need a hammer, trowel, and a paint scraper. You may also need a plane, a belt sander with fine sandpaper, a drill, and some nails.

> **Fix-It Phrase**
>
> In a window, the parts that hold the glass comprise the **sash**. In a window and door, the **jambs** are cases or frames that outline the door or window. Made of ¾" stock, they are as wide as the wall is thick. **Stops** hold the sash in its channel. Stops also prevent a door from swinging too far.

1. Slip a trowel in the cracks between the sash and the stops, and between the sash and sill. Run the trowel around the whole window, wiggling it and trying to move the sash. Don't gouge the wood.

Use a trowel to unstick the wood sash.

2. Press up with your hand at the middle of the lower sash. If the sash budges, concentrate your efforts where it's still stuck.

All Thumbs

Before applying megatons of force to a window, double-check that the lock is open, and that a nail or other security gadget is not holding it closed. Use caution with hammers, levers, and other bludgeons around windows. Sometimes a homemade wood lever can move a stuck sash, but be careful—there's glass here!

3. If the window refuses to move, remove one outer stop molding, using techniques described in Chapter 10.

4. Remove the sash. Prevent the counterweight ropes or straps from disappearing into their holes by tying a knot or grabbing them with locking pliers.

5. Clean the sash channels and lightly sandpaper or plane the edges of the sash where it binds. Remove paint buildup with a paint scraper or a light touch of a belt sander. Wax the channels with paraffin or spray them with silicon lubricant.

6. Reinstall the sash and reconnect the counterweights. Drill new nail holes and renail the stops tight (but not binding) to the sash. (If you use the old holes, the stops will return to jam the window.) In dry weather, leave the stop a bit loose, so the sash can move when the weather turns humid.

7. If you repaint the window, use paint sparingly. Move the sash while the paint dries to prevent sticking.

Toolbox Tips

Silicon spray is a miracle ingredient that can keep your windows moving smoothly. It's also great for greasing the skids under primitive wooden drawers.

Poor Counterweights

Suppose the window grudgingly opens, but you can't be bothered calling Bruce Willis every time the smell of fried catfish makes you yearn for some fresh air. The problem may be a detached counterweight. These metal weights, suspended in channels hidden behind the jambs, balance the weight of the sash, so it's easier to move. A double-hung window should have two counterweights (or two springs) for each sash, as shown in the drawing above.

To remove the counterweights, follow steps 3 and 4 in the preceding procedure for opening a jammed window. Detach the ropes from the sash and look for a removable rectangular cover (if it's painted over, you should still be able to see its outline). Pull the cover with a wood chisel and screwdriver, then rehang the weight with a new cord. Or install spring sash kits in the pulley slots and attach them to the lower sash.

If there's no cutout, you can't access the counterweights without at least tearing off the window trim. At this point, ditch the ropes and buy springs to support the sash.

If you've got an aging, drafty double-hung window, you can replace the sash, glass, and side channels with a kit that essentially gives you a new window, with spring supports, modern weather stripping, and the ability to clean all the glass from the inside. These kits must be ordered for your window size and are a comprehensive solution to window woes. They can be expensive, but they are much easier to install than a complete replacement window.

Paneless Glass Replacement

Whether it's *Complete Idiot's Guide* to-be authors playing baseball, current *Complete Idiot's Guide* authors swatting flies with hefty magazines, or kids practicing soccer, window panes do break. Fortunately, glass is usually pretty easy to replace.

Wood Sash

To replace broken glass in wooden sash, you'll need gloves, goggles, a small trowel, a hammer, new glass, glazier's points (the little fasteners that hold the glass in place), boiled linseed oil, a small brush, and glazing compound. If the window is accessible from outside, you might be able to fix it in place. Clean out all the glass, and start with step 5. Start here to remove the sash from the inside, and then replace the glass:

All Thumbs

Protect yourself when removing the broken pane with goggles and heavy-duty gloves.

1. Remove one outer stop (see Chapter 10 for advice on pulling molding).
2. Remove the lower sash and detach the counterweight ropes or spring lifts. Grab the ropes with locking pliers so they don't disappear into the jamb.
3. To repair the upper sash, remove the parting stop by repeating step 1 (even more delicately—this stop is tucked into a channel and harder to remove).
4. Wearing gloves and goggles, place the broken sash on a garbage pail. If the pane is mostly intact, lay a rag across it and beat it with a blunt object like a hunk of 2×4, then use pliers to remove the rest of the pane.

Be careful when removing the old pane. Be sure to wear goggles and heavy-duty gloves.

5. Scrape the seat (where the glass meets the wood) with an old wood chisel, paint scraper, or trowel. Remove any remaining glazier's points, highlighted in the photo.

A glazier's point holds the glass in place.

6. To cut a new piece of glass, oil the cutting wheel of a glass cutter. Hold a board or a square along the cut line, and run the cutter *once* along the guide. This creates the cracks that you will expand.

Cutting glass takes patience, but this technique actually works!

7. Using the knob end of the glass cutter, gradually tap below your cut line. Watch the crack grow gradually along the cut line—almost like magic! Work patiently, and you'll get the kind of controlled break that Alison, our expert, is getting in the photo.

Carefully tap below your cut line for a clean break.

Toolbox Tips

If you hate the idea of cutting glass, buy a ready-cut piece from a hardware store or glass company.

8. Paint the seat with boiled linseed oil or primer to keep the glazing compound flexible.

Linseed oil or exterior primer seals the seat for the new pane.

9. Press a small cylinder of glazing compound in the seat, then firmly press the new pane into the glazing.

Smooth the glazing compound with the trowel. Before the final pass, grease the trowel with a little boiled linseed oil so it doesn't pull out the glazing compound.

10. Push glazier's points into place with a trowel or wide screwdriver, so they hold the pane securely against the seat. Don't pull any Hercules imitations at this point!

11. Distribute glazing compound on the seat and press it to make a smooth coat. *Important:* Grease the trowel with linseed oil and glide it along the compound to leave a smooth layer of glazing.

12. Reassemble the window and reconnect the counterweight ropes or spring lifts. See "Unsticking Stuck Wood Windows," earlier in this chapter, to ensure that the sash moves freely.

13. Let the glazing dry for about a week, then prime and paint it.

Insulated Glass

Insulated—or double-pane—windows are a boon for people in northern climates—because they eliminate many of the leakage and cleaning problems of older storm windows. But when the seal between the panes leaks, the glass must be replaced. A glass company can do this, but you can save some money by measuring the length, width, and thickness of the pane (be sure to measure all the way to the edges). The glass company will probably have to order your pane. When you get the replacement, remove the weather stripping holding the sash, install the new pane, and replace the weather stripping.

Replacing Screens in Windows and Doors

Screens wear out. Here in Wisconsin, the mosquito capital of the world, that's an unpardonable sin. How to repair screens? For ultra-small repairs, cut a patch of aluminum screen that's about 1" larger in each dimension than the hole. Strip away a few wires from all sides and bend the remaining wires at 90°. Press these wires through the screen around the damage area, and bend them flat.

All Thumbs

For safety, doors must be glazed with Plexiglas or another clear plastic, or with safety glass, which breaks into harmless fragments. Safety glass is heavy and expensive, and must be ordered, since glass companies cannot cut it. Plexiglas scratches easily, but it's light, cheap, and easy to replace.

To replace the screen, place the door or window on sawhorses. Your repair technique depends on whether you are dealing with aluminum or wood.

If you have kids pushing through your doors, the screen is probably damaged around the edges, like this one.

For an Aluminum Window or Door

To replace screening in an aluminum window or door, you'll need a screen tool, which rolls screen *spline* into place:

1. Strip out the spline—the tube-shape vinyl holding the screen in place. If the old spline is brittle or chewed up, buy a replacement, as it will not hold.

Fix-It Phrase

A screen **spline** is a rope-shape piece of vinyl that squeezes into a channel to hold screen cloth in aluminum windows and doors.

2. Lay new screening on the opening, at least 1″ larger in each dimension.
3. Starting at the top, press the spline tool into the screen, making an indent. Follow the weave of the screen. Work gradually, or you'll tear the screen!

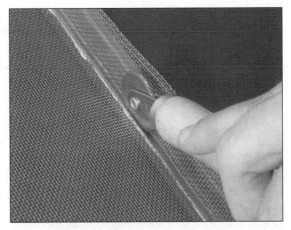

Press the spline tool into the screen.

4. Press the spline into the channel you have created and (a) roll it down with the spline tool or (b) press it into place with a scrap of wood. After forever tearing screen with a spline tool, I prefer a scrap of wood, as shown in the following figure. In any case, work slowly so you don't tear the vulnerable screening.

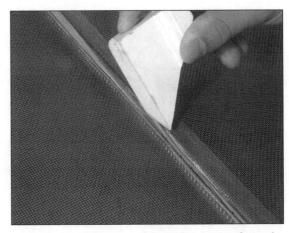

Or press the spline into place with a scrap of wood.

5. Repeat for the bottom. Pressing the spline into the channel pulls the screen tight.

6. Repeat steps 3 and 4 for the sides.

7. Cut off excess screen with a sharp utility knife, just outside the spline. Work carefully—the knife can cut in the wrong place.

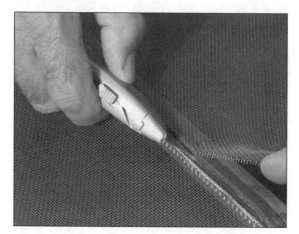

Cut off excess screen with a utility knife.

For a Wood Window or Door

To remove and replace screening in a wood window or door:

1. Remove wood moldings that hold screening into place. If you cannot salvage the molding, buy "screen bead" at a lumberyard.

2. Tear off the old screen and remove tacks and staples.

3. Lay the wood frame on a flat surface. Lay the screen material over the frame, overlapping 1" at each edge.

4. Fasten the top, using a ⁵⁄₁₆" staple every 3".

5. Pull the screen tight across from each staple and staple the bottom.

6. Repeat steps 4 and 5 for the sides.

7. Staple the center rail, and reattach the moldings with ⅞" brads.

8. Cut away excess screen with a utility knife.

Diagnosing and Curing Ill-Fitting Doors

Doors cause so many problems that I'm surprised nobody has figured how to eliminate them. But at least designers have invented ways to make them work more smoothly—better hinges, better hardware, even better doors. So if you're getting tired of shouldering your way into your house, let's look at some medicine for door diseases. We'll start with a bad fit and move to hardware problems, then show how to replace an entire door.

Doors are tricky, and tiny errors add up. Work slowly, and use sharp pencils. A utility knife makes the most accurate marks.

What's the Problem?

Plenty of problems can jam your door in its jambs—dry hinges, loose hinges, hinge *mortises* cut too deep, even oversize doors. But except for structural shifting, which can wrack a doorway out of square, every one of these problems is within idiot territory. So let's start salving a stuck door.

Fix-It Phrase

A **mortise,** for our purposes, is a shallow cutout that allows a hinge or other piece of hardware to rest flush with—not raised above—a surface. A **hinge plate** is half of the butt hinge typically used to hold doors. The **latch side** of a door is the side away from the hinge. The **hinge side** is, well, you get the picture.

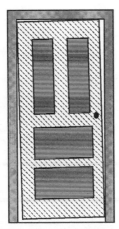

Typical door-fit woes caused by hinge problems are exaggerated here. Left: If the door binds high on the latch side, tighten upper hinge screws and/or recut upper hinge mortise. Right: If the door binds on bottom of latch side, tighten lower hinge screws and/or recut its mortise. If the door chafes against the entire latch side, both hinges may need attention or the entire latch side may need planing.

My Hinges Are Loose

To tighten or replace hinge screws, you'll need a screwdriver, screws, and maybe wood glue and splinters or wooden matches:

1. If you can tighten the screws, you're done.

2. If the screws slip, find some longer flat-head screws. Traditional flat-heads should be about the same diameter as the originals and slightly longer. I generally use 2½" Philips-head deck or construction screws, which are infinitely stronger because they grab the stud behind the jamb. If the screws hold, and the screw heads don't jam when you close the door, you're done.

Toolbox Tips

If you're having trouble getting the head of a big screw to lie flush in a hinge plate, enlarge the countersink with a countersinking bit—or ⅜" drill bit.

3. To reinforce the screw holes, pull the hinge pins as described in "Oiling Dry Hinges," later in the chapter, and remove the door. Leave the hinge plates screwed in place.

4. Coat big wood splinters or wooden matches with wood glue and tap them into all oversize holes. Cut the matches short, as we did at the center hole in the photo.

Tap glue-coated matches into oversize holes.

5. Let the glue dry. Carefully drill through the center of each hole in the hinge plates. Reattach the hinge, oil the hinges, and rehang the door.

Hinges Too Shallow?

Examine the hinges. The plates should be flush (level) or a hair above the jamb or door edge. Shallow mortises can cause the door to bind against the entire latch side.

If a hinge plate rides too high, unscrew it and chisel a deeper mortise. Take your time. Cut around the edge a bit with a sharp chisel, then make light cross-cuts with the chisel held vertically. Hold the chisel flat to remove the chips. Don't dig too deep: The hinge should sit flush, or slightly above, the door edge.

Take your time chiseling hinge mortises.

Hinges Too Deep?

If the door binds on the hinge *side*, and tends to spring open as you close it, your hinges are probably too deep.

1. Pull the hinge pins and remove the hinge plates. Place one plate on a few layers of thin cardboard, say a cereal box. Hold the plate firmly and use it as a template to cut several shims. Cutting on several layers of cardboard allows an easy, clean cut through the top layers.

2. Place the shims in the mortises, punch holes for the hinge screws, and rescrew. The shim should be invisible.

3. Test the door; if the cardboard is too thick, try several sheets of copier paper.

Shimming overcut hinges.

All Thumbs

"Hollow-core" doors are made of two sheets of thin paneling separated by strips of cardboard, with a frame of solid wood at the edge. To fasten a hook or a shelf to the perimeter, drill into the solid wood. To fasten at the center, use a spring toggle (see Chapter 5).

Repairing Old Hardware Damage

Many doors and door jambs are mutilated by mortises left over from old hardware. With a good sander, you can remove these marks quite rapidly. Here's how:

1. Clean out any loose stuff around the hole and fill it most of the way with wood filler, or putty (I like "Plastic Wood" brand).

Fill the hole with wood filler.

2. When the filler is dry, add another layer and let it dry.

3. Using a sanding block or belt sander, smooth the patch.

Smooth the patch before adding more filler.

4. Repeat the process, then prime and paint. When you're done, the patch should be almost invisible. (It's barely visible below the new striker plate in the photo. If I hadn't rushed the picture, you wouldn't see it at all.)

The finished patch is almost invisible.

Planing a Sticking Door

If none of the preceding suggestions help, your sticky door may need planing. But be judicious when removing wood, especially in wet weather. Once the weather turns dry, you may wonder why you cut the door so small.

Toolbox Tips

If you must plane end grain (at the door top or bottom) you'll need to buy or rent a power planer. In fact, a power planer is faster and surer for all door-planing tasks. The homemade, scrap-wood "door buck," shown in the following photos, is incredibly handy for working on doors.

To plane a sticking door, you'll need a hammer, screwdriver, pencil, and a sharp plane.

1. Mark the face of the door where it chafes against the jamb with a pencil (don't mark the edge, which you will be removing). If you can't locate the bind, slide a sheet of paper along the gap until it sticks.

2. Remove all hardware on the face you will plane (see "Oiling Door Latches and Locks," later in this chapter), and plane the edge. Holding a hand plane at a slight angle, as shown in the photo, seems to improve the cutting. Concentrate on the marked areas, and don't remove too much wood. Prevent splintering on end grain by planing from the edges toward the center.

3. Rehang the door and test. The door should swing absolutely freely, and the gap between it and the jamb should be uniform.

4. Seal the door edges (paying special attention to end grain) with a clear sealer or water-resistant paint, to slow the absorption of moisture. Reinstall hardware.

Hardware Problems

Let's say your door would open and close—if only the hardware would let it. Let's fix those squeaky hinges and balky locks and latches.

Oiling Dry Hinges

Cars have stickers to notify you when they need a lube job (don't tell me you ignore them, too!). Door hinges use an annoying screech to ask for an "oil change." Fortunately, the job is simplicity itself. You'll need an old flat-bladed screwdriver or a long nail, a hammer, penetrating oil if the pin is stuck, and an oil can and rag. Just follow these steps:

1. Examine the hinge. If there's a hole under the pin at the bottom, it's an "anti-rising" hinge—go to step 3. Otherwise, continue here.

A sharp hand plane (left) will work, but a power planer (right) is best for planing doors.

2. For a standard hinge, pound up on the lip of the pin with a screwdriver and hammer. Count on paint damage from this "el crudo" technique. If the pin won't budge, spray it with penetrating oil, swing the door to loosen it, and try again. Try twisting the head of the pin with locking pliers. Once the pin is out, go to step 4. (If the pin refuses to budge, unscrew and replace the entire hinge, oiling it as directed in step 6.)

3. For an "anti-rising" hinge, place a 3" finishing nail in the hole, and pound up with a hammer. The pin will rise slowly, then pop loose.

4. Leave the first pin partly in place, and release the other hinge pins.

5. Remove pins, then remove the door, taking care not to scrunch your fingers.

6. Oil each pin with motor oil, sliding it through a rag. Oil the faces of the hinge that rub against each other; then wipe off extra oil.

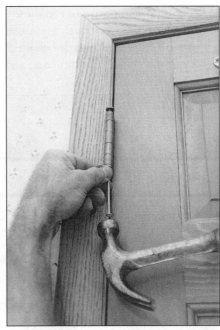

An anti-rising pin comes loose more easily.

7. Place the door in the opening, and start the top pin.

8. Insert other pins and drive them home.

Oiling Door Latches and Locks

Do your keys slip smoothly into your locks, and do the latch and lock mechanisms work freely? Surprise: They're supposed to. If they don't, grab your oil can: Metal doesn't like to meet metal without some lube. To take a latch or lock mechanism apart, you'll need a screwdriver, some motor oil, and a rag. As you take the gizmo apart, study the parts so you can reassemble the blasted thing without leaving too many parts on the table:

1. Start disassembling a latch or lock mechanism by removing the knobs or locks from both sides. First pull the shaft through the door to release the latch or bolt mechanism. The details depend on the type of mechanism:

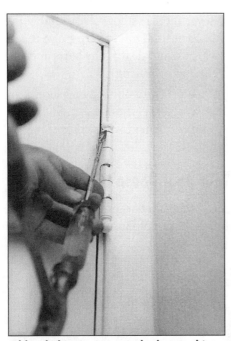

Old-style hinge pins must be battered into submission.

◆ On older doorknobs, loosen the screw on one knob; then unscrew the knob from the threaded shaft. Pull out the remaining knob and shaft.

To release an older-style doorknob, remove this screw, then unscrew the knob from the shaft. (Normally, the shaft would still be running through the door.)

◆ On newer doorknobs, push the tab coming up from inside the knob with a screwdriver while pulling the knob gently, and pull off the knob. The other knob should pull out attached to the shaft.

◆ On some doorknobs, the knob and face plate come off in one piece after you remove two screws from the inside.

◆ For deadbolts and other locks, remove the screws holding the inner faceplate, then pull the lock apart.

◆ On some locks you'll need to unscrew the tumbler assembly. You may need a long hex (Allen) wrench to loosen a set screw inside the mechanism.

2. At the edge of the door, remove any screws holding the latch mechanism and pull it out.

3. Oil all moving parts, turning them occasionally to get the oil between the metal parts. Put some oil on the key and work the lock a few times.

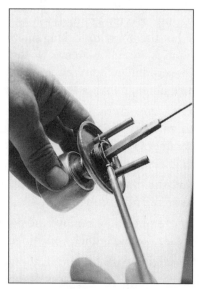

Put motor oil on the moving parts of the door mechanism, and rotate to get oil into the dry spots.

4. Reverse these steps to reassemble the mechanism. Don't overtighten the screws, which could distort the parts and cause binding or seizing.

5. Wipe off extra oil. If wood screws are loose, see suggestions in "My Hinges Are Loose," earlier in this chapter.

So Your Door Doesn't Latch?

Latches often slip because the spring-powered doohickey does not enter the *striker plate* on the jamb:

Fix-It Phrase

A **striker plate**, also called a "strike," is a metal plate in the jamb that holds the latch when a door closes.

◆ The latch is too sticky to move. See "Oiling Door Latches and Locks," earlier.

◆ The latch does not align with the striker plate. Look for off-center scratches on the striker plate. If the latch is slightly off-center, remove the striker plate and place it in a vise for filing. (If you try to move the plate without changing the screw holes, it will return to the same old location when you attach it.) If the striker plate is way out of line, you'll have to move it and cut a new mortise for it.

The latch struck too low on this striker plate, so we're filing on the bottom.

To make this striker plate work again, file some metal at A in the photo. If you have to close the door with a giant shove, you might need to remove metal at B.

◆ The striker plate is resting too deep in the jamb. Unscrew the plate and stick some cardboard shims under it.

◆ The pocket under the striker plate is too shallow, so the latch doohickey can't seat. Remove the plate, and drill and chisel a deeper pocket.

◆ If the latch won't grab without a major shove on the door, but the scratches show that the latch is centered on the striker plate, check for binding as described in "Hinges Too Deep?" earlier in the chapter. If that's not the problem, the door may not be able to close far enough to engage the striker plate. File some metal from the face of the striker plate at B in the previous photo.

Stormy Monday at the Storm Door

Door problems can also afflict the storm door, the lightweight door used to keep cold and mosquitoes out. If the following fixes don't work, it's usually easy to screw a new aluminum storm door to the door trim.

Sagging Storm Door

If the latch side of a wooden screen door is sagging, you've gotta love the screen door straightener—two rods joined by a screw-tightener called a turnbuckle. To use a door straightener:

1. Screw each rod four turns into the turnbuckle. Hold the straightener with one end halfway up the hinge side, and the other at the bottom of the latch side. Drill and start one screw at each end.

2. Drive the other screws and tighten all screws.

To adjust a door straightener, turn the big nut at the center.

3. Tighten the turnbuckle with a wrench until the door swings freely.

Storm Door Operator

Storm door operators are those tubes that slowly close storm doors—at least that's what they are supposed to do. In fact, they let storm doors slam and gouge innocent ankles, or fail to close during the storm of the century.

If the door closes either too fast or too slow, adjust the speed. The operator shown adjusts with a screw. With other operators, you detach one end, turn the tube, and reconnect it.

After years of abuse, a door operator can pull out of the jamb. The easiest repair is to buy a new house. Just kidding. Actually, it's easy to reconnect a door operator to the jamb:

1. Remove the operator and unscrew the jamb bracket. If the damage is all covered by the bracket, skip to step 4.

Adjusting the door operator.

2. Fill the gouged area with wood filler. Use several applications for deep gouges.

3. After the patch hardens, flatten it with a Surform planer or sandpaper. Prime and paint.

4. Hold the bracket ¼" from the door, and level with the closer. Mark the screw holes. Drill pilot holes, then drive 3" screws as Josh T. is doing in the following photo (these screws will grab the stud behind the jamb, making a strong repair).

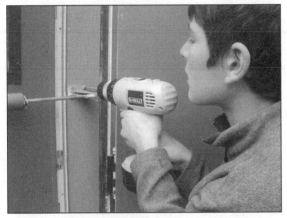

Attaching door-operator bracket.

Adding New Stuff

Let's face it: There are times when a door or its hardware just needs replaced. Warped, undersize, or ugly doors fall into this category, as do funky or worn-out hardware. In this section, I'll describe how to install a deadbolt and replace a door.

Installing a Deadbolt

Feeling insecure at home? At least you have company. The obvious solution is to replace your door locks with deadbolts. You need to work carefully and get some big drill bits. You'll need a screwdriver, hammer, chisel, electric drill (the beefier the better), the bits suggested on the lock package (usually ⅞" and 1½"), and lipstick or toothpaste (seriously!). Some lock-installation kits include a ⅞" spade bit and a

1½" hole saw. As a fringe benefit, the following procedure will also install a doorknob and latch. Here's how to install a deadbolt in a door:

Toolbox Tips

If your door has windows, an intruder can break the glass, reach through and open the deadbolt. I always place a new lock more than an arm's reach from the window in the door. Although these may be awkward to open, they are more secure, which is the whole point, right?

1. Tape the template supplied with the lock to the door. Using the ⅞" bit, bore in from the edge of the door to about 2" depth. Hold the bit square to the door.

Drill first hole from the door edge.

2. Drill a 1½" hole for the handle and latch mechanism. When the bit starts to show through the far side, remove it and finish the hole from the other side to prevent splintering.

Drill a 1½" hole through the side.

3. Slip the lock mechanism in the ⅞" hole and carefully trace its outline on the edge of the door. A utility knife gives a finer mark than a pencil. (Some mechanisms slip directly in the hole and need no chiseling.)

Slip the latch mechanism in the hole and mark.

4. Carefully chisel along the line, deep enough to receive the latch plate. Make the mortise flat, so the latch also seats well.

5. Punch holes for the two screws holding the plate, using a nail or an awl so the drill starts centered in the hole. Drill two holes, then screw the plate tight.

6. Assemble the mechanism per instructions. Make sure the bolt moves smoothly.

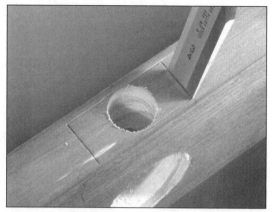

Carefully chisel along the line.

7. Put a blob of toothpaste or lipstick on the end of the bolt, close the door, and turn the bolt to mark the jamb.

8. Carefully position the striker plate over the mark and outline the mortise with a utility knife. Chisel out a mortise for the plate, then drill and chisel a deeper hole for the bolt. Screw the plate into place and test the bolt.

Take your time while positioning the striker plate—this is the only tricky part of the procedure.

Replacing a Door

Like cars, doors can reach a point where, due to damage, wear, or plain ugliness, they simply need replacement. If the existing door fits the opening, use it for a template. Buy a new door, or find an old, *straight* door at an architectural salvage yard. Lay the old door on the new one, and mark carefully, then saw or plane the new one to size. Pay attention to which face is which, and mark the hinge side so you don't get things backward.

If you don't have a door for a template, use this general procedure for marking and cutting the door. As you hang a door, go easy on your cuts—removing more wood is simpler than adding some back! Important: This procedure assumes that angle "A" is square. If your situation is different, adapt the procedure to start in a different corner. For a really screwy opening, don't feel ashamed to hire a carpenter.

To determine if an angle is square, (a) measure the diagonals of the door opening (they are equal in a rectangle), (b) use a square, or (c) use a level.

Doors are sold in feet-and-inches dimensions. Thus the common 32" wide by 80" tall door is called 2'8" by 6'8". Why? It's more complicated, that's why.

A 3° relief on the latch side, cut with a circular saw or plane, allows the door to close, but close enough is perfect enough: You needn't measure the angle.

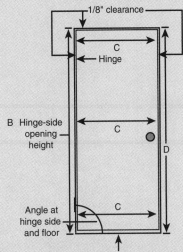

Hanging a door (suggested clearances are for interior doors).

Follow these steps to hang a new door in an existing door opening:

1. Measure the hinge-side opening height, "B." Subtract ⅝" for the top and bottom clearances to get the hinge-side door dimension. Measuring from the door bottom, mark this on the top of the door's hinge side.

2. Measure across the top, middle, and bottom of the door opening, "C." Subtract ¼" and use these measurements to cut the latch side. Set your circular saw for a 3° relief or plane the edge after sawing. Don't cut too much—you can always plane the door later.

   Hollow-core doors are (duh!) hollow. There's only solid wood around the edges—so you shouldn't trim more than about ¼" from any edge.

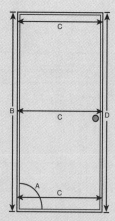

3. Repeat step 2 on the latch side to get the latch-side dimension ("D").

4. Check your measurements, then saw the top and test the door fit. Use a plane (see previous photos) to smooth your cuts and remove extra wood.

5. When the door fits, locate the hinges by matching the pattern in the room, or by using measurements from the following drawing. Mark the hinge location with a utility knife; it's more accurate than a pencil.

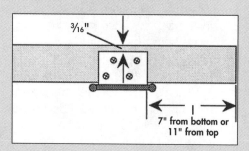

Positioning a door hinge (typical measurements).

6. To cut hinge mortises, see the earlier discussion called "Hinges Too Shallow?"

7. Hold the hinge plate in the mortise and dent the center of each screw hole with a nail. Drill pilot holes into these dents, and fasten the hinge plates.

Drill the hinge screw.

8. Shim the door in position using the top and bottom clearances from the above drawing. Carefully mark the bottom of each hinge on the jamb. Chisel a mortise on the jamb, affix the hinge, and attach the door.

Shim the door into position before attaching hinges to door.

9. Adapt the procedure for "Installing a Deadbolt," to install a door latch.

Weather Stripping

What's the best weather for stripping? A summer thunderstorm, when the cool rain relieves the muggy heat, and neighbors won't notice you splashing around, bare-bunned, in the cloudburst. But the best weather for weather stripping is a midwinter storm. Only then can you appreciate how fast frigid air moves through cracks around doors and windows.

Many varieties of weather stripping are sold these days; do yourself a favor and avoid ugly, ineffective foam tape and felt. Some of the better varieties are illustrated, but in many cases, you'll simply have to replace whatever you find on your door or window.

One of the most versatile weather strips is a V-shape strip of flexible plastic that's glued on one side. Apply the strip" to door and window jambs or stops. You cut it with a knife or scissors.

The gasket threshold (top) makes a good seal, but you may have to remove the existing threshold and/or saw the door to exact height. The vinyl strip compresses into the slot to make a flexible seal against the door bottom. An oak-and-aluminum threshold (bottom) reduces the frost buildup that plagues all-aluminum thresholds.

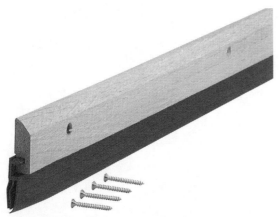

This vinyl door sweep, mounted to an oak trim strip, prevents wind and rain from gusting below your door.

The Least You Need to Know

◆ If humidity is jamming your windows, fight back with cleaning and carefully planing or sanding.

◆ Opening a window that's painted shut requires patience and a light touch.

◆ You can save big money, and look like a real hero, by replacing broken panes.

◆ Doors stick for a lot of reasons, few of which are serious enough to daunt an eager homeowner.

◆ Deadbolts are easy to install, although you may have to buy some jumbo drill bits.

◆ Balky door latches may call for some improvising, but you can usually revive or replace them.

In This Chapter

- ◆ Fixing talkative floors
- ◆ Replacing subfloors and floorboards
- ◆ Strengthening and raising sagging floors
- ◆ Sanding and refinishing floors

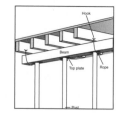

Chapter 7

Feet First on Fine Floors

If you got stomped on half as much as a floor, you'd be protesting too. Floors protest by talking back. In my house, the insubordination is worst in the kitchen, where the human equivalent of Hannibal's elephant-mounted army trudges past each day. And there's nothing I can do about it, because I stupidly had a parquet floor laid over the squeak before I "got around" to fixing it.

There's a lesson here: Fix problems, don't cover them up. Before a new carpet was laid over old linoleum in my bedroom, I renailed the floor to the floor joists. And that floor is quiet as a mummy. In this chapter, I will discuss cures for some of the most common flooring woes. We'll go from annihilating squeaks to fixing floor joists, repairing subfloors, repairing strip flooring, and refinishing wood floors. (For information on fixing tile, see Chapter 8.)

Squeakproofing Your Floors

Squeaks occur when wood rubs against wood or nails, in a floor that has loosened due to structural settling, poor carpentry, or alternating wet and dry weather. Squeaks are easiest to silence from underneath.

Working from Below

Use one of two techniques to cure floor squeaks from below:

1. Drill holes for a series of big wood screws that are ¼'' shorter than the combined thickness of the *finish floor* and *subfloor*. Floors and subfloors are usually each ¾'' thick. In this case, your drill should penetrate 1¼''. Put masking tape around your drill bit at this

point, so you'll know when you've drilled far enough. Ask a weighty go-fer to stand on the floor while you tighten the screws to bring the finish floor tight to the sub-floor. Use plenty of screws, and tighten gradually. Stop before you *strip* the holes.

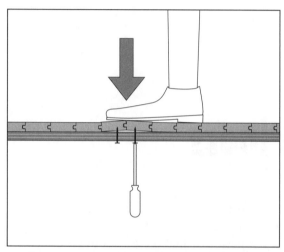

When repairing a squeaky floor from below, hold the board down and don't strip the screws. Be reasonable—the goal is silence, not punishment.

Fix-It Phrase

Finish floor is what's visible in a finished room (the logic, the logic!). **Subfloor** is the bottom layer of flooring wood. In fairly new houses, it's plywood or something similar. In older houses, it's ¾" lumber. You **strip** a screw hole when you tighten too hard. A stripped screw slips because it has enlarged the hole too much. A **floor joist** is a support member beneath the floor. Traditionally, they were 2×8s or larger. In new houses, various kinds of manufactured wood joists are often used instead.

2. The second method is to tap glue-coated shims into the gap between the *floor joist* and the floor. Don't use a sledgehammer—there's no point in raising the board any farther.

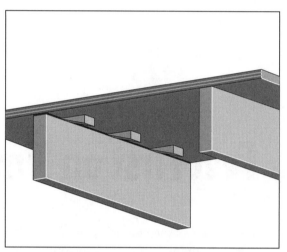

Shims underneath prevent the floor from moving—but use a light touch. Tap the shims into place.

Working from Above

If you can't work from below without tearing apart something important, like a ceiling, your first move will be to find the joists:

◆ If you don't care about the finish floor (maybe it's just particle board that you plan to cover with new carpet), locate a joist by drilling through the floor until you hit solid wood.

◆ Drill one hole and probe with a coat hanger.

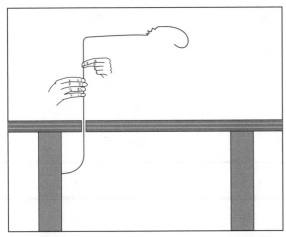

Find the joist by drilling and probing with a coat hanger.

- Pound on the floor; when the noise turns solid, you're likely to be near a joist.
- Take up some old floor covering and look for nails.
- Look inside a floor register for nails securing the floor to the joists.

Once you find one joist, the others should be parallel to it, at 16" (in rare cases, 12") *on center*.

Fix-It Phrase

On center, or OC, describes the spacing of repeated structural components. An extremely common spacing for studs and joists is 16" OC; 24" OC is common in rafters.

To fix a squeak from above:

1. Drill diagonal pilot holes and hammer long casing nails into a joist.

2. To tame a bad squeak, drive 2½" spiral flooring nails or 3" trim screws (see Chapter 5) diagonally into the joists—you need to grab more than just subfloor. Before screwing, it may help to pour a puddle of wood glue into the pilot hole.

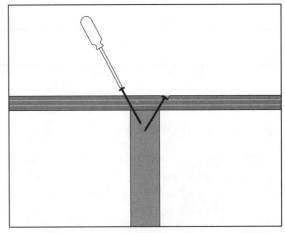

Wood screws—especially long trim screws—are much stronger than nails, but you'll need to hide a slightly bigger head with wood filler afterward.

3. When done, fill the screw or nail holes with wood filler, sand and finish (see Chapter 10).

Floor Framing Fixes

A bouncy spot in a floor can be due to a cracked, rotted, or just-plain-weak floor joist. It may be due to a weak beam supporting a series of joists. If a joist problem is local, splice a pair of joists to the outside of the wounded joist. If the splices are not connected to a supporting wall or beam, they should extend at least 18" past the damage. (The longer the splice, the better—but a longer splice is more likely to hit wires, pipes, or heat ducts.)

If the weakness is widespread, you may have undersize joists, and you're out of DIY-land. Time to call in a pro!

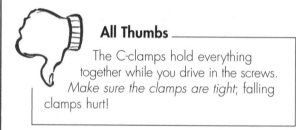

All Thumbs

If electric wires, plumbing, or air ducts must be rerouted before you can double a joist, the degree of difficulty immediately escalates. If you're intimidated by wiring or plumbing, call for expert help.

Joining Joists

Here's how to reinforce a joist:

1. Saw the *sister*—doubler—joists from the same size wood used in the original joists. Drill three rows of pilot holes, spaced 12" apart in each row.

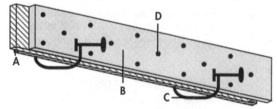

Take the sag out of a joist with this heavy-duty splice.

A. The weak joist is sandwiched between new joists.
B. The doubler joists should be the same material as the original joist.
C. The C-clamps hold everything together while you drive in the screws.
D. Space the screws 12" apart in 3 rows.

2. Apply lines of construction glue to one side of the damaged joist and clamp a sister joist into place.

3. Temporarily shore up the center of the weak joist with a jack post (see the following drawing). Extend the jack post, but see the warning in the following section about raising the floor too much.

4. Drive beefy 2½" construction screws into the pilot holes from step 1.

5. Remove the clamps and repeat these steps to fasten the second sister joist. Remove the clamps and post.

All Thumbs

The C-clamps hold everything together while you drive in the screws. *Make sure the clamps are tight;* falling clamps hurt!

Beam-Me-Up: Fixing a Weak Floor Beam

If the floor is sagging or bouncy, you may get away by simply supporting an existing beam with an adjustable steel jack post. (A beam is a heavy member that supports floor joists and runs perpendicular to them. Beams are typically found along the centerline of a house.) However, in many cases, you'll need to add a beam.

One jack post may be enough under a 3' beam. For longer beams, place a post every 4' to 6':

1. Adjust the jack post to the proper length. Support the post on a strong concrete floor, or on a 4" solid concrete block. To support a very heavy load, you may need to pour a concrete footing—about 18" square by 8" high.

2. Using a level to hold the post plumb (vertical), screw the upper plate into the beam.

3. Snug up the post, then tighten it ⅛ turn every couple of days. Don't shock your house with sudden moves! Watch the floors above—if the plaster starts cracking, or windows or doors start binding, back off. The post is mainly designed to stop the decline, not to undo 50 years of settling.

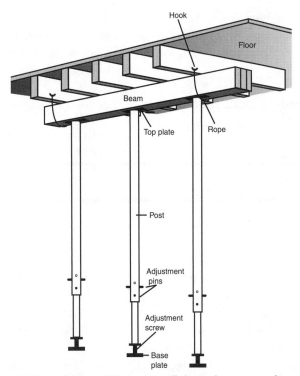

To prevent the beam from falling while you install the jack post, (a) place temporary 2×4 posts at each end; (b) tie a rope to one substantial hook screwed into a joist at one end, position the beam, and tie it to a second hook; or (c) find slaves to hold each end while you work. Slaves are probably most trustworthy, but whatever technique you use, make sure you don't wind up with a beam falling on your head!

If a group of joists is sagging, you may need a new beam. As a rule of thumb, a triple thick beam is a strong beam. To assemble the beam, see "Joining Joists," earlier in this chapter. Let the glue dry for two hours before installing it. You can screw diagonally through the beam into the joists, using 3" construction screws.

All Thumbs

Replacement beams and jack posts are both heavy and awkward. *Don't trust the post to support the beam during installation.* Get help from willing accomplices and/or use the ropes or 2×4s shown in the drawing. *Toe nails will not support a beam during assembly.* I'd suggest getting a helper to hold a 2×4 brace until the job is done.

Stepping Stones to Silent Stairs

In older houses, the squeaks seem to concentrate on the stairs. Most people want to fix them, but not my in-laws, who realized that their horribly squeaky stairs made a perfect alarm for signaling the after-hours return of the elegant teenager I later married. If you don't need to monitor errant, elegant youths, there are several ways to silence squeaky stairs.

Many of these fixes reflect the same techniques you've seen for fixing freaky floors:

◆ Drill pilot holes and drive long trim screws through the *treads* into the *risers*. Drill diagonally near the end of the tread into the *stringers*. Drill a countersink (recess) for the screw head and fill with wood filler.

Fix-It Phrase

Treads are the horizontal boards you walk (tread) on. **Risers** are the vertical boards that rise between two treads. **Stringers,** the slanting framing lumber at each side that support the stairway, are almost always covered by trim wood.

◆ If you have access from below, coat two sides of a 1×3 with wood glue or construction adhesive, and screw it to the risers and treads, where they meet at the side of the stairway. Drill pilot holes and, while somebody stands on the tread, screw from below. Use large-diameter screws, but make sure they do not poke through the tread!

◆ Pull off the molding (see Chapter 10) between a tread and a riser (if it's present) and insert glue-coated wedges in the gaps. When the glue is dry, remove the visible part of the wedges with a wood chisel or utility knife, then replace the molding.

Wood Subfloor Repair

You may need to patch your subfloor due to rot or the removal of an old floor register. The subfloor under a wood floor is usually ¾" boards, plywood or the equivalent. Subfloor under a ceramic tile floor may be some kind of sheet concrete material. A house built on a concrete slab may have no subfloor. Or you may see rigid insulation under the finish floor.

To patch or repair a wood subfloor, you'll need a variable-speed drill, jig saw or keyhole saw, boards or plywood as thick as the subfloor, 2×4 blocking, construction adhesive or wood glue, and construction screws (1½" and 3"). Then follow these steps:

1. Remove finish flooring wider than the damaged area. To take up strip flooring, see "Replacing Strip Flooring," later in this chapter.

2. Mark a rectangular cutout around the damaged area (if you're repairing a hole left by a floor register, skip this step). Drill starter holes for the jig saw blade near the joist, and insert the blade. I cut toward the joist, and when the saw hit heavy resistance, I knew it had hit the joist. That's where I marked the cut line.

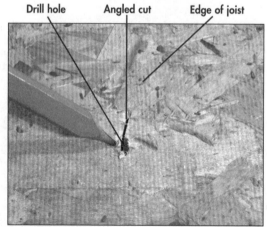

Drill hole   Angled cut   Edge of joist

Finding the joist with a drill.

3. Saw out the remaining subfloor. Saw alongside the joists, and then between the joists, to make a rectangular hole. Renail adjacent subfloor to the joists if it's loose.

This example shows a subfloor with no finish floor. You'll use these techniques after you've gotten through the finish floor, as described next. To cut smoothly across staggered remnants of strip flooring (not shown), rest the jig saw on a piece of plywood.

4. Saw 2×4 blocks to support the patch at each joist. The blocks should extend 3" beyond each edge of the hole, if there's room. Coat one side of the block with glue and screw it to the joist. Hold the block tight to the bottom of the existing subfloor, so it's at the right height.

Screwing nailers to the joist.

5. Cut a piece of subfloor to size. Put glue on top of the blocks you just screwed into place, and screw the subfloor patch down. Drive the screws deep enough so the heads lie flush to the subfloor; you may have to countersink to accomplish this.

Sears sells the neat two-in-one bit I'm using in this photo. First, the bit cuts a countersink. Then, it drives the screw into the countersink. A real timesaver if you drive lots of screws.

6. If there's a gap around the repair, carpet, vinyl tile, or linoleum may settle into it. Squish floor filler into the cavity, following directions on the package. Be warned—this stuff will not adhere if the floor is loose and shifting. That's one reason your patch must be solid to begin with.

Replacing Strip Flooring

Let's say you want to replace damaged or stained *strip flooring*. You'll need replacement floorboards. The size of strip flooring has long been standardized—¾" thick by 2¼" wide, but if you can't find what you need at a lumberyard, contact somebody who salvages old buildings. Measure the flooring carefully and try to identify the wood species. It's best to bring a piece of flooring to the store. (Having said all this, the size of the tongues and grooves may vary, forcing you to do some fancy carpentry, as we found while making the repair you see in the next figure.)

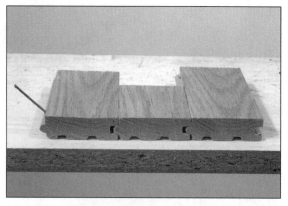

End view of tongue-and-groove flooring, showing nail placement.

On square-edge flooring, you can usually see the nails or screws (or the plugs or fillers concealing them). Square-edge is easy to repair, because you can find the fasteners, and it's easier to remove boards without disturbing adjacent ones. Tongue-and-groove is hard to repair, because the boards are keyed together at the sides and ends. A good patch will emulate the "staggered joints" in your existing floor (the end joints are randomly placed, not lined up).

To avoid gaps due to wood drying and shrinking, keep replacement boards indoors at least 24 hours. Don't work in humid weather, because the slightly swollen boards may resist going into position.

All Thumbs

Strip flooring is narrow boards nailed individually to the subfloor. A newer product that looks like strip flooring is actually plywood with a hardwood veneer. You can recognize this stuff because it looks perfect—there are no gaps between the boards. The repair technique listed here will not work on this material.

Wood flooring is made with square (flat) edges, or more commonly with tongue-and-groove (T&G) edges, which key together to make a very strong floor. Hardwood (oak or maple) flooring is generally tongue-and-groove. T&G is "blind-nailed" through the tongue—you won't see the nails when the floor is completed.

How to Fix Strip Flooring

To fix strip flooring, you'll need a circular saw, a square, prybar, wood chisel, hammer, nail set, drill, nails, and replacement flooring. I found the RotoZip tool to be extremely useful for the difficult cross-cuts needed for an invisible repair. For a really large repair, you might want to rent a flooring nailer (shown later in the chapter), which holds the boards tight while it blind nails them. If the nails don't grab the subfloor very well, remove any paper from the subfloor and squirt on carpenter's glue (it's cheap when bought by the gallon) before nailing the finish floor.

Follow these steps to fix strip flooring:

1. Eyeball the repair. The goal is to remove the minimum number of boards, but leave the same staggered pattern you see in the rest of the floor. Remove good boards that end within 2' of the damaged area, so the new boards can "key" into the old floor.

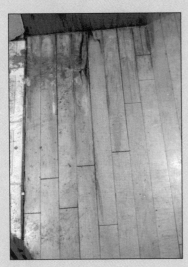

This strip flooring needs serious repair.

2. Instead of removing longer pieces, cross-cut them to limit the overall size of the repair. Cross-cuts are cut at 90° to the grain—across the short dimension of a board. The highlight color shows where I'll be cross-cutting for this repair. Cross-cutting is the toughest part of the procedure, and by far the best tool among many I've tried is the RotoZip. I had an assistant stand on the big square, to give me a good guide for the cut. I cut twice. The first cut went halfway through the board, and the second cut finished the job. A second-best alternative is to use a jig saw and a fine-tooth blade. Break the blade so it cuts only as deep as the finish floor. Drill a pilot hole for the blade, and run it along a square as I did with the RotoZip. Use a chisel to cut where the blade does not reach. In any case, don't butcher good boards around the repair.

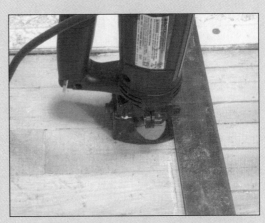

Strip floor being cut with RotoZip tool.

3. If your flooring is buried by a cabinet, remove the base from the RotoZip and freehand cut along the cabinet. If you confront this problem, you definitely ought to consider investing in a RotoZip—no other tool will even come close to this cut. The only real alternative, if you have the time and patience, is some serious chiseling ...

Cutting the corner with a RotoZip.

4. Rip-saw down the middle of several of the longest boards in the repair with the circular saw. If your floor is face nailed, just stay away from the nails. Face nails are visible, because they go through the face of the board. If it's blind nailed, the nails should go through the tongue, so you won't wreck the saw blade by cutting down the center. Blind nails are invisible, because they go through the tongue of the board. Set the saw shallow enough to graze the subfloor. Cut close to the cross-cuts made in step 2, but don't cut good boards. The highlight color shows

which boards I'll be rip-sawing.
Parallel cuts allow you to remove damaged boards.

5. Force a prybar into a rip-saw cut, and pry out the board. Continue prying, taking care not to damage boards you'll be leaving. Remember: Old wood can

be fragile and prone to splitting.
After the parallel cuts are made, pry out the damaged boards.

6. Remove the rest of the damage (ripsaw more boards if needed), and pull all

nails.
With more prying, the damaged area is almost out.

Removing the damage takes more work than replacing the boards. At this point, you're

more than halfway home.

7. Start replacing flooring at the side of the repair where the tongue shows. Lay in a piece of new flooring so its groove swallows that tongue. Carefully mark the other end and saw it, preferably with a power or hand miter box.

8. Matching the pattern around the repair, blind or face nail the strips into position. To blind-nail with a flooring nailer, follow the directions for the unit. To blind nail by hand, drill each tongue diagonally. Hammer the nail most of the way into place, and complete the job with a nail set. Keep the joints tight as you nail, using a rubber mallet or by pounding a scrap block of wood with a hammer. This is especially important when face nailing; blind nailing tends to

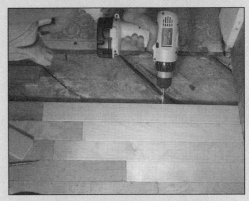

tighten the joints.
It's almost impossible to nail maple or oak

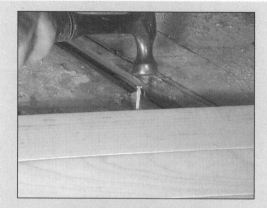

flooring without drilling first. Use a bit that's slightly smaller than the nails.

Don't be a fool—stop nailing with ¼" standing out from the board, and use a nail set from there.

If you have a lot of floor to repair, consider renting a flooring nailer. *(Photo by Porta-Nails Inc.)*

9. Saw or chisel the bottom of the groove from the last board, slip it into place, and face-nail (nail vertically—leaving the nailheads visible). If you're cagey,

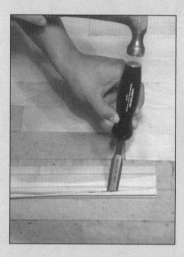

you can nail in a place that will be covered by baseboard or base shoe. Fill and stain the nail holes.

Chisel bottom of groove and remove it.

10. Sand the entire floor.

Here's the completed patch. After a good floor sanding, it will be invisible.

Super Sanding Techniques

Once in a while, wood floors like to suffer the punishment of sanding. Sanding flattens the floor and prepares it for staining or varnishing, which I'll cover in the next section. Although floor sanding looks easy, it's not for everyone. The key problem is that you can gouge the floor by contacting a rotating but stationary sander with the floor. A floor sander can cause a lot of damage in very short order if it's running at high RPMs, a problem that particularly affects variable-speed sanders.

You may need these tools to sand a floor:

◆ A *belt* or *drum* sander rotates a wide piece of sandpaper on the floor. Few rental

shops handle belt sanders, so we'll focus on drum sanders, which remove wood with a rotating, cylindrical drum that's covered with abrasive. This is your main tool, used everywhere except at the edges.

A drum sander covers the main part of the floor. Sand parallel to the grain. *(Photo by Essex Silver-Line Corporation)*

◆ Sand the edges with a disk sander, a heavy-duty version of an orbital sander.
A disk sander cuts around the edges. *(Photo by Essex Silver-Line Corporation)*

◆ To simply remove old finish (not stain or wood), rent an *orbiting pad sander* or a *floor polishing machine*. These machines can also clean up after the heavy artillery—

Toolbox Tips

If you rent on Saturday morning, you may get the machine until Monday for the price of a one-day rental.

the drum sander. A polisher is also useful between coats of finish.

◆ A *hand scraper* can remove finish in corners, where neither sander will reach. It can also remove localized gouges.

The general routine for floor sanding is to

move a drum sander with the grain over the main area of the floor—in other words, wherever it can reach. Then work around the edges with the disk sander. Change sandpaper in unison on the sanders: Start with coarse paper, and work toward finer grits.

Observe these do's and don'ts of floor sanding (see more details online at www.nofma.org/finishing.htm):

◆ Do protect yourself and the rest of the house from dust (see Chapter 2).

◆ Do remove base shoe and baseboard, to avoid leaving a line with the disk sander (see "Yanking up Molding" in Chapter 10).

◆ Don't sand if the floor is thinner than ½" (look inside a heat register to gauge its thickness), or lots of nail heads are showing. Either condition indicates that the floor has been sanded enough. Also, use extreme caution sanding prefinished flooring—you may go right through the thin veneer on this stuff.

◆ Don't *ever* put a running sander down unless you're moving it across the floor—this leaves gouges.

◆ Do move the sander at a steady pace across the floor. At the end of the pass, ease the sander up from the floor before stopping.

◆ Do each pass twice—lift the sander as you reach the wall, start moving backward, and lower the sander. Move sideways (with the sander off the floor) at the middle of the room.

◆ Do start with the least aggressive grit that will level the floor and remove the finish. A good starting point might be 20 grit.

◆ Do work your way down through the grits—through 40, 60, and 100 (on both sanders). If you skip too many grits, the finer paper won't remove rough marks left

Toolbox Tips _____

It's usually best to sand with the grain. If the boards are cupped (warped in a concave fashion), diagonal sanding on the first and possibly second pass is more effective for flattening. Diagonal sanding is also useful with parquet flooring, but start with a finer abrasive.

by the coarser grade.

◆ Do consider renting a floor polisher. This light-duty sander (either orbital or rotary) removes the last traces left by the other sanders.

◆ Don't let the abrasive get clogged—that can burn bare wood. Change abrasive when needed.

◆ Do hold a light close to the floor and look for odd reflections left by imperfect sanding. Blemishes that are invisible during sanding can become painfully obvious after staining.

◆ Do scrape with a sharp chisel or wood scraper in the corners, where the disk sander won't reach.

Finishing Up

Once you've finished the onerous task of sanding, you come to the more delightful stage of staining and varnishing. Vacuum the room thoroughly, paying attention to window sills and other dust catchers. Rub the floor down with a tack cloth (a rag dampened with mineral spirits).

It's best to stain and/or varnish immediately after the dust settles, before the floor can be damaged. The choice of whether to use a stain is strictly aesthetic. A homeowner can get hung up on stain color, and for good reason. Floors are a major element in a room's overall color scheme. Test stain colors on a scrap of the same species of flooring. Paint stores can mix stains if you don't like any of the premixed stains.

One option is to use penetrating oil, sometimes called Danish oil finish. These oils sink nicely into the wood and display the grain most handsomely, so long as you protect the surface with paste wax.

Most do-it-yourselfers protect floors with polyurethane varnish, which comes in various levels of gloss. "Poly" is best applied with a

All Thumbs

After the first coat of varnish is dry, be sure to lightly sand the floor with extra-fine sandpaper to remove bubbles. Vacuum and tack-cloth the surface again to remove dust before recoating with varnish.

wide brush or a paint pad—a roller will leave hideous bubbles. Read the can before mucking around with polyurethane or any other floor finish. In some cases, you must recoat within a certain time period, or the finish will become

so hard that the varnish won't stick to itself.

Use adequate ventilation; consider using an organic solvent respirator for close quarters (see Chapter 2). The fumes—combined with the nasty solvent cleanup—are more good reasons to consider water-based poly varnish. You might need more coats, but they apply faster because the varnish dries faster, and that means less dust gets trapped in the finish. Although a waterborne finish has less resistance to heat and chemicals than a solvent-based one, they are about equal in terms of all-important scratch resistance.

Because many varnishes get stronger with age, delay walking on your beautiful new floor for a few days, if possible.

The Least You Need to Know

- ◆ Some floor squeaks are easy to silence, especially if you have access to the bottom side of the floor.
- ◆ Patching subfloor is fast and easy.
- ◆ You can make a seamless patch in tongue-and-groove flooring if you know how it's put together, and work patiently with the right tools.
- ◆ Floor sanding requires a few tricks, but

In This Chapter

- ◆ Recaulking bathroom tiles and fixtures
- ◆ Drilling ceramic tile
- ◆ Repairing ceramic tile
- ◆ Cutting tile

Chapter 8

Tile in Style!

Take it from the Romans: Ceramic tiles are a dynamite material for floors and walls. Independent, flinty, and waterproof, tiles are the ultimate in durable, cleanable surfaces, ideal for bathrooms and kitchens.

But like every other part of a house, tiles occasionally need first aid. Sooner or later, almost everybody confronts the need to replace caulking around a bathtub or sink. Maybe your ceramic tile is broken, or the grout is disintegrating. Perhaps you need to install a grab bar in the shower. All these repairs require some familiarity with tile. And while tiling can call for some special tools, many of the hand tools are cheap, and you can rent a power saw for major projects. Ready to get started?

Caulking the Lines

One of the best ways to keep ceramic tile happy is to keep it dry. If the caulking around a tub enclosure, sink, or tiled corner is coming loose:

1. Cut away the caulking with a utility knife. Change the blade often to keep it sharp, and hold it as close to the tile as possible.

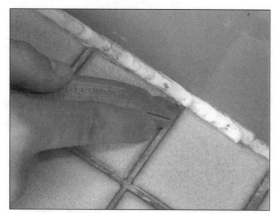

Cut away old caulking with a utility knife.

2. Use a window scraper, scouring powder, or rubbing alcohol to finish cleaning the surfaces.

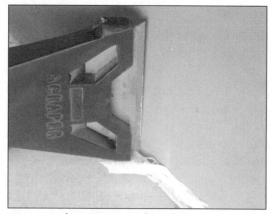

Use a window scraper and/or cleanser to remove the last traces of caulk.

3. Caulk with a good silicone tub-and-tile caulk. To caulk a small crack, cut a small opening in the tube, making a narrow line of caulking.

Toolbox Tips

Buy colored caulk to harmonize with gray, black, or colored tile. The standard, bright-white caulking can look hideous against a subdued tile color.

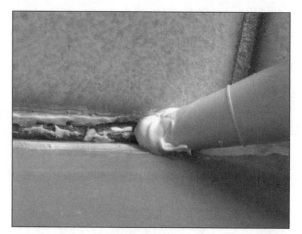

Apply caulk carefully, working forward if possible.

Fastening to Ceramic Tile

Some things you may want to attach to ceramic tile, like towel bars, can be glued in place. But you've got to screw safety or grab bars to the studs in a tub or shower. Start by finding the studs (see Chapter 9). When you buy the grab bar, get a tile drill bit large enough for the screws that come with it. If your tile is set on a thick *substrate*, use long deck screws; they're strong and rust-resistant.

Fix-It Phrase

Substrate is tile-ese for the backing material that supports the tile.

When drilling the tile, switch to a wood bit once you get through the substrate. The screws will drive easier if you put dry hand soap on the threads.

Drill ceramic tile with a special bit.

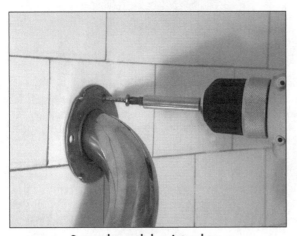

Screw the grab bar into place.

Tile Repair

Ceramic tiles are inflexible, and flaws in the substrate will cause them to break or fall off. If the underside of a floor is accessible, see the floor-strengthening techniques in Chapter 7. You can stiffen a wall by ripping off the tiles and substrate and doubling up the studs—definitely a job for an experienced home fixer. If you can't firm up the surface, call a pro before repairing the tile.

Toolbox Tips

To make an invisible tile repair, you must get hold of matching replacement tiles. With luck, you'll find some stashed in a basement, attic, or garage. Otherwise, a tile store may have a reasonable match. Matching the grout (the stuff that fills the gap between tiles) should be easier—good tile stores stock plenty of colors.

If you've neglected the grout or ignored the caulking in a tub enclosure, the tiles may be sliding off your waterlogged walls. Once water loosens the tiles, you have two choices. You can sell the house. Or you can remove the tiles, repair the wall, and reset the tiles.

To replace rotten drywall or plaster in a tub enclosure:

1. Remove all tiles from a rectangular area with a stud at each end (generally, the entire lower part of a tub enclosure will be rotten). Be thorough—the idea is to repair everything the first time.

2. Soak the tiles in water and scrape off the adhesive to make room for new adhesive. Use a solvent if necessary.

3. Replace the rotten plaster with a waterproof cement-based backing board (such as Durock or Wonderboard brand). Follow the instructions on "Cutting Back to the Studs and Starting Over" in Chapter 9. Then proceed with the suggestions for "Replacing Ceramic Tiles."

Replacing Ceramic Tiles

If you're dreading a tile repair, you're not alone. But if you have access to replacement tiles and work cautiously, the job is usually pretty simple. First you have to remove the old tiles.

or you'll loosen too many tiles, and curse the day you read these instructions.

The "before" shot. Photographer's assistant Alex T. practices anger management on our photo prop. The result is the kind of cracking that you might see after somebody drops something heavy (like a hammer?) on a floor tile.

Once you've broken the tiles, follow these steps:

1. Carefully remove all broken tiles (wear goggles). To protect good tiles surrounding the repair from damage, saw the grout with a fiberglass-reinforced blade designed to cut brick—*not* with a regular wood blade. You may have to cut an "X" shape in the damaged tile to facilitate removal. If you don't have a circular saw, use a hammer and a metal or stone-cutting chisel. Work cautiously,

The saw is set to cut just through the tile—about ⅜" deep. Notice the toothless, abrasive blade—it's designed to cut masonry.

Sawing removes grout around the damaged tile.

2. Clean out mortar or tile adhesive. (Mortar is a cement material holding the tile to the substrate; some tile is secured by a chemical adhesive instead.) Don't pull up—that could loosen adjacent tiles.

Clean out mortar or tile adhesive.

3. When all the old grout and tile mortar are removed, place the new tiles (or old ones that survived the removal) in position. The tiles must rest a little below the surface, leaving room for mortar or adhesive.

4. If you need to cut tile, see the next section, "Cutting Ceramic Tile."

5. Select a ceramic tile cement or mortar according to the instructions on the package. Use waterproof adhesive on countertops and tub enclosures. Apply the cement or mortar with the correct notched trowel (again, read the package). The notching allows the tile to settle a bit into the mortar.

Use a notched trowel to apply cement or mortar.

6. Notice that we've protected nearby tiles with masking tape. Using even pressure, embed replacement tiles. Tap them down with a trowel handle or hunk of wood until they are flush to the floor. Check flushness with a level or straightedge.

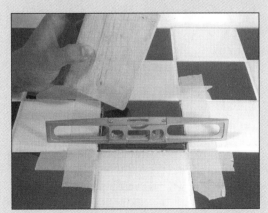

Tap new tile until it's flush with the others.

7. Carefully clean out mortar from the joint with a screwdriver, then a damp rag, and allow the mortar to set.

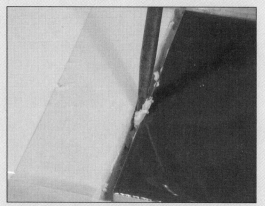

Clean and remove excess mortar with a screwdriver.

8. Mix grout. To push it into the joints, either hold the grout on one trowel and push it in with another (see photo) or push the grout in with a rubber grout squeegee, a rubber float, or a damp sponge. With the second method, smear the grout diagonally to fill all the joints evenly. The new grout is highlighted in the photo for clarity.

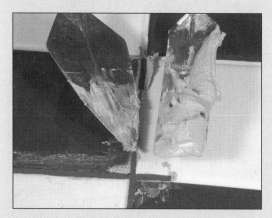

To apply grout, this two-trowel method works great.

9. Remove the masking tape and compress grout with the trowel. Make sure the joints are full.

Compress the grout with the trowel.

10. Strike (shape) the joint with a piece of wood that you've carved with the right profile. I whittled the end of a carpenter's pencil with a utility knife. Why a carpenter's pencil? Because it happened to be handy.

Shape the joint before the grout sets too hard.

11. Brush tiles diagonally with a coarse brush to remove extra grout. Don't gouge grout from the joints.

Brush tile to remove extra grout.

12. Wipe tiles with damp rag or sponge, cleaned occasionally in water. Wipe periodically until the tiles are clean and the joints are uniform. If necessary, use a grout remover to clean any haze left on tiles.

13. If desired, apply a silicon grout sealer to protect against staining. The container will tell you how long the grout must set before treatment.

Tile repair calls for some judgment calls. Around the edges of the repair, you may find tiles that shift just slightly. If you have large areas like this, my advice is to leave these tiles alone. Otherwise, a small repair can spiral out of control.

The toughest part of replacing tiles is getting the level right. Don't press down too fast or too hard, or you'll have to remove and remortar the tile. Using a notched trowel gives the mortar some "give" so you can press them down far enough.

Cutting Ceramic Tile

You bought ceramic tiles because they are so indestructible. But when you lugged them home, you realized that they are also impossible to cut. How can you trim them to size?

Straight Cuts

Tile cutters come in two varieties—hand cutters and power saws. A hand cutter scores the tile and breaks it along a straight line. This tool works, but I'd buy extra tile to allow for breakage while you learn. And your cuts will be a bit more jagged than cuts made with a wet saw, described next.

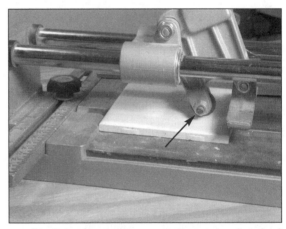

Set the tile in position. Score once by running the wheel (arrow) away from you while pushing down firmly.

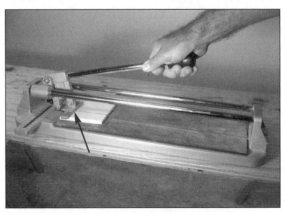

Without moving the tile, put the flat plate (arrow) into position above the tile and press down.

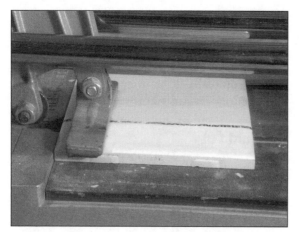

This close-up shows the tile broken exactly where it was scored by the cutter wheel.

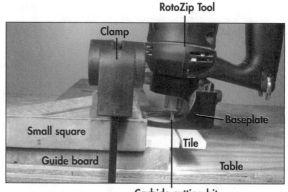

Making a straight cut with a RotoZip tool.

Far more effective (and expensive) is the wet saw. You don't need to buy one of these beauties, but they are handy to rent for a big or complicated tile job. The circular, diamond-impregnated blade is water cooled, and it can cut tile and stone. It will also spray tile soup out the back, so it's best used outdoors. Place the tile on the sliding tray and move it through the saw blade. A wet saw can trim ⅛" from a tile—something you can't do with a hand cutter. Most will cut tile at an angle, and some at a bevel.

A versatile tool called the RotoZip can also cut wall tile (floor tile is usually too hard to cut). RotoZips use a bit that resembles a drill bit, except that it also cuts on the side, which explains why it's called a spiral saw. Press down, work slowly, get good support under the tile, and read the instructions. If you clamp a straight guide board to the tile, as I've done, leave the clamp loose enough to avoid breaking the tile. And do wear ear protection—this baby shrieks!

Curved Cuts

A wet saw will also make crude curves. Make a series of parallel cuts through the area to be removed, and then break off the scrap with long-nose pliers or tile nippers.

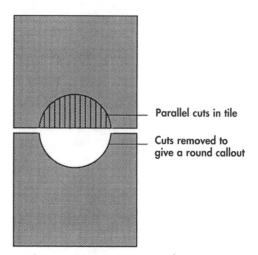

One way to cut a curve in tile.

The RotoZip is ideal for cutting curves in tile. To start the cut, simply push down at an angle through the tile (this is called a "plunge cut"), then follow your guideline.

A better way to make a circular cut in soft tile.

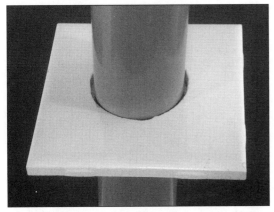

Any irregularity in this freehand cut will be hidden by caulking.

Scribing: A Quick Trick for Fitting Tiles

I cut my teeth in home repair on an 1854 farmhouse, where the peculiar geometry reflected a serious shortage of levels and squares. I wish I'd known a superb method for working with irregular surfaces called "scribing." You can scribe to mark cuts in tiles that touch an unsquare wall. You can scribe to fit baseboard against a sagging floor, or in countless other finishing touches in a house not burdened by right angles.

In this example, our young assistant is marking a floor tile to fit along a wall that is not parallel to the tiles. He's using a compass, or divider, a grade-school gadget normally used to draw circles.

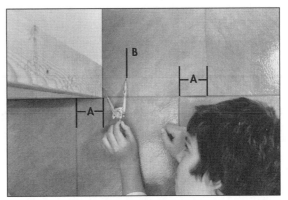

Fitting an irregular tile.

1. Push the tile as far against the wall as it can go, while holding it square to the tile pattern (in other words, don't let it rotate).
2. Set the divider equal to the overlap of the new tile on the tile beneath it. You can take this measurement, "A," at two locations; it is the amount you will remove from the tile.
3. Without moving the tile or changing the divider setting, scribe the line "B" as Alex is doing in the photo. The point of the compass touches the baseboard, and the compass stays perpendicular to the wall.
4. Cut along this line.

The Least You Need to Know

- ◆ Ceramic tile is easy to drill.
- ◆ A successful tiling job depends on good surface preparation.
- ◆ Tile is easy to lay on a flat, rectangular surface—with the right tools and techniques.
- ◆ The key to tile repair is removing all loose and damaged tile, without loosening good tiles.

In This Chapter

- ◆ Choosing the right materials is half the battle
- ◆ The seven commandments of wall repair
- ◆ Fixing damaged drywall and plaster
- ◆ Finding a stud
- ◆ Hanging and finishing drywall

Chapter 9

Flatland Revisited: Drywall and Plaster Repair

I am a recovering plasterer, and it's been a long time since I felt the insane urge to grab a plastering trowel and smear a heavy, abrasive glop on the walls—the very thought, in fact, puts a twinge in my shoulder. No wonder they invented drywall—it's faster, easier, and cheaper than plaster, and nobody seems to mind that it's not as hard or durable. I bet even the plasterers who have been pushed out of business are kinda grateful for drywall …

Still, no matter what they are made of, walls attract their share of drywall diseases and plaster pathology. In the course of making innumerable plaster and drywall repairs, I learned the tricks of the trade. And I am eager to pass them along, if only so you won't think about calling *me* to fix your walls! But I've got good news for your wailing walls: As long as the wall isn't actively shifting, almost any flaw in plaster or drywall can be fixed.

Meet Plaster and Drywall

Plaster and drywall are the two standard materials for interior walls. Both are made of ground-up gypsum rock with various additives. Plaster is troweled on as a stiff goop that sets rock hard. Drywall is softer stuff sandwiched between heavy paper and sold in sheets that are cut and fastened into place.

Most drywall is ½'' thick; although the ⅝'' sheets used in high-class construction are stronger and quieter. The sheets are 4' wide by 8', 9', 10', or 12' (oh boy, that's heavy!) long. Use water-resistant drywall for bathrooms and kitchens. Use cement board ("Durock" or equivalent) in shower and bath stalls.

To appreciate the number of blights, blues, and blisters that afflict plaster and drywall, just glance at the shelf of wall patchers at a building supplier. After long experience, I would avoid spackling and patching plaster entirely in favor of these materials:

◆ **Drywall joint compound:** The standard goop for installing new drywall is also great for shallow repairs. You can buy it premixed or dry.

◆ **Fast-setting compound:** Sold dry, as "Durabond" and similar brands, this stuff sets fast, making it ideal for deep cracks.

◆ **Finish plaster:** Sold dry, Kal-Kote Texture Finish or equivalent is essential for patching sand-finish plaster. Buy it at a drywall suppliers—a 50-pound bag should last a lifetime if you store it dry.

It's hard to photograph, but this is a typical floated finish, used on many plaster ceilings and some walls. Patching this finish requires the special technique to be described shortly.

◆ **"Spakfast":** This stuff, from 3M Corp., is a godsend. Made of tiny beads, it's a non-shrinking, water-based, interior or exterior patching compound that needs no priming. You can even paint shallow repairs immediately. Like the texture finish just mentioned, it's worth going out of your way to find Spakfast.

Toolbox Tips

Materials make all the difference in wall repair. I've mentioned some stellar patching compounds not because the manufacturer paid me, but because they work far better than the junk most people use. Patching plaster sets too quickly. And while drywall joint compound is okay for some purposes, it's a nightmare in a deep hole, let alone when you need to match sand finish.

The Tools of Your Trade

The tools for repairing plaster and drywall are basic—you could even say primitive. Be sure to use a dust mask (see Chapter 2), a basic requirement for the many dusty parts of wall repair.

Fix-It Phrase

Trowel, drywall knife, putty knife. What's the difference? They will all apply various patching compounds. Your choice depends on what you have available, and what you are doing. The margin trowel shown in Chapter 3 is also extremely handy for small repairs. In this book, when I say "trowel," I mean whichever tool is handy—but never a putty knife! They're too flexible, and essentially useless.

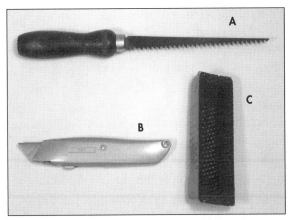
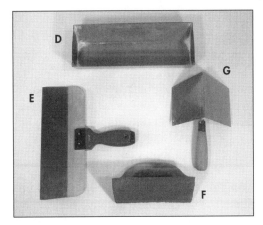

Essential drywall tools.

The photo on the left shows some of the fundamental tools of drywall repair:

A. A drywall saw cuts odd shapes for repairs, and openings for electrical boxes.

B. A utility knife plays a major role in drywall repair, and in most other home-fixes.

C. A "Surform" brand plane trims cut edges of drywall.

To handle mud, the tools shown in the photo on the right should find their way into your tool kit:

D. A mud tray (mud box) holds the patching material; it's ideal for loading up a drywall knife without spillage.

E. A drywall knife (12" model shown in photo; it's also available in 4", 6", and 8" widths) is used to patch walls and apply mud.

F. A rubber float applies finish coats, creates a sand-finish texture, and smoothes mortar.

G. A corner knife is essential for mudding corners, generally in large repairs.

Drywall sanding screen, held in a sanding block, is the best way to sand drywall mud. The abrasive mesh resists clogging.

A Wall-Fixer's Seven Commandments

Before we plunge into the gritty task of repairing walls, let's meet the seven commandments of wall repair (if you're repairing a sand finish, make sure to read the following section, "A Finish Made of Sand"):

♦ Don't allow patching material to build up above the surrounding surface. Scrape or sandpaper anything above the wall surface. Otherwise, your *mud* will build up and you'll have jumped from the frying pan of broken plaster into the fire of a globby patch.

Fix-It Phrase

Mud, to anybody who works with plaster, drywall, or masonry, is the general term for a soft substance that will turn hard: plaster, drywall compound, mortar, and the like.

♦ Skip the usual home-repair-book-advice to "undercut" the damaged edges so the patch will hold tight by "keying" into the hole. If you can undercut brittle plaster without wrecking the wall, you should be *writing* home-repair books, not reading them. And if you follow my suggestions, your patches will bond to the wall both chemically and mechanically.

♦ Remove all crumbling or rotted junk until only solid wall surrounds the repair.

♦ Dampen the edges around the patch before using water-based, "setting type" patching, so it won't dry before setting. *Do not moisten* if using drywall compound and other materials that harden by drying.

♦ Fill deep holes with one or two layers of fast-setting material before filling the surface.

♦ Use thick consistency for deep holes and soupier stuff for thin finishes.

♦ Stir the patching thoroughly, and keep crumbs and grit out. They inevitably rise to the surface, causing hideous streaks and reminding you to heed these seven commandments next time around.

The Question of Texture

Some walls, usually made of drywall, are almost as flat as marble. But others feature various kinds of texture, and to repair these walls, you really have to know what you are doing.

A Finish Made of Sand

Most old plaster was surfaced with sand finish, a finishing plaster that—amazing but true—contains fine sand. Sand finish has a gritty, regular texture that is best patched with the floating technique described in a moment. A second-best alternative is to mix sand finish additive (sometimes sold as an anti-slip paint additive) in the patch material or paint primer. If the surface is still too smooth, add more sand to the paint.

Before repairing sand finish, scrape sand from around the injury with a trowel or paint scraper. Otherwise, your trowel or drywall knife will ride up on this sand, leaving an el-grosso corrugated effect.

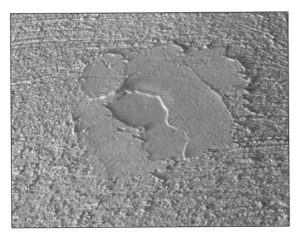

This sand-finish plaster was repaired with smooth patching material—leaving this obnoxiously obvious "repair."

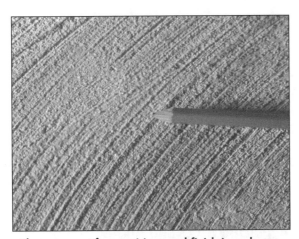

The pro secret for repairing sand finish is a plastering float, which is made of foam rubber and costs about $10 at a plastering supplier. Finding a float is worth the trouble, since nothing else will invisibly patch sand-finish plaster. Pencil points to a floated patch. Made with Kal-Kote texture finish, it's still wet, but already invisible.

Floating moves the surface but not the body of the patching. It also avoids those hideous jagged lines formed when a trowel rides across the rough surface on textured plaster.

Here's how to use a float to finish a repair:

1. Using fast-setting mud, fill the hole to ⅛" below the final surface. Let the mud set hard, but not dry.

2. Mix a small amount of Kal-Kote Texture Finish or equivalent according to directions.

3. Moisten the patch area if it's really dry. Trowel on the texture finish and allow it to harden for a few minutes. Don't fuss getting the surface perfectly flat at this point.

4. When the mud has stiffened, dampen the float and flick a bit of water at the patch with a paint brush. Work the float over the patch in a circular motion to flatten the surface. If the mud won't move, wet it further. If it moves too much, delay floating for a few minutes.

When you're done, the patch should closely match the texture and level of the surface. Clean the float well with water so it won't get stiff.

Fix-It Phrase

A **float** is used to float the surface of mud in a floating motion. It's a great trick to know, because you are moving only the outer surface of the mud—filling hollows and smoothing high spots—which is what you need to finish a wall repair. In short, only a float can float.

Other Textures

If your walls are truly mangled, but you don't feel up to replacing them with new drywall, consider creating a texture with texture paint or drywall compound. Both can hide major damage. A thick-napped paint roller makes a nubbly surface akin to sand finish. Play around to get a texture you like:

◆ **Homemade stucco.** Joint compound can be used to replicate several common interior textures, including stucco.

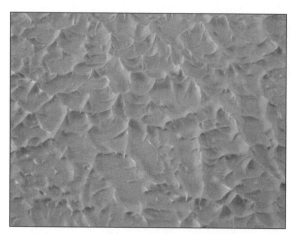

For the stucco look shown on the left, apply drywall joint compound, then pull it away with a large trowel (like a plastering or brick trowel). For the smoother texture shown on the right, let the mud set for a few minutes, then lightly press down the peaks.

◆ **Still streaking.** You can streak drywall compound with a brush.

Trowel mud on a wide area, and use a coarse-bristled 6" brush to make a forgiving texture that can hide grotesque gouges.

Small and Large Fixes

Enough on texture. What if the drywall has holes or breaks? We'll take the repairs from smallest to largest.

Toolbox Tips

Why not list the tools and materials for each repair? Because, as I've explained, the patching technique depends on the circumstances. And because many tools do the same thing—apply mud. For these reasons, I'll use general terms unless a repair requires a specific tool or material.

Repairing Nicks and Gouges

If your wall suffers from a series of little defects, follow these steps:

1. Clean out loose or raised junk. Cut off loose drywall paper with a utility knife.

2. If using patching plaster or another setting-type material, dampen the repair area, especially where it's shallow. Allow the water to sink in while you mix mud.

3. Apply the patching material, which we've tinted in the photo for emphasis.

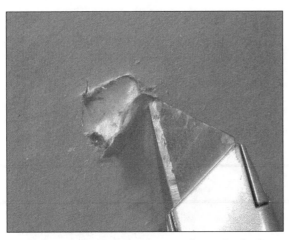

Before repair, clean the gouge with a utility knife.

Apply patching to gouge.

4. Clean off extra patching. For a smooth patch, scrape with a trowel held at 60° to the surface. For a rough (sand-finish) patch, see the earlier section, "A Finish Made of Sand."

5. A few minutes later, wipe the surroundings (not the patch) with a damp rag. The more mud you remove now, the less you'll have to sand later—that's tedious work.

6. Sand (unless you used a texture), prime, and paint.

Toolbox Tips

One of the many benefits of floating is the ability to remove extra mud around the patch.

Covering with the Metal-and-Mesh Repair Gizmo

Instead of going to heroic measures to repair a medium-size defect, you can buy the clever repair gizmo shown in the photo, available in 4×4" and 8×8" sizes. The metal covers the wound, the fiberglass mesh sticks to the wall, and you simply put mud over the patch, usually in two applications.

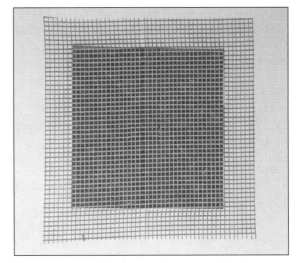

The metal-and-mesh patch can save a lot of time.

Covering with Drywall Tape

You can cover a small hole with several layers of drywall tape (it's sold for covering joints in new drywall) and patching. The repair is fast and easy, but you'll have to avoid leaving a visible mound of patching on the wall. Here's how to do it:

1. Clean off all loose and ragged material for at least 12" around the hole. Your patch will extend far beyond the hole, and this area must be clean and flat.

2. Stick several strips of drywall tape across the wound, extending 4" to 6" past the damage. Either use self-adhesive Fiberglass tape (as shown), or place paper tape over wet mud, add more mud, and stick more tape on top.

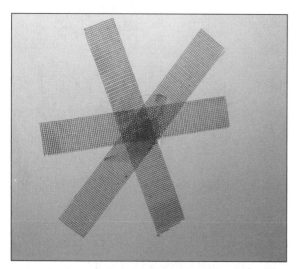

Tape the damaged area before patching, keeping the tape as thin as possible.

3. Cover the tape with a thin layer of patching.

The first coat of mud covers the tape and starts to taper at the edges.

4. When that mud is dry, add a second coat of mud and feather the edges. By now, you've probably covered far beyond the original damage, since each coat must extend beyond the previous one.

5. When the last coat is dry, sand to blend with surroundings.

Cutting Back to the Studs and Starting Over

Let's say the damage is more like a disaster—the plaster is rotten, the drywall is crumbling. Say the wall was used for darts or a teenager slammed it with a hammer. What to do? Cut out the whole disaster, that's what. Removing entire hunks of drywall or plaster sounds dramatic, but it's often easier than trying to repair something truly rotten. You'll need a hand or power saw, replacement drywall, shims (possibly), power screwdriver and drywall screws, drywall compound, and drywall tape. Follow these steps:

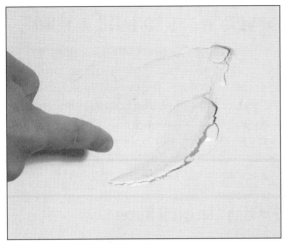

Damaged area.

1. Mark the damaged area at the inside edge of the nearby studs (see the next section, "Seven Ways to Find a Stud"). Use a level to mark a perfect rectangle. For strength, the patch should be 6″ to 8″ high.

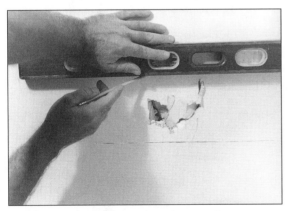

Use a level to mark a perfectly rectangular cutout—your patch will fit much better.

2. Screw the existing wall material (either drywall or plaster) to the stud at both sides of the cutout. In plaster, drill a pilot hole and a countersink for the screw head, and don't overtighten the screw.

All Thumbs

It's hard to cut brittle old plaster without damaging nearby plaster. Duct tape along the edge may reduce cracking as you cut. Press the jig saw hard against the wall to minimize vibration. The best way to cut plaster is with a circular saw, but this will wreck the saw blade and start a real dust bowl in your house.

3. Cut out the damaged area alongside the stud with a drywall saw, keyhole saw, jig saw, utility knife, or circular saw.

4. Screw a 1×3 blocking—6″ longer than the height of the cutout—flush to the front of studs at each end of the patch.

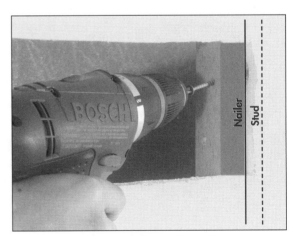

Screw a nailer to the studs.

5. Cut a piece of drywall about ¼″ smaller than the repair in each dimension (see "Making the Cuts" later in the chapter for instructions on cutting). *Important:* If needed, shim the patch with wood or asphalt roof shingle so it's flush with the surface.

6. Screw the drywall into place.

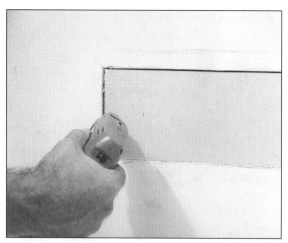

Screws cause much less damage than nails, but nails will work for traditionalists.

7. Fill deep holes with quick-set compound.

8. Stick drywall tape to the edges and cover with joint compound.

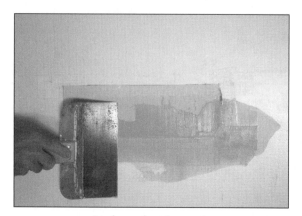

Apply mud to the patch.

9. When the mud is dry, scrape off ridges and high spots with the drywall knife. Apply another coat of compound, and feather it to meet the wall surface. Sand, apply a third coat if needed, and sand again. Prime and paint when dry.

Seven Ways to Find a Stud

In fixing walls, hanging shelves, or making electrical repairs, you'll face the homeowner's nightmare: Where's the stud? (Studs, you'll recall, are the 2×4 or 2×6 framing lumber that support walls.) There are plenty of ways to find these elusive characters. The problem is worst in old walls, where studs are obscured behind thick plaster and/or drywall.

Finding Electrical Boxes

Most electrical boxes are mounted on studs. Generally you can just tap with a hammer (see next hint) to figure out which side the stud is on; if you're baffled, shut off the circuit, open up the box, and look inside for the fastenings, as indicated by the pencil in the photo.

A stud is next to most electrical boxes.

Tapping with a Hammer

This was my dad's favorite technique. If you tap carefully, and if your ear is good, you'll hear the noise change from a hollow sound between studs to a tighter sound on top of the stud. Don't bother trying this method with thick, plaster walls, although it may help you find the general location.

Drilling

You can find a stud by drilling (use a $\frac{1}{16}$" bit) the wall and looking for increased resistance. Or drill an $\frac{1}{8}$" hole at an angle toward the suspected stud location and probe with a cut-off coat-hanger, much like the joist-finding technique shown in Chapter 7. I usually drill to double-check a less intrusive method—or when nothing else will work.

Drilling will find a stud, but it leaves tracks.

Measuring

Studs are usually located 16" (or, less commonly, 24") apart. Once you've found one stud, measuring should find the others—unless the carpenter was drinking brandy that day, or you found an out-of-pattern stud.

Baseboard

The top of the baseboard—the trim along the floor—should be nailed to the studs. (Nails at the bottom of the baseboard enter the sole plate rather than the stud.) These nails should be visible even under a gob of hole-filler, but you can also use the magnetic studfinder, described next. Use a level to locate the stud higher up the wall.

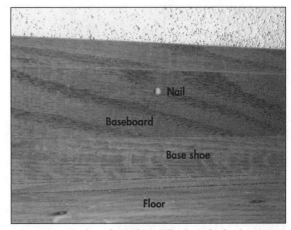

A nail in the baseboard usually reveals the location of the stud.

Magnetic Studfinder

These gizmos hold a magnet that, theoretically, will pivot when attracted by a nail going into the stud. Magnetic studfinders work better in drywall than in plaster, whose thickness tends to block the magnetic field. If you can't find nails in the wall itself, search in the baseboard as just described.

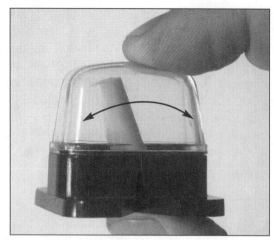

Magnetic studfinder.

Electronic Studfinder

Sadly, this battery-operated gadget is not a surefire solution to the stud-seeking snafu. Success takes a bit of a knack, and depends on the wall construction. I find this electronic "wonder" no panacea.

Installing Drywall

Let's say you want to hang a whole wallful (or even roomful) of drywall. Maybe your spouse has butchered the existing drywall while removing wallpaper (history proves this can happen!). Maybe you need to replace some "el-hideoso" paneling. What follows is a basic procedure for tackling this "edge-idiot" job, starting from the bare studs. While this is not the easiest task in this book— you did notice it comes before plumbing …

Aside from the tools and materials listed earlier in this chapter, you will need a 4' aluminum drywall square and a variable-speed drill with screwdriver bit (see "A Fascination with Fastening," later in this chapter).

Drywall is sold in 4' panels that are 8', 9' 10', or 12' long. Long sheets are heavy and may not pass through stairwells, but they do reduce your taping chores. Order a little extra *rock*. You can get a large amount delivered, sometimes even through a second-floor window.

> **All Thumbs**
>
> Drywall installation is a nightmare if you make mistakes early on. Before hanging the first piece, make sure the studs are all perfect, and that every vertical edge of drywall can be screwed to something. And remember that the process drags on for days during the taping and finishing phase. Finally, sanding drywall makes a real mess. See Chapter 2 for advice on protecting your house from the talcum-like dust you'll be creating.

Drywall installation has three phases. Planning and preparing, "hanging rock," and taping and finishing the joints.

> **Fix-It Phrase**
>
> Drywallers call the sheets of material **rock** for a couple of reasons. Sheetrock is a common brand, and the stuff is made of, you guessed it, rock. In fact, sometimes drywallers refer to themselves as rockers. Hear that, Mick Jagger?

Planning and Preparing

Scan your room, in all its bare-studded glory, and follow these suggestions for preparation:

◆ Your layout should aim to simplify taping and mudding. Run ceiling sheets perpendicular to the joists, so end joints meet on joists. To simplify taping, the long, tapered edges of sheets should meet each other.

◆ Make sure all old screws and nails are out.

◆ If you want more electrical outlets and phone jacks, this is your best chance to add them (see Chapter 16).

◆ Check that you have enough "nailers," or "blocking," the 2×4 blocks that support drywall from behind. If the rock wanders while taping or mudding, you're headed for disaster. 10d sinker nails or 2½" construction screws are plenty strong for blocking.

Taking the time to nail blocking in place can really simplify your life when it's time to tape drywall joints.

◆ To avoid cracks, don't put a joint at the top corner of a window or door.

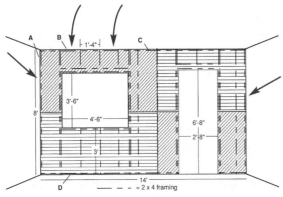

Blocking is often needed at the arrows. If you don't support joints, the drywall will wander during taping, and you'll never get a decent joint.

A. Extra nailers are often needed here.

B. Nailers are needed here unless joists are parallel and adjacent to the wall.

C. Plate.

D. Sole plate.

Toolbox Tips

Drywall is unforgiving. At every stage, make sure surfaces that should be flush actually are flush. Get all fasteners below the surface level. A good drywaller is a closet anal-compulsive.

◆ Exterior walls need a vapor barrier just beneath the drywall. If you've insulated with waterproof foam panels, seal the joints with vapor-barrier tape. Otherwise, staple 4-mil poly sheeting to the studs, using a minimum of staples.

Making the Cuts

With the planning out of the way, it's time to cut and hang rock. There are three kinds of cuts: straight, compound, and for openings for electrical boxes.

Straight cuts are a no-brainer. Using a square, cut the paper on the face of the drywall with a utility knife. Make a second cut deeper, if needed, then bend backward to break the gypsum. Finally, cut the back paper from behind. Allow ¼" leeway on cuts to avoid recutting. If your piece is slightly oversize, trim with the Surform plane shown earlier in this chapter.

Toolbox Tips

Which is the face (good side) of new drywall? If it's not obviously whiter than the back, look for the shallow region along the long sides. These cutouts, intended to simplify taping, are on the face.

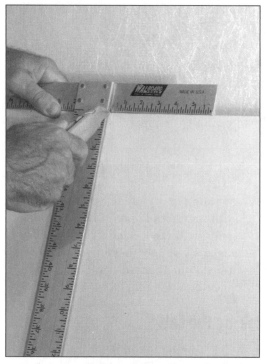

Make a simple drywall cut with a utility knife and a straightedge.

Cutting the hole for an electrical box using the RotoZip.

Sheets that go above windows or doors need an "L-shape" cut. Saw the first cut with a hand saw. Make the second cut with a utility knife, as already described. (To cut a curve, or complicated shapes, use a hand drywall saw, a jig saw, or a RotoZip spiral saw.)

Most walls have electrical boxes for outlets or switches. Measure carefully before cutting these boxes. Or use the toothpaste trick: To locate an electrical box cutout on a piece of drywall, first cut the sheet to size. Then smear toothpaste on the edge of the box and push the sheet into position. The toothpaste will mark the box location. Make openings no more than $\frac{1}{8}$" oversize; otherwise the box cover will not hide the hole. Cut with a jig saw, a hand drywall saw, or the RotoZip saw used in the photo. If you press the drywall against the wall, a RotoZip will follow the outline of the electrical box.

A Fascination with Fastening

After fastidious preparations, the hanging should be easy. Pencil in fastener lines with a drywall square while the sheets are against the wall. Find a beefy friend who owes you a favor (everyone needs at least one) to help lift the sheets.

Support ceiling sheets with a home-made crutch made from 2×4. Nudge the crutch into place to hold the rock, but don't let it fall!

Once upon a time, rockers used nails. Today, the game is all screwed up—I mean—drywall is always screwed up. Screws are stronger, easier to work with, and less damaging to the framing and rock. Since screws should bite only $\frac{3}{4}$" of the wood (longer screws will eventually pop out), $\frac{1}{2}$" drywall calls for $1\frac{1}{4}$" screws.

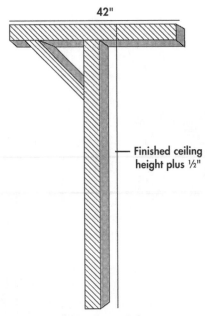

42"

Finished ceiling
height plus ½"

**Use a homemade drywall crutch for accurate instal-
lation on ceilings.**

**When screwing rock, increase your pressure as the
screw enters the stud.**

The trick in screwing rock is to set the screw
just under the paper without fracturing the
gypsum core. The screw gun shown will shut
off at whatever depth you select. When using
a drill, test the drywall screw gadget shown in

Chapter 3. If using a standard Phillips bit in a
drill, angle the drill when you reach the right
depth to release the screw. If you set a screw
too deep, drive another screw 2" away.

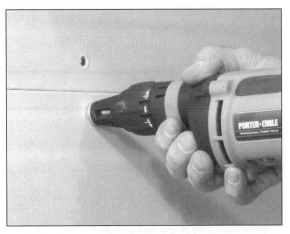

**Driving screws with a foolproof drywall screwgun.
For big jobs, I'd recommend renting this time-saver.**

These suggestions will help you screw drywall without screwing up:

◆ The ends of adjacent sheets share a stud
or joist. Screw them at a slight angle.

◆ Always press hard with your other hand
while screwing—screws alone cannot pull
the sheet tight. This is not needed with a
screw gun, which presses the rock tight.

◆ Screws go 8" apart along the edges, and
12" apart on the inside framing.

◆ Near windows, doors, and baseboards,
screws should be covered by molding, so
you won't have to tape them.

◆ When finished, run a drywall knife over
every fastener. Wherever you hear a
"zing," drive the screw deeper.

Finishing Joints

If you've done a good job of hanging and fastening, mudding and taping should be a breeze. The various kinds of tape and joint compound are discussed earlier in this chapter. Taping creates a dust storm; see Chapter 2 for suggestions on protecting your home and body.

All Thumbs

Never allow gritty stuff into the mud. Heave out old and caked mud and get new stuff. Otherwise, the new mud will be covered with gouges, you'll drive yourself to distraction, and still get a lousy job.

Fill all deep spots, holes, and corners with quick-setting compound. Keep mud below the surface. Slap some joint compound on the screw heads with a narrow trowel. Either stick Fiberglass tape onto the seam before mudding, or apply mud with a 4" or 6" knife and lay paper tape into it, as shown in the photo.

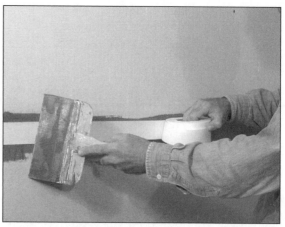

With the mud still wet, embed paper tape into it.

Cover the tape with mud (preferably 6" or less in width), and smooth the edges.

All Thumbs

Paper tape only sticks to wet mud. Trust me: Tape will pull away from dry mud, air bubbles will form beneath it, or both.

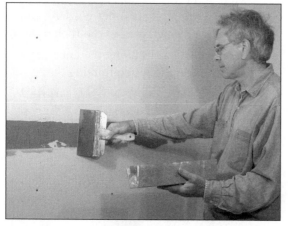

Quickly put a narrow band of drywall joint compound along a seam.

When the first coat is dry, lightly sand (using the drywall sanding screens shown earlier in this chapter) the edges to remove ridges. Apply a second coat of drywall joint compound with a broader knife. Smear mud across the first coat, working wider and concentrating on low areas. Hold a light bulb near the wall to identify low spots, and continue sanding and mudding until the wall is perfect enough. On ceilings, be especially fastidious near ceiling lights—the low-angle illumination will "show off" any flaw.

The procedure is similar in a corner. Using a 6" or 8" knife, spread mud in the joint. Fold paper tape at the score in the center, and press it into the mud. When applying the second coat, concentrate on building up the corner. Using an 8" knife, work from the corner, then use the corner trowel to smooth the corner. Fill areas further from the corner using a third coat.

Corners can be tricky. The first two coats concentrate on the corner itself; the third coat makes the mud match the nearby surfaces.

The Least You Need to Know

◆ Using the right materials for repairing plaster and drywall is the only way to do a good job.

◆ Floating is the best way to repair sand-finish plaster.

◆ Don't undercut plaster or drywall before a repair; this only causes more damage.

◆ The technique for repairing drywall or plaster depends on the construction and the scale of the damage.

◆ Finding a stud is easy if you know the right techniques.

◆ Drywall replacement is not too complicated for the ambitious homeowner.

In This Chapter

- ◆ Learning the often confusing language of molding
- ◆ Do's and don'ts of working with molding
- ◆ Painless molding removal
- ◆ Top tricks for installing molding around windows, doors, and floors
- ◆ Making tight molding joints that stay tight

Chapter 10

Holding Your Own with Molding

Molding is trim that joins windows, doors, and floors to walls. Ranging from plain to ornate, molding can give an interior style, character, and elegance. It can also keep out drafts and cover gaps between walls and windows or doors.

Installing molding is exacting work but not tedious. It's a handy knack to learn, whether you want to replace bent, spindled, or mutilated molding, or plan on restyling a room inexpensively. You'll want to know the art of molding if you're installing a new door or window, or want to refinish a wood floor.

Molding Lingo

To work with molding, you need to know some terminology. Here are some terms for joints and cuts:

- ◆ **Butt joint:** A meeting of 2 square (90°) ends.
- ◆ **Bevel:** A cut with angle visible when seen from the edge (the top in the following photo). Much better than a butt joint if you have to join baseboard; nailing through the face of the right-hand piece in the photo will fasten both pieces.
- ◆ **Miter:** A cut so the angle is visible when viewing the face of the molding. We'll use miter cuts in door trim later in the chapter.
- ◆ **Compound miter:** A cut that combines a miter and a bevel.
- ◆ **Cope:** To cut a profile on the end of molding; better than miter joints at inside corners of baseboard (see photos later in the chapter).

Butt joint.

Molding bevel cut (scarf joint).

Finished miter joint.

Molding comes in a million styles, or patterns, but fortunately, it is only found in a few common places. Each of these location gets its own name:

◆ **Baseboard:** Molding around the edge of a floor, flush to the wall. Usually 3" to 6" high.

◆ **Base shoe:** A molding (usually rounded) that joins baseboard and floor.

◆ **Casing:** Molding flat on the wall, around a door or window.

◆ **Crown:** Molding at the joint between wall and ceiling. Often gets a compound miter cut.

◆ **Jamb:** Wood that encases a window or door; it's perpendicular to the wall.

◆ **Head:** A piece that goes across the top; a "head jamb" or "head casing."

◆ **Reveal (setback):** A narrow shoulder showing on a jamb after a casing is nailed.

◆ **Stop:** A molding nailed to a jamb to prevent a door from swinging too far, or to hold double-hung windows in place.

Mark the reveal lines with pencil ³⁄₁₆" from the inner edge of the jamb to align the casing. As a shortcut, mark reveal lines at top corners and eyeball your way to the bottom while nailing the molding.

Molding Do's and Don'ts

Since molding must seal gaps and look great, installation is mainly a matter of appearance. Take it from me: Replacing the molding actually makes a place look better. I've just finished dressing up my house by replacing the hum-drum, painted molding with nicely stained oak. I worked on one room at a time, and by now, the old home place is about ready to pose for a home magazine (just kidding).

Here are the do's and don'ts of working with molding:

◆ Do mark your cuts with a utility knife—or at least a sharp pencil.

◆ Do predrill nail holes, especially in hardwood. Go all the way through the molding, but don't go far into the jamb or wall. Nails don't need help going through them, and you could weaken their grip.

◆ Do stain (or prime and paint) molding before installation.

◆ Do place the longest and best pieces in the most visible places.

◆ Do clean up the edges of old jambs before reattaching casing. Use a plane (if necessary) and sandpaper, then paint, stain, or varnish the face of the casing.

A rag works great for staining molding that is fairly flat. Use a paint brush or paint sponge on heavily textured molding. Either way, rubber gloves are a must.

◆ Don't make miter joints on inside corners of baseboards—they will always separate. Use a coped joint, as explained later in this chapter.

◆ Don't drive any nails home until the molding really fits. If the nail heads are up, you can always remove pieces that bother you.

◆ Don't overfasten. In most cases, nails can be about 2' apart.

Toolbox Tips

The miter joints found at the top of many windows and doors are tricky, because they love to pull apart when you drive in the last nail. The only sure-fire way I've found to make tight miter joints requires a nifty tool called a plate joiner (also called a biscuit cutter). The plate joiner allows strong glue joints between flat surfaces, which normally cannot be glued effectively. It has a small, circular blade that cuts to a predetermined depth. The size of biscuits depends on how deep you set the joiner and how strong the joint must be. I'll show you more later in the chapter, if you promise to consider begging, borrowing, renting, or buying a plate joiner.

Yanking Up Molding with Scarcely a Split

Let's say you're planning to sand a floor the right way, which requires you to remove the baseboard and base shoe. We'll assume you're the sensible type, and would rather not buy, cut, and stain new molding. How can you pull off the molding without harm? By slowly and carefully punching through some nails, and then prying with two slender, low-impact tools. (Come to think of it, even if you will deep-six the old molding, this technique will minimize damage to your wall and jambs, minimizing your installation problem.)

In molding removal, here's the #1 rule: Always remove the top piece first. You'll need a nail set, wood chisel, flat prybar, hammer, locking pliers, and wood scraps. With brittle or crooked-grain wood, expect some breakage. If you're careful, you may be able to glue broken pieces together (see Chapter 5).

To remove molding, follow these steps:

1. Starting at an end or corner, hammer the nails straight through the molding with a nail set. Do this along 3' of molding.

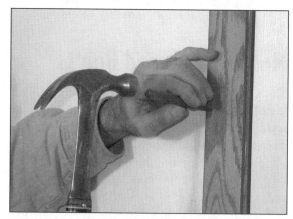

Punch out nails to start loosening the molding.

2. Slip the flat blade of a chisel or prybar under the molding (which should be rather loose at this point), protecting the wall with a trowel or scrap wood. Using a second tool (hammer or a prybar), gradually pull up the piece.

Remove the molding with two tools to minimize damage.

3. If a nail head pops up, pull it out with the hammer (protect the molding from hammer marks with scrap wood). Slowly remove the entire molding.

4. After the molding is off, do not pound out the remaining nails from behind—this damages the face of the molding. Grab the nail from behind with locking pliers and pry down to pull the head through the wood. When you renail the molding, drive larger-diameter nails into the same holes. If the larger diameter are ridiculously long, shorten them to about 2" with cutting pliers.

Pull the nails from behind to lessen damage to the face of the molding.

Cutting and Installing Molding

Now that power miter boxes (described in Chapter 3) are relatively cheap and common, I can't see any reason to cut molding with those hand miter boxes. They might have worked well for those mythic, meticulous Swedish carpenters, but in the real world, they are almost unworkable. If you are forced to use a hand miter box, at least screw or clamp it to a workbench so it doesn't wander while you cut.

Mitering molding.

When mounting new molding, start with the windows and doors, then attach the base moldings. If you've got unlevel, unsquare floors and walls, see Chapter 8 for a tip that will help you make moldings match miserably misshapen walls.

Installing Door and Window Molding

Nailing new moldings to windows and doors is tricky because every flaw will be visible. The commonly used miter joints, for example, have a nasty tendency to pull apart. Cutting a 45° miter (the kind you see at the corners of door trim) requires some practice—just take it from somebody who has repeatedly cut them backward. Now I hold the molding up where it will eventually be nailed, and lightly mark the angle of the cut on the molding. Then I cut—works every time.

Work slowly and exactly, and make sure you can buy replacement molding at a building supplier or salvage yard before you break anything crucial! If your molding is more complicated than what's shown in the following procedure, take your time with disassembly.

You can adapt the following general procedure for nailing casing to doors or windows. Nail the inner edge of the casing to the jambs with 4d finish nails. Nail the outer edge to the

studs with 6d or 8d finish nails, depending on the thickness of your wall and molding. If the finish nail gets 1" of purchase (grab) in the stud, that is plenty.

Be sure to predrill all nail holes, especially in hardwood trim, and do not pound the nails home until everything is perfect! With the heads raised above the trim, you can always go back and fix your mistakes.

The numbers shown in the figure indicate steps in the procedure:

1. Mark the reveal lines $\frac{3}{16}$" from the inner edges of the jambs, as seen in the previous photo, and in the drawing.

2. Make a butt cut at the bottom of the left casing.

3. Hold the left casing in place and mark the miter cut at the spot meeting between the two reveal lines.

4. Drill pairs of nail holes $\frac{1}{2}$" from the inner and outer edges and tack the left casing into place.

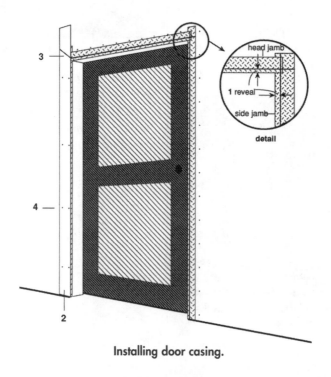

Installing door casing.

Drill before nailing casing. You'll save a lot of bent nails and frustration!

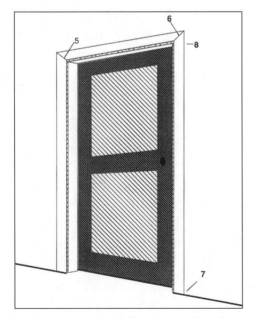

To finish a door casing, follow the numbered steps.

5. Miter the left end of the head casing at 45° and hold it into place. If the joint is not tight, recut the miters slightly to fit.

6. Miter the right end of the head casing, drill nail holes, and tack casing in place.

7. Make a butt cut on the bottom of the right casing and stand it in position, so it overlaps the head casing.

8. Mark the inside and outside of head casing miter on the right casing. Saw the miter and test the fit. Recut if the joint is not tight.

9. When both miter joints are tight, remove all casings and cut two slots for a biscuit joint in each miter joint, as shown in the photo.

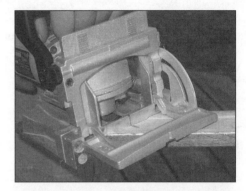

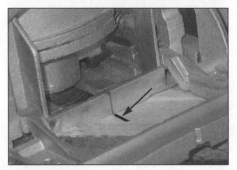

The mark on the plate joiner aligns with a mark on the molding (see arrow on bottom figure). Use a #0 (small) biscuit and experiment on scrap wood so the slot does not cut through the front or back of the molding.

10. Put carpenter's glue into each biscuit slot and insert the biscuit.

Some glue should squeeze from the biscuit joint after it's assembled.

![All Thumbs] **All Thumbs**

While nailing upper parts of door and window molding, do not over-nail! You can pull the joints apart.

11. Assemble the joint and tack (lightly nail) the casings into place. Place a pipe clamp over the top and tighten it.

Watch that pipe clamp! It can fall on your head, especially when you pound the nails.

To protect the molding, set the finish nailing with a nail set.

12. Using a nail set, set the nails below the surface. First set the outer nails, then the inner ones—this tends to pull miter joints closed.

13. Wipe off glue and allow to set. Remove clamp.

14. Fill the nail holes with wood filler, as described in Chapter 11. Wipe off extra filler, sand, and then stain to match.

Fill the nail hole with a bit of wood filler.

Casings have a habit of pulling back and opening up miter joints. If the joint opens when you press back on the outside of the casing, stick wood or cardboard shims behind the casing. Leave a tab hanging out so you can pull shims that are too thick. Cut off the tab when finished.

Basic Base Moldings

Now that you've installed the window and door casings, it's time to cut and fasten the base moldings: first the baseboard, then the base shoe. Using the longest pieces on the longest stretches, lay out the baseboard. Remember to predrill nail holes and don't nail anything home until you've tacked everything into place!

Toolbox Tips

Coping is a hand-sawing technique that sounds like a lot of work, but most people can cope with it. If you cope, when you nail the baseboard, you'll see a tight joint, not an ugly gap. Anybody can cope with that!

Starting at an inside corner, follow these suggestions to cut and nail baseboard and base shoe:

1. To cut molding at an inside corner—where two baseboards meet in a corner of the room—don't do the obvious. Don't cut each piece at 45°. Instead, cut a square (butt) end on the first piece and tack it into place.

2. Saw a 45° miter cut on the second piece and mount it in a vise or clamp.

3. Using a coping saw—a kind of hand jigsaw—saw along the edge of the cut from step 2. (This is easier than it sounds if the blade is sharp.)

4. Lightly sand the edges. Tack the molding into place, starting at the inside corner.

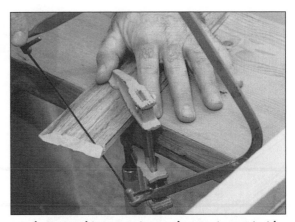

A clamp is a big convenience when coping an inside corner.

A completed coped joint.

To cut an outside corner joint, follow these directions:

1. Make sure the joint is 90°. Cut 2 pieces of scrap wood at 45° and position them where the baseboard will go. If the joint is not tight, adjust your saw a degree or so, and retest.

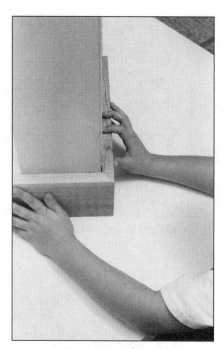

Testing an outside corner.

2. Once the baseboard is nailed, repeat the process with the base shoe. Nail diagonally into the floor. A scrap of sheet metal or thin plywood can protect the floor from the hammer.

A Handy Caulking Trick

Even well-installed molding may show gaps where it's supposed to meet the wall. You may have tried to pound the molding back into place, but naturally that failed—in home repair, anything so simple is doomed. But in this case, something even simpler will actually work: Fill the gap with a paintable caulking compound (or white caulking in a white room). Cut a small hole in the tip of the cartridge. Apply sparingly, in one smooth motion. Smooth the stuff into place with a moistened finger. Paint when dry if you want. Done.

The Least You Need to Know

◆ By working carefully, you can remove molding intact, without mauling the surrounding walls and trim.

◆ Molding repair and replacement is slow, methodical work. Always predrill nail holes, and don't attach the molding too tightly.

◆ A power miter box is an enormous help in molding installation.

◆ Don't assume your room, windows, and doors are all square. Test each piece of molding first!

In This Part

Part 3

Looking Outside

By this point, I trust that the inside of your home is looking as sleek as a movie star. But what has the weather done to the siding, paint, foundation, and roof? Are the boards on your deck rotted and cracked? Sadly, the skin of most "mature" houses shows way too many wrinkles, sags, leaks, and blemishes.

If an aging Hollywood star can buy annual facelifts, doesn't your home deserve the same treatment? In this chapter, I'll talk about exterior problems that, if left unattended, can add up faster than royalties on a James Bond movie. Consider the bonus: A face-lift should help your house live longer. Not even a Hollywood plastic surgeon dares make that claim …

In This Chapter

- ◆ Three categories of wall coatings
- ◆ Figuring out how much paint you need
- ◆ The whys and wherefores of paint preparation
- ◆ The right tools make a faster job
- ◆ The do's and don'ts of rolling, brushing, and spraying
- ◆ Painless paint cleanup

Chapter 11

Avoiding Pain in the Paint Department

Paint has changed plenty since I first opened a can of evil-smelling, lead-based oil paint. By the time the paint dried, it was dotted with insects that had mistaken my wall for bright blue flypaper. When it was all over, the brush-cleaning ceremony involved buckets of nauseating thinner. Painting was literally a nerve-wracking one-two punch: Both the solvent and the lead pigment in that paint were toxic to the nervous system.

Today, the lead is gone and water has largely replaced organic solvents. A range of specialty finishes for wood, masonry, and metal have solved many of the traditional painter's pitfalls. These days, painting can actually be a lot of fun.

Meet the Coating Family

The boatload of wall coatings can be pigeonholed in three categories:

◆ Surface preparers (primers, fillers, and sealers) get the surface ready for the coating.

◆ Film formers (paint and varnish) sit on the surface and protect from above.

◆ Penetrating coatings (stain, water repellent, and preservative) seep into the surface and protect from within.

After you open a new can of paint, punch holes in the rim with a finishing nail. The paint will then drain from the rim, and you'll actually be able to reseal the can.

Surface Preparers

Surface preparers look inward, toward the substrate (the coated material), while topcoats (the final coats) look outward, toward destructive sun, rain, and dirt.

Primer penetrates the substrate to create a paint-friendly surface. It may also kill mildew or prevent rust. You'll need primer on unpainted drywall, plaster, wood, and metal, but usually not on sound paint. Priming a few areas is called *spot-priming.* After extensive repairs, it's better to prime the whole area.

Filler is used to fill pores on rough masonry, concrete, and some woods. *Sealer* covers stains—crayons, oil, and pitchy knots—that could otherwise bleed through the paint.

Toolbox Tips

The ultimate authority on paint, preservative, and primer is the label on the new stuff. It's not Stephen King, but still worth reading.

A relaxed grip gives the best combination of comfort and control.

Film Formers

Sad but true: You have to pay extra for high-quality paint. Good paint has a high proportion of pigment (solids), giving better longevity and better odds of one-coat coverage. Pigment proportions are listed on the can if you wish to compare paints.

Alkyd paint has replaced oil paint as the heavy-duty option for trim and exteriors. Alkyd is more washable and durable than latex, but you need paint thinner, or mineral spirits, to thin the paint and clean the brushes.

All Thumbs

Scraping, sanding, or stripping paint that was made before 1978 can bring you face to face with lead, a nerve poison that's particularly dangerous to children. Unless a reliable test tells you otherwise, assume that there's lead in old paint. Some municipalities restrict the washing or scraping of lead paint; ask a building inspector. A mask and respirator will do something to protect yourself against leaded paint, but you may want to hire a pro to remove it.

Latex paint is the water-thinned workhorse of interior painting, and increasingly for exteriors as well. Latex paints produce almost no fumes, and they even work on damp surfaces. Latexes are permeable to moisture, making them ideal for masonry, but are difficult to wash. Contrary to rumor, you can paint latex over alkyd, and vice versa. As long as the old surface is rough, well-bonded, and clean, you'll get good adhesion.

Acrylic paint is generally water-based, and a step up from latex in coverage, color retention, and glossiness.

Enamel paint is glossy, durable stuff for high-stress areas, like kitchens, bathrooms, and outdoor metal. Industrial enamel is best for tough jobs, like repainting cabinets in a bargain-basement kitchen remodeling.

Varnish is a clear finish used to protect wood while showing off the grain. *Spar varnish* can be used outside; it has protection against ultra-violet light. For floors, most homeowners use *polyurethane varnish* because it's so easy to use, as long as you don't get too vigorous while stirring—that makes hideous bubbles.

All Thumbs

Unless you like getting loopy on solvents, use good ventilation and wear a respirator when using solvent-based paint. The charcoal filters in today's respirators are highly effective if the mask has a tight fit and the filters are fresh.

Penetrating Finishes

Penetrating finishes protect from below. Although stains and water-repellents tend to splatter while being applied, they have a couple of advantages over paint:

- They can't peel or crack, because they become part of the top layer of wood.
- You can skip the primer.
- You won't need to scrape before the next repainting—just wash and restain.

These advantages appear only if you observe the cardinal rule of penetrating finishes: They've got to penetrate. The surface is porous enough for a penetrating finish if a few drops of water will sink in. If not, wait.

Opaque or *semi-transparent stain* is an excellent option for exterior wood. Opaque stain will cover many paints (although a light-colored stain may not cover dark paint). Stain is the best choice for rough wood, since the large amount of stain absorbed gives good protection. On smooth plywood, paint is a better choice, since little stain will be absorbed.

Interior stain is sold in many hues, to simulate various species of wood. When choosing stain color, bring a wood sample to the store—use the back of some molding, if you must. Still, the results on your wood might not be identical to the color sample.

Water repellent sinks into wood so it will shed water. Some water repellents contain preservative, to make life miserable for any fungi waiting to eat your house. Paintable, water-repellent *preservative* is an excellent base for painting new, exterior wood.

How Much Paint Do You Need?

Paint cans may promise to "cover 400 square feet per gallon," but actual coverage will reflect these factors:

- A rough surface can soak up twice as much paint as a smooth one.
- Second coats usually go further than first coats, especially if you're covering a cheapo paint.
- End grain is thirsty, especially of primer and penetrating finish.

End grain needs a lot more paint or stain.

Preparation: The Key to Success

Whether you are painting a single closet or a whole house, painting requires obsessive preparation. You may have to do any or all of the following:

- Repair trim, siding, gutters, windows, and so on.
- Patch plaster or drywall.
- Scrape peeling paint.
- Sand alligatored (cracked) paint.
- Attack rust with a wire brush or steel wool.
- Sand glossy surfaces.
- Kill fungus with diluted household bleach.
- Prime nail heads.
- Fill holes.
- Mask and protect the surroundings.
- Wash the surface.

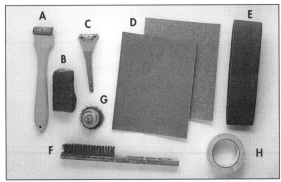

Paint prep tools and supplies.

Common tools and supplies for paint prep, as shown in the photo, include:

A. A paint scraper is the number-one enemy of peeling paint.

B. Steel wool removes rust from metal.

C. A window scraper cleans fresh paint from windows, saving endless masking.

D. Sandpaper removes or roughens old paint, smoothes wood or filler, and smoothes first coats of paint or varnish.

E. A sanding belt in a belt sander will quickly smooth wood, but will clog if you sand too much paint.

F. A hand wire brush removes peeling paint and rust.

G. A drill-mounted wire brush removes paint and rust more quickly.

H. Masking tape keeps paint off light switches, outlets, and baseboard; attaches other masking. (Use duct tape to hold plastic drop cloths.)

Toolbox Tips

To get a smooth surface with high-gloss paint, after the first coat is dry, lightly polish it with extra-fine sandpaper or steel wool to remove bubbles and dust.

Filling Holes in Wood

Like people, wood can show its age. But you don't need a plastic surgeon to repair the occasional hole, scratch, or dent in wood. Instead, you need wood filler and a couple of tricks. If the surface was stained, choose a filler that absorbs stain. (See Chapter 6 for a view of how to repair a larger hole in wood, and Chapter 9 for a treatment of hole-filling in walls. If you have hideous gashes in your siding, see Chapter 14 for repair techniques.)

Toolbox Tips

You may not need filler for small nicks and scratches. Rub some wood stain onto the blemish and forget it. If the surface is varnished, revarnish when the stain dries.

To deftly fill a hole in wood, follow these steps:

1. Clean raised, loose, or damaged wood with a utility knife, small trowel, or sandpaper. If you leave anything above the surface, the patching will bulge.

2. Firmly push wood filler into the hole. If you'll be staining the patch, also smear a thin coat on scrap wood to test the stain color when dry.

3. Scrape the patching flush and parallel to the wood grain. Notice that the trowel is held at a very high angle, which removes most extra patching. Allow the patching to set.

Fill the hole only after you've flattened the surface.

4. If needed, apply another coat and scrape flat.

5. When the patch is partly hardened, wipe the area with a rag dampened with water for water-based filler (or with solvent for other fillers). Repeat a few minutes later to remove any filler haze left on the surface.

At this point, just lightly sandpaper the dried patch, and paint.

Preparing for an Inside Job

In general, interior painting starts with the ceiling, then moves to the walls, trim, and floor. Here what you'll need to do to prepare:

◆ Remove everything portable. Pile heavy furniture in the center of the room and cover with a doubled drop cloth.

◆ Assemble your ladders, tools, lights, and paint.

◆ Scan for defects by holding a light bulb close to the wall. Patch, then prime if needed.

◆ Clean surfaces with a trisodium phosphate substitute (sold at paint stores), then rinse and dry. Keep the solution out of electrical boxes.

◆ Remove outlet covers, switch covers, and light fixtures. Put masking tape across outlets, switches, and anything else you don't want to paint.

◆ Cover the floor with plastic and/or cloth drop cloths. If you're painting the ceiling, cover the entire floor. For walls only, cover 3' to 4' out from each wall. For the best floor protection, put a cloth drop cloth over plastic.

◆ Before roller-painting a wall, rip newspaper into 4" strips, and tape them on top of the baseboards and door and window frames. If you're also painting the ceiling, mask the entire area of windows and doors.

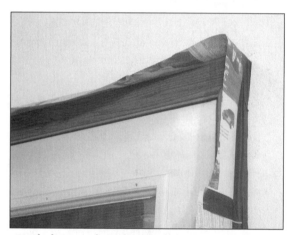

Mask doors and windows with newspaper and tape before rolling paint.

◆ If you're brush painting, masking tape should be enough around doors and windows.

◆ When painting a window, don't bother masking each pane. Shortly after the paint dries, scrape the glass with a window scraper.

◆ Set up lights and open the windows for ventilation.

Mask with tape only before brushing.

Use a window scraper to remove paint from glass.

Preparing for an Outside Job

The general sequence of preparing for exterior painting and staining is scraping, patching, cleaning, masking, and painting. Start with a hand scraper. A sharp scraper will remove more paint (and gouge more wood if you're not careful). If you have a vise and a metal file, it's worth the effort to frequently sharpen the blade. Place

the blade as close as possible to the vise, and recreate the angle the manufacturer put into the blade.

Use a vise and a metal file to sharpen the paint scraper.

If scraping fails, try a wire brush, as shown later in this chapter (you may want to rent a portable grinder and drive a wire brush or sanding disks). Be sure to wear safety goggles.

If that fails, the options for stripping paint get nasty: chemical stripper, a heat gun, or a propane torch. Chemical stripper is toxic and expensive, a heat gun is slow, and the propane torch is dangerous. As we used to say, "It's a free country." Translated: I'm not choosing for you.

When the scraping and patching are done, wash your house by hand or with a power washer. Follow the instructions with the power washer. A simple but effective hand washing uses a TSP substitute, a bucket, and a stiff-bristled brush or broom. Dip the brush into the cleaning solution, work it on the wall, and then rinse. The technique sounds crude, but it works fast, and is vastly more effective than simply hosing off the wall. (TSP, or trisodium phosphate, was one of the phosphate cleaners that caused gross blooms of algae in surface water. It's largely been banned, but TSP substitute works fine.)

Where and When to Caulk

After scraping, washing, and repairs, it's time for caulking. Caulking is flexible material that seals between different building materials, which expand and contract with changes in temperature, creating cracks that only caulk can seal.

A good way to learn about controlling heat and moisture, and where better caulking is needed, is to obtain a home energy audit, courtesy of any utilities that still care about energy conservation. Or spend an hour on a particularly hot or cold day looking for drafts.

Outdoors, caulk the following areas:

◆ At the joint between the foundation and siding (if you can reach it).

◆ At cracks in the foundation (see Chapter 15 for more on foundation repair).

◆ Around windows, doors, faucets, vents, and other openings in siding.

All Thumbs

In brick houses, don't caulk the small, regularly spaced holes just above the foundation, doors, and windows. These "weep-holes" allow moisture to escape the wall, and must be left open.

Indoors, caulk the following areas:

◆ At cracks around windows and exterior doors.

◆ At entry points of pipes and wires, such as under a sink or tub.

◆ To hide gaps between molding and walls.

◆ At floor joints near a tub or toilet, to prevent spills or condensation from damaging floors and walls.

Spring and fall are ideal caulking weather, because it's warm enough to meet the minimum temperature requirement of caulking, surfaces are dry, and you won't get broiled. Unfortunately, some caulking won't flow or adhere in cold weather, even though winter is when you may be most motivated to cure drafts.

Caulking has improved greatly over the past couple of decades, and there's no excuse to buy low-grade caulking. Many reasonably priced silicone caulks on the market promise Sphinxlike longevity.

Caulking Cracks

Caulking is real idiot-proof work. First, you clean the crack. Then you pump the caulk into place. Finally, if you're feeling ferociously fastidious, you smear it flat. While many home-maintenance tasks sound easy, this one truly is easy! About the only complication is deciding that caulking is more pressing than paddling a canoe or reading a book.

Read the caulk tube to see the limitations on application temperature and the size of crack the caulking can fill:

1. Clean the crack with a trowel, screwdriver, and/or stiff plastic brush. If you want really smooth caulking, remove all bumps near the joint. Drive in raised nailheads, and remove dust.

2. Put the tube in the gun, cut the tip at an angle (a bigger opening is best for wider cracks), and pierce the seal with a long nail.

3. Start caulking. Hold the gun at an angle and press the tip against the crack. While the caulking gun in the photo leans away from the new caulking, some people prefer leaning it the other way, so the caulk is pushed in front of the nozzle.

Keep steady pressure on the caulking gun, and try not to let bulges form when the gun snags on obstacles. Remember, it's much easier to make a smooth application than to fix it afterward.

4. Move the gun steadily along the entire crack, gradually squeezing the trigger. Release pressure just before the end of the crack, since the caulking will ooze out for another second. Release the pressure by turning the push-rod or clicking a button on the caulking gun.

5. Optional: Smooth the caulk and press it into place with a moistened finger, the handle of an old toothbrush, or a rag dampened with whatever solvent the manufacturer specifies.

Painter's Tools

Just because painter's tools are basic doesn't mean you should buy them in the bargain bin. When I finally bought a pro paintbrush, I discovered that it laid paint down much faster, with less spattering and streaking. Why did I wait so long?

Toolbox Tips

Three millimeter plastic is the lightest weight to buy as a painter's drop cloth. Anything lighter will just blow around and snag on your feet.

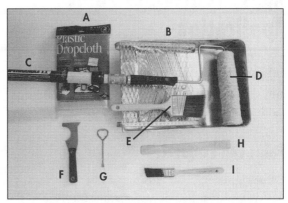

Brushes and rollers are the painter's best friend.

Here are the basic painting tools, as shown in the photo. You may also need scrapers, ladders, newspaper, and a fan for ventilation.

A. A plastic drop cloth protects walls, floors, windows, and furniture.

B. A roller tray holds paint for the roller. The optional screen helps load the roller evenly.

C. A roller extension is an adjustable pole that helps when painting walls and ceilings. I always use an extension, not just because it improves my reach, but also because it reduces bending and saves the wrists.

D. A 9″ roller is the basic tool for covering walls. A smooth nap covers a flat surface; a heavier nap covers a rougher surface.

E. Use a 2½″ brush for "cutting in"—painting where the roller won't fit. The angled bristles reach tight spots.

F. A painter's tool scrapes, loosens brushes, and cleans rollers like nuttin' else.

G. A paint-can opener is much better than a screwdriver; paint stores often give them away.

H. A stirring stick; well, need an explanation?

I. Use a 1" trim brush for fine trim.

Apply Yourself to Paint Application

Now that you've taken care of the dirty business—paint prep—it's time for the fun: buying paint and splashing it on. (If you need advice on using ladders, see Chapter 2.)

Paint Can Etiquette

Opening, using, and closing paint cans seems basic, but most people make a mess of it. See the earlier photo of making holes in the paint can rim, and follow these suggestions:

◆ When pouring paint, immediately swipe up the drips with your brush.

◆ Before closing a can, brush out the rim and hammer the lid closed. No need for a Neanderthal act—if the rim is clean, tapping works fine.

Before closing the paint can, brush out the rim to remove excess paint.

◆ Before closing a can of solvent-thinned paint, save some mineral spirits from the brush-cleaning ceremony and dump them into the can to prevent a skin from forming.

Toolbox Tips

Don't use a brush to stir paint. A brush that's soggy with paint is a hazard and a nuisance. Use one of those wood stirrers that paint stores give away, or a scrap of wood. Also, keep the paint toward the front of the bristles for maximum efficiency.

Brushing

Even kindergartners think they know how to brush paint, but most people make a bosh of it—all for the want of a few good suggestions. Let me paint a word picture of what I've learned in the course of painting a dozen houses:

◆ Use a paint bucket or another smaller container—don't drag the entire gallon up the ladder. It's easier on your wrist, and reduces the consequences of dropping the can.

◆ When working on a ladder with hollow rungs (like most aluminum ladders), cut notches in both ends of a 4' broom handle. Slip the handle through the rungs, and put the bail of the paint can into a notch on either side.

◆ When painting complicated things like windows, start in a corner. Press in a loaded brush and shimmy from side to side (see arrows on the following photo) to paint both surfaces. Pull away from the corner as the brush empties.

Painting in a corner.

◆ On complex shapes and vertical areas, quickly rebrush the paint after a couple minutes. This catches drips.

Left: I lightly brushed this molding 2 minutes after painting. Right: The drips at lower left formed because the molding was not brushed out.

◆ Move the brush rapidly; don't smooth the paint until you have applied enough to cover a relatively large area.

◆ Paint wood with the grain, not across it.

◆ To brush a broad area, paint stripes across the grain with a full brush. Then paint with the grain to merge the stripes. Work quickly.

◆ Lightly sand wood with fine or extra-fine sandpaper between coats to eliminate roughness.

Toolbox Tips

Painting with glue? You may think you are if you don't thin sticky paint. Depending on temperature and other factors, some paint gets gloppy rather quickly; however, paint from a new can should not be thinned.

This trick lets you quickly paint a large area with a brush.

Rolling

Rollers are the king of interior painting—it's hard to imagine painting walls with a brush. Still, rollers spatter, leave a stippled pattern, and stir up bubbles in some coatings.

For basic rolling, you'll need roller, pan, a trim brush, a stepladder, and preferably, a roller handle extension. Here's the basic routine for rolling paint:

1. With a 1½" to 2½" brush, *cut in* the edges and corners of the section you will roll.

2. Evenly load the roller. (Don't leave the roller soaking in the pan, where one side will get heavily gooped. Rest it in the shallow end of the pan.)

Fix-It Phrase _____

Cutting in is painter-speak for painting around the edges before or after rolling.

3. Make your first strokes as a long W, gradually increasing the pressure. (Normally, you would be painting alongside fresh paint. In the following photo I'm painting out in the open to show the technique more clearly.)

4. Roll perpendicular to the first strokes to fill in the area. Press more lightly so ridges don't form at the edge of the roller.

5. Roll horizontally near the baseboard, windows, and doors to blend with the cut-in areas.

Make your first strokes in a long "W" shape.

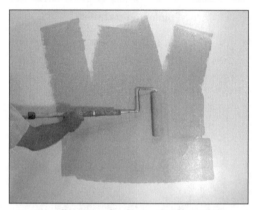

Now roll perpendicular to the first strokes.

Little-known fact: Rollers are also great for painting siding and floors. Quickly roll an area about 2×4', then brush it out with a 4" brush. The brush smoothes the nappy surface the roller would normally leave, and paints the siding lip.

Spraying

Even if you're not a graffiti artist, spray paint cans can be handy stuff, particularly for small jobs, intricate surfaces, and metal. You don't need a Ph.D. to spray paint, but these suggestions may help:

◆ Start spraying before the can starts to pass over the surface, and continue spraying until it's past the surface.

◆ Move your hand parallel to the surface.

◆ Keep moving, spraying light, sag-proof coats. Cover the whole surface, giving each part a moment to dry.

◆ When done, hold the can upside-down and spray until the stream is clear. Then wipe the spray nozzle with a rag. With this treatment, the can can actually work next time you need it.

Test Your Mettle Painting Metal

As the ad said, rust never sleeps, and the better you scrape and wire-brush iron and steel, the longer your paint will last. (Aluminum is much easier to paint because it oxidizes into a thin, self-protective layer, as long as you use a primer made for aluminum.)

To paint iron and steel, get the surface as clean and dry as possible, and then apply a rust-inhibiting primer. You'll need a scraper, an electric drill with a wire brush, goggles, and primer and paint. If you've got lots of rust, rent a high-speed grinder.

All Thumbs

A high-speed grinder with a wire brush or sanding disk is incredibly effective for removing bad paint and rust. Wear work gloves and safety goggles, and *use this brawny tool with extreme care!*

Don't paint on a windy, rainy, or cold day. Here's how to clean up rust and spray paint onto metal:

1. Put on gloves and goggles and wire-brush all loose rust. Run your drill at top speed. Use a two-handed grip to prevent the drill from wandering.

Wire-brush all loose rust.

2. Sandpaper the edges of the repair to smooth the existing paint.

3. Mask the surroundings as needed.

4. Warm the metal, particularly in damp conditions, to remove trapped moisture. If you use a propane torch, move it rapidly so you don't scorch the paint. Get the metal warm but still touchable.

5. Spray metal primer onto the warm, bare metal, overlapping onto painted areas.

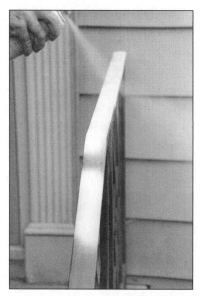

Spray metal primer onto the warm metal, using quick, light applications to avoid sagging paint.

6. When the primer is dry, apply finish paint.

Cleaning Brushes and Rollers

Darn few painters look forward to cleaning brushes, but it's much easier once you know what you are doing:

◆ Clean or soak brushes and rollers immediately after painting.

◆ Add a bit of dish soap to water when cleaning latex paint from brushes and rollers.

◆ Flick a brush against a log or board to remove the last bit of paint.

◆ If you'll paint tomorrow, work some water or thinner into the brush or roller, and store in a double layer of plastic bags.

◆ Use a painter's tool to squeeze extra paint from a roller into the can. If you wish, clean water-based paint by stroking the roller with the painter's tool, now under a stream of water. I would dry a roller filled with solvent-based paint, and throw it out. Once the paint is dry, it's no longer hazardous.

Roller cleanup is easy with a painter's tool.

◆ Store dry, clean brushes with bristles straight.

◆ Cut off stray bristles with scissors before using a brush.

Are You Ready for This Job?

Painting can be an enjoyable diversion, or an endless drudge that drags you away from biking, canoeing, and other summer fun. Consider these pointers when evaluating a painting project:

◆ Preparation is the wild card. How much heavy-duty repair (rotten soffits or window frames, moth-eaten trim) is required? How much scraping? Do you have the tools, skills, and time for it?

This kind of peeling paint demands serious scraping and sandpapering. If you just paint over this crud, your paint will look hideous and die young.

◆ Renting a power washer can save cleaning time, but be sure to allow drying time.

◆ A big paint job may call for a lot of ladders, which you'll have to buy, beg, borrow, or rent. (Scrimping on ladders can be dangerous if it causes you to overreach or use unsafe ladders!)

◆ Exterior painting is mostly a spring and fall sport. In any case, you can't work on rainy days.

The Least You Need to Know

◆ Painting has become much less painful with the advent of fast-drying, water-based products.

◆ Primer looks inward; paint looks outward—so you'll usually need both. Stain and other "self-priming" products serve double duty.

◆ Preparation is nine-tenths of painting. Don't open a paint can until everything is clean, exposed, patched, primed, or covered.

◆ A few basic brushing and rolling techniques can save significant time and make the new paint last far longer.

◆ Iron and steel are the biggest challenges in home painting. Rust may win in the end, but the cleaner the surface, the slower its victory will be.

In This Chapter

- ◆ The importance of maintaining your deck

- ◆ Cleaning and preserving decks and other outdoor wood

- ◆ Replacing deck boards—easier than you think!

- ◆ Replacing a rotten joist under an outdoor deck

  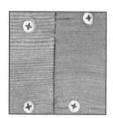   

Chapter 12

Step Up to the Deck

If you think you can shirk your home repair obligations just by lounging in the backyard, I've got news for you: sunlight, snow, rain, and fungus exact their heaviest toll outdoors, and the yard is ideal territory for rot, decay, and rust (did anyone mention moral decrepitude?). But it's also a place to save money—in tomorrow's repair bills, and in next year's replacement bills.

Even if you'd rather be napping in the hammock, or just plain asleep at the switch—the forces of decay are happily rotting, rusting, and ruining your outdoor possessions. So slurp down that beer and let's get down to some yard work.

Treating a Deck

Ah, wooden decks—the delightful replacement for front porches, the staging ground for innumerable barbecues, the whining ground for mosquitoes, and the battleground of your home's struggle with the elements.

Chances are your outdoor deck or stairway is made of treated lumber—the faintly green stuff that's so full of poison that even bugs and fungi won't sink the fungal equivalent of teeth into it. Treated lumber is great stuff. It lasts forever. It never needs painting. It's like, permanent. Isn't it?

Outdoor wood needs protection from the sun and rain. A paint roller is one good way to apply stain and preservative.

All Thumbs

The sad news is that exterior wood needs care. When water seeps in, wood expands and cracks. Sunlight does dry wood, but its ultraviolet rays also destroy wood fibers.

Wrong. Treated lumber may be repellent to insects and fungi, but it won't last forever unless you paint or stain it. Just as you need sunscreen at the beach, your deck (and other outdoor wood) needs sunscreen, too. So if you want it to last a long time in good condition, you'll have to do this every year or two. All of this is a good reason to buy the wood-substitute material now being sold for decking. It's a tradeoff more people are willing to make—trading nasty maintenance chores for one less bit of real wood in your life.

Swab the Deck!

If you're like me, you've shirked your duty to protect your backyard deck (or other outdoor wood). And now you've got a dirty deck. So you've got to do what I did—use deck cleaner to brighten and clean the wood before staining.

(Although deck cleaner may sound like a backyard version of Love Canal, the stuff I used was pretty nontoxic once mixed with water. Still, it's expensive, and if I am more diligent about protecting the deck next time, I won't need to use brightener again.)

To clean a dirty deck, you'll need a hose with spray attachment, a bucket and a brush with stiff bristles, or a garage broom. (Must I remind you to read the instructions on the deck cleaner you buy?) Then follow these steps:

1. Sweep the deck with a broom.
2. Put on safety goggles. Mix the cleaner according to the instructions and apply to a small area at a time. Work the cleaner back and forth with a brush. A garage broom is fast and easier on the back than a hand brush.
3. If the cleaner doesn't remove stains, try removing them with diluted household bleach. (Never mix the cleaner with bleach unless the cleaner's directions say it's okay—you could create toxic fumes.)
4. Hose off the deck and allow the wood to dry for at least 24 hours before staining. Heed the manufacturer's advice about getting the chemical on your lawn or into your pool.

A Real Treat for Your Deck

Now that you've cleaned the deck, it's time to protect it. Paint is not flexible enough to expand and contract as wood responds to changing humidity and temperature. Instead, use a penetrating, water-repellent treatment—a stain, in other words—to protect against water absorption and ultraviolet light and forestall warping, swelling, and cracking.

I suggest a product with a low percentage of volatile organic compounds (VOCs), which cause ozone smog. Low-VOC coatings are not just good for the environment, they're good for you—you won't suffer that refinery stench while using the stuff, and you should be able to clean your tools in water instead of paint thinner.

Toolbox Tips

Deck treatment is pretty simple, both in technique and tools. You'll need a 2" paintbrush, a roller and roller pan, and a garage broom (or the short-bristled broom sold to coat asphalt driveways). Save your back with a roller extension handle. A low-pressure sprayer will work, but may be an extravagance unless you have other uses for it.

Outdoor wood needs a new protective coating as soon as raindrops start to sink in. Choose a warm day when leaves are not falling and rain, dogs, and children are not in the forecast. The wood should be fairly dry (although some products do not require bone dryness). Follow these steps to treat your deck:

1. Clean the deck with a brightener, as described earlier in this chapter, if necessary.

2. Using the 2" brush, cut in near the house and other nonrollable areas. Do not get too far ahead of the roller.

3. Apply the coating as indicated on the can.

4. After 2 to 5 minutes, brush away puddles and drips with a wide brush.

5. Roll stain on the end grain again. These thirsty board ends absorb lots of coating.

6. Clean up tools and keep traffic off the deck. Do not recoat unless the label directs.

Brush out the coating to smooth the coat.

Renailing Deck Boards

Between all those feet and all those years of sun and rain, deck boards—and especially the nails that used to hold them in place—can start to lose their grip. You can renail with galvanized, 8d spiral-pattern deck nails. Unfortunately, as you can see from the photo, a lot of nail heads will be visible.

Renailing the deck leaves a lot of nail heads showing.

You can also tear off and replace the deck boards, as shown later in this chapter. An intermediate option is to set the nailheads, and then try to hide them with big screws:

1. Set heads of existing nails well below the wood surface.

Set the nailhead in the deck before hiding it with a screw.

2. Drill countersinks close to each head.

Countersink for the new screw head.

3. Drive in rustproof deck screws. With a bit of luck, they will cover the nail heads.

Drive in a rustproof deck screw.

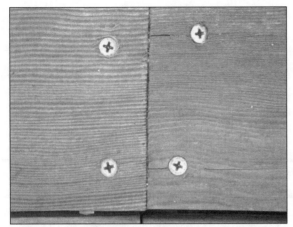

These screws hide four nailheads and greatly strengthen the attachment.

Hoisting a New Joist

Virtually all new outdoor construction is built of wood that has been rot-proofed either with chemicals or plastic. But there's plenty of rotting wood around from earlier construction. We'll cover the replacement of damaged deck boards shortly. Here's how to replace the rotten *joists* that are supposed to support them.

Fix-It Phrase _____

A **joist** is a piece of framing—2×6 or larger—that supports a deck, floor, or ceiling.

For this joist replacement, you'll need a drill, standard hand tools, treated wood of the same dimensions as the existing joists, ⅜" carriage bolts, scraps of 1" wood for spacers, and a scissors-action car jack. Also, you'll need at least 2' of access below the joists. Before starting, make sure you will be able to sneak the new joist into position, either from the end, or from below. If framing gets in the way, this technique won't work.

Instead of going to the effort of removing the damaged joist, we'll install a *sister* joist ¾" away from it. We'll leave a gap to prevent leaves from accumulating and soaking the pair of joists. Once you've used this technique, you can later trash the rotted joist by removing the bolts and puling the nails, but you'll have less destruction at first, and the result will be stronger than removing the rotted joist first. However, if your existing joist is totally rotted, install a new joist with this procedure, then remove the rotten joist.

1. Cut spacer blocks from 1" material, *mitering* the top end at 30° so water will run off.

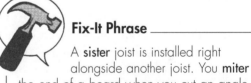

Fix-It Phrase _____

A **sister** joist is installed right alongside another joist. You **miter** the end of a board when you cut an angle across the broad side. The pointy tops of a picket fence have two miter cuts. You might see bevels in the edges of tables or counters.

2. Saw the new joist ¼" shorter than the existing joist.
3. Using 6d galvanized box nails, nail spacer blocks to the new joist. Nail a block 1' from each end. Place the others 3' to 4' apart. Apply black roofing tar to the top to keep water out of the thirsty end grain.

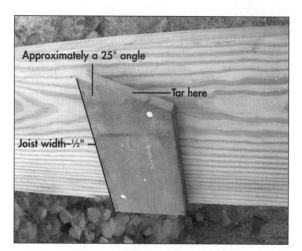

Nail spacer blocks to the new joist.

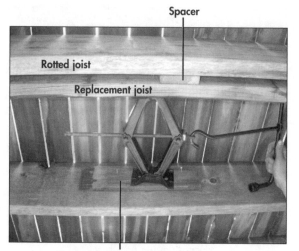

Board tacked into position to hold jack

With the jack expanded, the joist is ready for fastening.

4. Lay the new joist flat in the gap alongside the damaged joist. Tack a piece of scrap wood as shown in one of the following photos, so the jack does not dig into the damaged joist.

5. Place the car jack on its side, and tie it to something so it can't fall. Because the new joist is the same dimension as the old one, you must force it into position by expanding the jack. You may have to jack in several places to get the joist in place.

6. Clamp the joist in place and drill a ⅜" hole through the center of each spacer.

Clamp the joist in place while you drill for the bolts.

7. Push one ⁵⁄₁₆×5" carriage bolt through each hole. Slip a flat washer on the bolt, and thread and tighten a nut.

New joist being jacked into position   Note damaged joist

Jacking the new joist into position. Move the jack if the joist gets stuck.

Wrench tightens the nut

Bolting the joint.

All Thumbs

You've got to know when to hold, and when to fold. If you see massive rot in your joists, don't hesitate to take them out. With time, that rot will likely infect your decking.

8. Using right-angle truss plates, secure the joist to the framing at each end. Use deck screws long enough to penetrate the framing (1½" to 3"). If the deck screws don't grab the house framing, try ¼" lag screws.

3" rustproof screws fasten bracket to house.

Attaching the joist to the house framing.

Replace Rotten Deck Boards

Deck boards can go bad for any number of reasons—from poor original quality to subsequent abuse and neglect. If the deck is *screwed* down, you're in luck: simply unscrew the damaged board, cut a replacement to the same length, and screw it down. You'll need rustproof deck screws, a power screwdriver, and a pilot drill bit.

Deck boards that are *nailed* down are more difficult to remove and replace. You may need a saber or keyhole saw, a triangular square, a pencil, a hammer, a prybar, a chisel or cat's paw, replacement board, scraps of treated 2×4 or 2×6, and galvanized deck nails or deck screws. It will be very handy to have a circular saw and a C-clamp.

Toolbox Tips

Decks are one of the many places where screws are pushing nails into the dustbin of construction history. Because screws are even more noticeable than nails, however, it pays to place new ones carefully, in the same pattern as existing fasteners.

Start by sizing up the problem. It's easier to remove whole boards, but if the damage is small, you can replace only a portion of a board (for stability, any board should span at least three joists). Removing part of a board is more complicated than yanking up the whole thing, so I'll describe that process:

1. At the end of the section to be replaced, mark a square cutting line. Sight from above and make the line directly above the *near edge* of a joist. Sawing at the edge gives room for the saw blade while leaving the good piece of decking nailed to the joist.

Cut straight and square along the line. Don't let the square slip.

2. Cut along the line, preferably with a jig saw (shown in the preceding photo) or reciprocating saw. Use the square for guidance in making a straight, square cut.

3. Pull as many nails as possible. If you have a cat's paw (see Chapter 3), hammer the hooked end under the nails and pull them. Otherwise, gouge around the nail head as shown with a wood chisel (don't hit the nail), then pull the nail with a hammer or wrecking bar (prybar).

Pull the nail after you have exposed the head with a chisel.

4. Once most of the nails are out, pry the board loose with the wrecking bar, using scrap wood to protect nearby boards.

5. Cut a section of pressure-treated 2×4 or 2×6 about three times as long as the *width* of your decking. (If the board you removed was sound 2" lumber, use a piece of it.) C-clamp this "nailing block" against the joist where you sawed out the old board, with the top tight to the bottom of the decking. Screw the block to the framing with 3" deck screws, or nail as shown.

Attaching nailer block.

6. Cut the new board to length and nail or screw into place. To prevent splitting, drill holes before inserting the end fasteners. Finish per suggestions in "Treating a Deck," earlier in the chapter.

Screwing replacement deck board into place.

The Least You Need to Know

◆ Treated lumber needs protection from rain and ultraviolet light—use a water-repellent, ultraviolet-resistant coating. Most people call this stuff "deck stain."

◆ If water soaks into the surface of outdoor wood, it's time to renew the water-repellent treatment.

◆ You can easily reinforce broken or rotted joists—if you have access to the underside.

◆ Rotted deck boards are easy to replace.

In This Chapter

- ◆ The parts of a roof
- ◆ Detecting, isolating, and repairing roof leaks
- ◆ Replacing damaged shingles
- ◆ Gutter maintenance
- ◆ The best way to prevent a wet basement
- ◆ Attic and roof ventilation

Chapter 13

Dry Is Beautiful: Roof Repair

When we talk roof, I don't have to convince you about the value of preventive maintenance—everyone understands why a house needs a working roof. But roof leaks can be sneaky; by the time you recognize one problem (a leak) you may have a bigger problem—damaged drywall and framing caused by that silent but deadly drip, drip, drip. Call it the homeowner's water torture.

Roofs are one place where it pays to look for trouble, since that's the best way to avoid water torture. As you search, follow a veteran roofer's advice: Think like a raindrop. Because water flows downhill, roofs are formed of overlapping layers of shingles, helped along by various pieces of metal flashing.

Roofing Lingo

Before we start thinking like a raindrop, we'll get our feet wet learning the anatomy of roofs. Roofers, like everybody else, have their own dialect. Refer to the following illustration to see these parts of a roof:

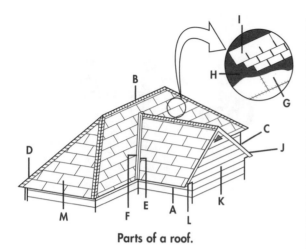

Parts of a roof.

A. **Eave:** The lower, horizontal edge of the roof.

B. **Ridge:** The horizontal line along the peak.

C. **Rake edge:** The slanting edge.

D. **Hip:** Where two roof planes meet in a convex angle.

E. **Valley:** Where two roof planes meet in a concave angle. Valleys are "open," if the flashing is visible because the shingles are cut, or "closed," if the shingles cover the flashing.

F. **Valley flashing:** Metal used to seal the valley. Should be used in open and closed valleys.

G. **Sheathing (decking):** The plywood or boards nailed to rafters.

H. **Roofing felt (underlayment):** Gives a final seal in case the shingles leak.

I. **Shingle:** Usually 12×36" total size, with bottom 5" showing (5⅝" show on a metric shingle: check the package).

J. **Fascia:** Vertical face of rake edges and eaves.

K. **Gable:** Area under a peaked roof.

L. **Soffit:** Horizontal section under an eave or rake edge.

M. **Course:** A horizontal band of shingles.

Fix-It Phrase

To roofers, a **square** is 100 square feet of roof surface. Three bundles of shingles, generally weighing 80 pounds apiece, cover 1 square (shingles made to last 40 or more years require more bundles per square). A **course** is a horizontal layer of shingles.

The Foundations of Roofing

Water runs downhill. That's why the upper shingles overlap lower ones. Pitched (sloping) roofs are really that simple—except where they meet a chimney or another roof.

Because shingles, flashing, and everything else on a roof expand and contract with changing temperature, a repair that looks solid today may leak in a year or so, particularly when strong wind blows the rain almost horizontal. Thus, a bit of overkill is wise in roof repair.

Roofers don't talk about slope in degrees. Instead, they talk about "roof pitch" (this is not what happens when a roofer tries to sell you a shingling job you don't need). Pitch is measured in "rise over run," the number of inches in height gained every time you move 12" horizontally. Knowing pitch can help you decide whether you want to walk on a roof. (The 4-12 pitch found on ranch houses and many new homes is pretty flat. If the pitch is much steeper than 6-12, get a pro to do your roofing.)

To measure roof pitch you'll need a ladder, a level, and a carpenter's square. Stand on a ladder leaning against the rake (slanting) edge of the roof. Place the 12" mark on one leg of the square against the rake edge. Use the level to make this leg horizontal. Read the rise where the vertical leg meets the roof (4-12 pitch is shown in the following illustration).

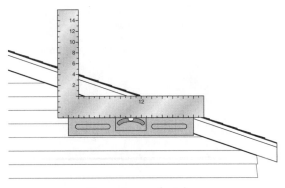

Measuring roof pitch.

Special Tools and Materials

Roofing requires simple tools. You could get fancy and rent a nail gun to put on a new layer of shingles, but for repairs a hammer works fine. Here are some other tools and materials you'll need (refer to the following illustration):

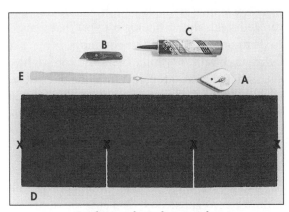

Roofing tools and materials.

A. **Chalk line:** Used to draw long straight lines, for starting or finishing shingling. Stretch the string tight above where you want the line, pull it up, and release.

B. **Utility knife:** Cuts shingles (preferably from the back).

C. **Roof cement (tar):** Seals gaps and nail-heads, and holds old shingles down. Sold in 1-gallon cans.

D. **Roof shingles:** Most roof shingles are made of a fiberglass mat, soaked in asphalt, and covered with colored, sunlight-resistant mineral granules. These shingles last 15 to 40 years, depending on quality and the environment on your roof. (Xs show nail locations: about ¾" above the slot between the tabs. These nails will be covered by the next course of shingles.)

E. **Paint stirrer (for applying tar):** Trowels work, but you won't have to clean a stir stick afterward.

Looking for Trouble: Finding Leaks

If you're lucky, a roof leak will announce itself. Maybe a section of the ceiling will fall into your living room when your boss is starting dessert, or some black crud will start oozing down the chimney on Christmas Eve.

But you can also spend a lot of time searching for leaks, which may originate when wind-blown rain enters under flashing around a chimney or other opening. Windy rain is nasty, because it negates the basic principle of roofing by blowing water sideways, even uphill.

Scanning Your Roof from Inside

Many leaks are obvious once you look inside your roof. Even if your attic is only accessible through a hatchway, I'd suggest you occasionally visit the dust and cobwebs, preferably after a downpour. Pay special attention to brick chimneys, which are a major source of leaks. If the chimney is connected to a wood-burning stove or fireplace, it may bleed a disgusting, evil-smelling, flammable form of liquefied creosote. Creosote, or discolored brick or wood, indicates either a water leak or a dangerous flaw in the chimney. Either is a good reason to phone a mason for a chimney rebuild. Fortunately for your wallet, chimneys generally only need rebuilding above the roof.

Looking directly above any wet spot on your ceiling—or further up the roof—search for that dampness and mold that signify an active leak (simple discoloration may indicate a past leak that was repaired). Poke around with a flashlight to find the precise leak. If you're going to fix the leak right away, pound a 16-penny nail up through the leak, and locate the nail from outside. Or measure diagonally down from the peak, and horizontally across from a wall, chimney, ridge, or other landmark.

Scanning Your Roof from Outside

If you did not find trouble from inside, head up to the roof to search for the flaw. If your roof is shallow (4–12 to 6–12 pitch), get a ladder and haul yourself up (see Chapter 2 for tips on using a ladder safely). If it's steeper, use binoculars from the ground, or climb a ladder and look from the eave. Look for broken, buckled, or missing shingles, and rusted or detached flashing (see the photo of decayed shingles in Chapter 1). Mineral granules in the gutter indicate that the top surface of the shingles is deteriorating. Pay special attention to junctions between the roof and dormers, chimneys, vents, skylights, or another roof.

If none of this works, wait for a dry spell. Ask a helper to spray water on the roof while you scan from the attic. Your helper should start spraying the bottom of the suspect area, then gradually work uphill until the leak shows its miserable self.

Spraying water on the roof to find a leak.

Flashing Is Trouble

Flashing is the rust-resistant, flexible metal (galvanized steel, aluminum, or copper) that joins roofs to other roofs, and to chimneys, vents, skylights, and walls. Flashing keeps the roof tight even when the various parts move due to expansion or contraction from changes in temperature. But flashing can get sick—through rust, perforation, or simply separating from whatever it once joined.

Generally, the nails securing flashing are covered by shingles—except those at the lower end of chimney flashing. Replace loose flashing nails with rust-resistant screws, then coat the heads with roof tar. (For copper flashing, use copper nails—galvanized fasteners will cause rapid corrosion.)

Toolbox Tips

Flashing is a seriously annoying source of leaks. Even if your leak is several feet below the flashing, don't rule out the flashing until you've used the hosing technique described in the previous section.

Damn Ice Dams

In colder regions, one of a roof's worst enemies is the ice buildup, or ice dam. Ice dams usually occur near the eave, where melted snow from higher up tends to freeze. Water trapped by the dam can build up and enter the roof, severely damaging the shingles and sheathing.

Try these solutions to ice dams:

◆ Insulate the attic or roof to prevent heat from escaping and melting the snow.

◆ Increase ventilation through the attic and roof (see "Roof Vents" later in this chapter).

◆ Install electric de-icing tapes (sold at building suppliers or hardware stores) near the roof edge.

◆ Install special ice-dam membrane under shingles at the eave. (This good solution is only possible during reshingling, because the dam underlies the first six courses of shingles. In cold areas, roofers should always use an ice dam.)

Quickie Shingle Fixes

When you think about it, the blights that afflict old shingles sound suspiciously like the diseases of aging people: buckles, bald spots, blisters, even premature curling. For all of these ills, a bit of attention now can save serious woes later on.

◆ If a corner of a shingle curls up, wait for a warm day and smear roof cement under the curled portion. Nail it flat with a couple roofing nails and tar the nail heads.

◆ If a shingle is cracked, smear roof cement under and on top of the crack.

◆ If a shingle is torn, treat it as a crack, but nail down the loose parts and goop the nail heads.

After you tar a loose shingle, sun should heat and soften the tar.

◆ If a shingle is broken or otherwise mangled, slip a rectangular piece of aluminum flashing as far as possible underneath it, nail it into place, and tar the nail head. It may be better to replace the shingle, as described next.

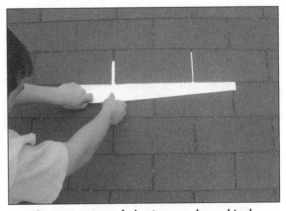

Slipping a piece of aluminum under a shingle.

Toolbox Tips

Dry roof tar is murder to remove from tools. For your next roof repair, apply tar with a paint stirrer or scrap wood, then just toss it out.

Replacing Shingles

If a few shingles on your roof have lost their mineral coating, are curled beyond repair, or are split, missing, or otherwise AWOL, you'll have to replace them with new recruits (but see "Starting Fresh" later in this chapter).

Even in black-and-white, you can see that these shingles are starting to lose their protective coating of mineral granules. This roof is due for replacement—now!

Before you get started, take note of these roof repair cautions:

- Bend old, brittle shingles carefully, particularly in cold weather.

- Use care on the roof—wear nonslip shoes and rig a safety line if needed.

- In hot weather, spray water on the roof *below the repair* to cool the shingles so you won't damage them (you'll also be more comfortable).

- Use common sense. If you're not feeling secure on the roof, get down and get help.

To replace a few shingles, you'll need a ladder, hammer, prybar, trowel, utility knife, roofing nails, new shingles, and roof tar. Use a tool belt so tools don't roll down the roof, and follow these steps to make your repair:

1. Examine the area and figure out how many shingles need replacement (one bundle of new shingles usually covers 25 or 33⅓ square feet). Seriously curled, bare, or broken shingles are all candidates.

2. Separate the uppermost damaged shingles from the good shingles above them with a trowel like the brick trowel shown. Slide the trowel back and forth to break the seal. Don't be in a hurry or you'll mangle good shingles.

Use a trowel to separate shingles.

3. Work downward, releasing shingles as you go. Use a hammer or prybar to pull nails. Treat old shingles that you want to preserve with respect, so you don't break any around the edge of the repair.

4. Remove bad shingles down to the bottom of the repair area (you can see a photo of deteriorating shingles in Chapter 1). To remove part of a shingle, cut from the top. (The step flashing is shown along the right edge in the following photo. Step flashing is a series of folded rectangles used to seal walls, chimneys, and skylights in a roof. If water gets under one step, it will drop to the next step, and flow down on top of the shingles.)

Old shingles cut easily, even with a dull utility knife.

5. Clean out loose nails and scrap shingles.

6. Starting from the bottom, nail down the replacement shingles, matching the old pattern. Score new shingles from the back, then fold to separate them.

7. Continue nailing shingles all the way up. Stagger the seams so they are at least 6" apart, from one course to the next.

8. Follow the old pattern when nailing the new shingles. Never allow the vertical joints between shingles to line up vertically. Always offset them at least 5".

Follow the old pattern when nailing new shingles.

9. Nail the last replacement shingle with the side of the hammer so you don't curl the old shingle too much.

To minimize damage, nail the last replacement shingle with the side of the hammer.

Smear roof tar on exposed nail heads, under broken or split shingles, and under the first course of new shingles (see the earlier photo showing how to do this). The new shingles may not lie flat until they are softened by the sun.

Starting Fresh

There's little point in fixing a roof that's basically shot. You know when a shingle roof is a total loss if you are seeing lots of mineral granules in your gutters, or lots of tired, bald, cracked, or curled shingles, or even leaks inside the house. (Remember, drywall does not get dark and damp all by its lonesome.) But whatever the reason, at a certain point, you just plain need a new roof.

Getting Ready

Building codes and common sense both limit the buildup of shingles on a roof to two or three layers. Multiple layers of roofing material can collapse the framing or wrinkle up and collect water. Many good roofers insist on tearing the roof down to bare wood before starting. Unless you're a real masochist, or have lots of energetic friends, that's a pro job.

You may be able to count layers from the rake edge. Or estimate, based on the age of the house, using 20 years as the average lifetime for asphalt shingles. (If the first layer contains wood shingles, figure it lasted 30 to 40 years.) Thus, a 40-year-old house that's approaching a reroofing job probably has two layers of asphalt shingles, and needs a tear-off (a complete stripping of the old shingles).

All Thumbs

If you contemplate a tear-off, be aware that a small percentage of old shingles contain asbestos, a known cause of cancer. If you suspect your shingles do contain asbestos, a firm that recycles roofing material or a public-health lab may be able to test them.

Laying It On

Once you have the roof cleaned off, you are in a good position to repair any damage, or simply to make sure the sheathing is in good shape. After that, all roof processes work from the eaves toward the ridge (highest part of the roof).

All Thumbs

Smart roofers—even pros—follow the instructions printed on the shingle package.

1. For a really good job, renail old decking with 8d sinker nails, spaced 8" apart.

2. Staple the roofing felt to the deck. Start at the bottom, and overlap each course 3".

Notice how ace roofer Ken Schuster breaks the rule by working from the top down. He's trying to avoid stepping on the slippery roof felt until it's stapled into place. He's using a hammer tacker. A staple gun will do the same thing, but it's slower.

3. Nail roof edging over the felt, starting from the bottom. Overlap top pieces over bottom ones by 3". If you are bashing your fingers, hold the nails with pliers.

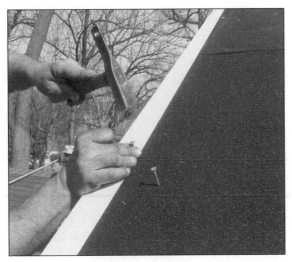

Nailing roof edging.

4. In cold climates, unwrap ice dam material and roll it out, so it covers the edging.

Toolbox Tips

If you're shingling a steep roof, buy or rent the "roof jacks" shown later in this chapter. Nail these brackets through the decking into the rafters as you work your way up, and bridge between them with good 2×6 planks. When the roof is finished, pound upward on the jacks and they will slip out from the nails.

5. Lay out valley flashing, meeting at a valley (concave angle between adjacent pieces of roof). Cut the bottom edges to match the eaves, and nail at outer edges of flashing. Place the nails about 2' apart.

6. Lay down a starter course of shingles, nailed every 12". The starter course has adhesive to secure the first true course of shingles. Follow the manufacturer's directions, as the position of the starter course varies with different shingles.

Nailing starter course.

7. Nail one whole shingle at the rake edge, with the bottom edge upward. Nail 1" above the slot between tabs, and at the ends, as shown in the drawing of roofing materials, earlier in the chapter. The nails must be long enough to penetrate roof decking.

8. Nail the second shingle alongside the first one, with the end touching but not jammed together. The photo shows that other courses have been started; the second course will slightly overlap the white line.

Nailing the first course.

9. Start the second course: Cut a piece (see shingle instructions for length) from the rake edge-end of a new shingle, and nail it into place, 6" up from the first course. Cut each shingle from the back, flip it over, and break the end free.

The second course is started with a trimmed shingle.

10. Nail the cut shingle with four nails to start the second course, leaving 6" of the first course exposed.

Continue nailing successive courses. Seth Schuster is power-nailing the fourth course. Normally you will work upward, diagonally, but Seth is nailing full horizontal courses so he can place shingles under the roof jacks, and then he'll start up diagonally.

Roof jacks are the metal brackets holding the plank used for a walkway. When the roof is done, Seth will remove the jacks by pounding upward.

11. Continue nailing successive courses. After every 4' of vertical progress, snap a chalk line across the roof to keep the courses straight. Do this by measuring down from the peak at each end of the roof and snapping a line where the top of the next course should go.

12. To make the cap shingles, cut a shingle in three pieces, as shown in the next photo.

Make cap shingles by cutting whole shingles into 3 pieces.

13. Mark a chalk line 6" to the side of the ridge. Starting at one end, nail cap shingles so the edges touch the chalk mark. Use nails that are ½" longer than before. These nails will be covered by subsequent cap shingles.

Nail capping with one nail at each arrow.

14. Continue capping to the end. Cut the last cap shingle in half. When done, tar the two exposed nails.

Gutter Talk—Maintaining Eaves Troughs

Gutters, or eaves troughs, always look so—well—optional. All they do is collect water that's already run off your roof and dump it on the ground. The water would end up there anyway, so why bother? Because they save your siding from the stress of shedding all that water. Because they

route water away from the foundation (see "Can We Discuss Your Soggy Basement?" coming up next). And most important, because they give you one more thing to fix!

Toolbox Tips

Gutter problems are a major cause of leaking basements. That's a good reason to clean them regularly, which is a great reason to own rubber gloves! If you do this once or twice a year, organic litter won't have time to ferment, so the task will be far less disgusting than if you wait until Bonsai trees are sprouting from your gutters. Clean gutters are also less prone to overflowing, icing up, or falling off. Best of all, they will actually carry water away from the house, which should help your soggy basement.

Follow these hints for a healthier relationship with your gutters:

◆ Keep leaves out of gutters by installing protective screens. Some screens even have hinges so you can clean out crud that filters through them. To prevent rust, attach the screens with aluminum rivets.

◆ If the gutter is not draining, check for a plug at a downspout connection. Then check the slope by holding a level against the gutter at several places. The gutter should slope consistently toward the downspout, about 1" per 20' of run. Remove and reattach gutter nails, straps, or connectors to correct the slope.

◆ If the gutter is leaking at connectors or through holes, use gutter repair goop (sold for caulking guns).

Drill an ⅛'' hole, push a rivet into place, and squeeze the handle of the riveter.

◆ Repair broken gutter straps with sheet metal screws or rivets.

◆ To refasten or repair gutters, use sheet-metal screws or a hand riveter. Most gutters are aluminum; use rivets for them.

Can We Discuss Your Soggy Basement?

In the masonry business, I was often called to fix a wet basement. I usually started by explaining that most of these problems did not require expensive waterproofing, trenching, or sump pumps. Instead, they required a low-tech solution—routing the water away from the foundation so it could not sink into the ground and cause a problem. (Ever wonder why you don't hear this solution from people who sell waterproofing, trenching, or sump pumps?)

So when someone asked me to dry out a waterlogged basement, my first response was to roll my eyes to the sky. I wasn't being rude; I was looking for the problem, which was usually traceable to balky gutters. The lesson for you, dear homeowner-plagued-by-a-soggy-basement, is that it's easier to remove the water than to make your basement as watertight as a boat.

Follow this script for a "dry-is-beautiful" basement:

1. Stand outside, near where the water is entering, and examine the gutter. Is it leaking or plugged? Then reread the previous section on "Gutter Talk—Maintaining Eaves Troughs."

2. Check the downspouts, which deliver water from the gutters to the ground. If the spouts empty near the problem area, you've got to route that water elsewhere.

3. If you have underground piping to route run-off away, try to clean it out with a high-pressure hose. Or replace it with flexible black plastic pipe sold at lumberyards.

4. Look at the grading (slope) of the ground near the wet spot. Is the water simply doing what comes naturally—running downhill toward your house? Then add topsoil around the house, and grade it so the water runs away. You may need to (a) build a low berm to divert water to a place where it won't cause harm, or (b) caulk cracks between a driveway and a foundation with heavy-duty caulking.

Although these fixes usually work, you can always install a sump pump or hire a water-proofer if they don't.

Roof Vents

As houses are built ever tighter, a problem with moisture buildup has emerged. Insufficient ventilation can cause rot and mold. It can cause paint to peel or insulation to become wet and useless. Roof ventilation is simple: Air enters soffit vents and leaves through vents near the peak. (A soffit is the horizontal section under the eave, or horizontal edge, of a roof.) The vents allow moisture to escape from the roof, cooling the house, keeping the insulation dry, and helping prevent mold.

Any do-it-yourselfer can vent a shingle roof that's not too steep. The ventilator package should explain how many ventilators your house needs, based on square footage.

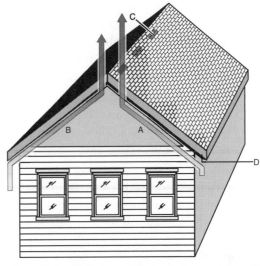

The attic or roof above any heated room in a cold climate must be ventilated. Air enters at soffit vents and leaves at ridge or roof vents. Roof vents are shown. Ridge vents run along the ridge of the roof.

A. If the attic is living space, air flows above the insulation, between the rafters.

B. If the attic is unused, air can flow through the attic.

C. Roof vent.

D. Soffit vent.

Aluminum soffit is usually vented with narrow slits cut in the aluminum at the factory. In wood soffit, install round ventilators with a rented hole saw or right-angle drill. Line up the holes with string. Drill between each rafter and push the vent into the hole. You'll need good ladders and goggles to shield your eyes.

To insert a roof ventilator under the shingles near the ridge, you'll need chalk or a pencil, a hammer, a saber saw or keyhole saw, a drill and bit, a trowel, the ventilator, roof cement, and roofing nails.

1A. If you can enter the attic: Locate the first ventilator by punching a nail upward, through the midpoint between the rafters, and about 18" below the ridge. This nail marks the hole's center. Go to step 2.

1B. If you must work from above: Locate the rafters by pounding on the roof. At a place with maximum bounce, mark the center of the first ventilator.

2. Place the ventilator on the roof—centered on the nail from step 1A or the mark from step 1B—and mark the opening (not the outer dimension) on the shingles with chalk. (Some ventilators include a template for this hole.)

3. Drill a ⅜" hole to start a saber saw (you'll need a ½" hole for a keyhole saw). Cut through the entire roof and remove the disk.

Cut the hole with a jigsaw.

4. Slip the trowel under the shingles above the hole to loosen the cement holding shingles together. Clear away debris.

Lift the shingle.

5. Coat the bottom of the ventilator base with roof cement and slip it under the upper shingles.

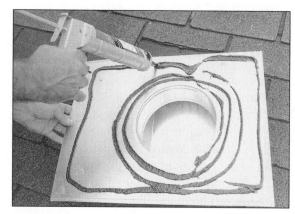

Seal the vent.

6. Nail the ventilator in place and coat visible nail heads with cement. Squirt a line of cement under the shingles you loosened in step 4 and press them down.

Ventilator installed.

The Least You Need to Know

◆ Keeping an eye on your roof is one of the most effective types of preventive mainte-nance, and it can save you big money on repairs.

◆ Most roof leaks occur where a roof meets a chimney, vent, skylight, or another roof.

◆ Wood shingles and shakes need protec-tion from sunlight, dampness, fungus, and moss.

◆ Many roof problems are repairable if you understand the basic principle of roofing.

◆ The best way to prevent a wet basement is to route the water away from the foun-dation so it can't sink into the ground and cause problems.

◆ Most competent homeowners can handle a simple roof replacement if the roof is not too high or steep.

In This Chapter

- ◆ Dealing with moisture in your siding
- ◆ Maintaining vinyl, aluminum, wood, shingle, hard-board, and plywood siding
- ◆ Fixing popped nails to prevent rot
- ◆ Replacing damaged plywood, aluminum, and vinyl siding

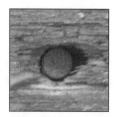
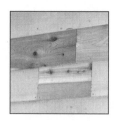

Chapter 14

Gliding Into Siding

Siding may seem dull, but it can conceal nasty surprises. Shortly after I moved into a house with new aluminum siding, a board blew loose. Then, a few days later, I received further proof (was any needed?) that Murphy's law also applies to siding: The stuff started peeling off the whole side of the house. It turned out that the contractor had saved time and money by using nails that didn't quite reach the studs—a brilliant bit of false economy that forced my wife and me to waste a beautiful evening renailing siding.

Still, not much goes wrong with siding that's properly installed and maintained. But if you fail your house-painting auditions, or let moisture build up behind the siding, you can expect trouble. With siding, as elsewhere, it's smarter to prevent problems than to solve them.

Wood Shingles

Wood shingles—usually made of red or white cedar—are a traditional siding material in the East. Shingles are sometimes left unpainted; near the ocean, they weather to a beautiful gray. But if you want longevity, it's probably better to give shingles occasional treatment with a water-repellent, ultraviolet-light inhibitor. To replace wood shingles used for siding, adapt the technique for replacing asphalt roof shingles (see "Shingle Replacement" in Chapter 13). Shakes, incidentally, are a type of wood shingle that is split instead of sawed. They are bigger and rougher, but respond to the same repair technique.

Wood shingles.

If you don't protect siding from water, it can rot.

Wood Lap Siding

Wood lap siding, also called clapboard, comes in various styles and is often made of cedar or redwood. Like all wood, lap siding needs paint, stain, or a water-repellent treatment every few years. Good eaves and working gutters will definitely reduce damage and peeling paint caused by water dripping down the siding. Splitting, drying, and separation are due to excess moisture, combined with a routine failure to put paint, preservative, or stain on the siding. (And I could add one more deficiency: galvanized corner caps, seen in later photos, would hold those ends tight and prevent more water entry.)

All Thumbs

Peeling paint, mold, and carpenter ants in your siding all indicate one thing: moisture. Excess humidity, whether it comes from outside or inside, is probably the biggest danger to your siding (and the structure beneath it). Moisture is a lurking disaster that must be fixed before you repaint or reside.

Hardboard lap siding is a form of particle board, formed to resemble wood siding, and primed at the factory. You can repair it with the same technique shown for wood siding, below.

Water is the most common cause of damage to lap siding, and you should isolate and cure that problem first. In the following photo, Gage is taking a last look at an outmoded kitchen ventilator on his house. To repair lap siding, you'll need a saw, prybar, hammer, nail set, wood scraps, replacement siding, and rust-proof deck screws and/or siding nails:

Young Gage gazes at lap siding—with unused kitchen ventilator.

1. Mark out the replacement area so vertical joints are at least 8" apart. In general, they should lie above a stud, but since I was short of replacement siding, I attached a horizontal 2×4 to hold a joint in the upper course (horizontal strip) of siding. Mark the cut lines at the center of studs, using a level or a small square.

2. Punch nails through in the boards you'll be replacing. Don't forget nails on the cut lines, and in the course above siding you'll replace.

3. Carefully pry away the loosened boards, using a scrap to protect good boards. Notice that Johan is carefully loosening the corner trim by prying directly beneath the nails. He's leaving the second nail, which holds the trim on the other side of the corner.

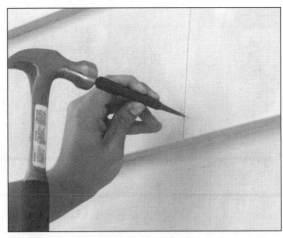

To loosen siding, punch the nails through the boards. The pencil line shows where we'll cut the siding.

4. Stick a block of scrap wood behind the siding, near your cut, to give the saw blade some room to travel. Using locking pliers, break off a jigsaw blade so it will only cut as deep as the siding, and carefully follow your line on all cuts.

Hole left by punched-through nail

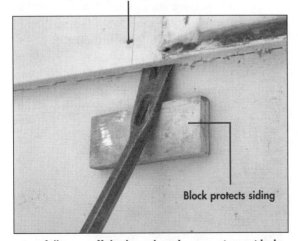

Block protects siding

Carefully pry off the boards; take your time with the boards you want to save.

Working slowly, remove the corner cap.

Cut line

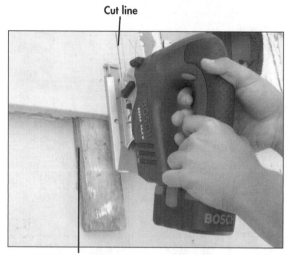

Block lifts siding

Make accurate cuts with a jigsaw.

5. Remove all old wood and all old nails. Search carefully under the course above your repair and pound in or pull any nails that will block the last course of replacement siding. Use a nail set, locking pliers, reciprocating saw, or any other tool to destroy these nails. This step is a pain, but it will save time in the long run.

6. Measure and cut replacement pieces of siding. If cutting with a circular saw, hold the siding face down to get a cleaner cut. To get a perfect cut with any hand saw, guide the saw along a square, as shown in the following photo.

Cut replacement pieces of siding.

7. To avoid splitting, drill holes for nails or screws in the end of new and old pieces.

Drill holes for nails or screws.

8. Nail or screw the new siding, working up from the bottom. Notice that I don't complete the nailing until I'm sure everything is in the right place. I'm using 6d galvanized box nails—you could also use the thinner galvanized siding nails. Nails should be long enough to grab the stud by 1". If the nails are too long, you're likely to damage the siding with the hammer.

Nail the new siding into place, working upward.

9. To fill the big holes left where I punched through the nails in the top course, I drive in 2" siding screws.

All Thumbs

Don't let nails or screws dig in too deep—siding doesn't need to be fastened as tightly as a floor joist!

Screw the old siding tight, but don't overdo it—that could cause splits.

10. When it's done, your repair should be practically invisible!

Finished lap siding—ready to paint.

Plywood Siding Repair

Plywood siding comes in several textures and thicknesses. About the only way to wreck this stuff is to neglect your obligation to paint or stain it. Once water gets inside plywood, delamination and destruction are sure to follow. Pay special attention to cracks between the sheets, since end grain absorbs an outsize share of water.

To repair plywood siding, you'll need a circular saw with a plywood (fine-tooth) blade, a carpenter's square, a level, a pencil, a nail set, a hammer and chisel, tin snips, galvanized siding screws or nails, aluminum "Z-bar" flashing, and replacement siding. If you can't locate the Z-bar flashing (shown in the drawing that follows), make it from flat aluminum flashing, which you can buy in rolls at a lumberyard, over two scraps of 2×4.

Follow these steps to repair plywood siding:

1. Mark out a rectangular cutout around the damaged area. Vertical cuts should run down the center of studs (nail holes reveal the stud locations). Use a level to mark all lines so the cutout is rectangular.

2. Punch nails on the cutting lines beneath the siding with a heavy nail punch so they won't wreck the saw blade. (If you have a cat's paw, try to pull the nails with it, but don't damage any siding you're planning to keep.)

3. Fit a circular saw with a plywood blade. With the saw adjusted just deep enough to penetrate the siding, saw along the lines. The saw won't go to the end of the cut, so finish the cut with the wood chisel.

4. Pull any nails holding the damaged piece and remove it.

5. Cut a piece of new siding about ⅛" smaller in each direction, matching the grain and pattern.

6. Cut Z-bar flashing to prevent rainwater from seeping into the plywood through the joint above it. Or make the flashing from strip aluminum, using dimensions from the drawing: Mount a 2×4 in a vise. Hold the sheet metal over the 2×4 and bend it with a second block of 2×4.

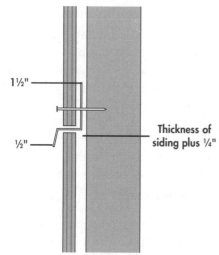

1½"

½"

Thickness of siding plus ¼"

Z-bar flashing keeps water out of plywood siding. Note the bottom is slightly away from the siding, so water will run away from the siding. Paint the flashing to match the wall.

7. Slip the flashing under the existing siding above the repair, and nail it into place through at least two studs.

8. Slip the new plywood under the flashing and fasten with galvanized screws or siding nails.

9. Caulk the seams, allow to dry, and stain or paint the siding and flashing.

Popped Nails

You won't see nails at all in aluminum and vinyl siding, but you may see them in wood siding. And if they "pop" above the surface, or if they are enlarged, and open to water and rot, you'll see them all too clearly. What to do?

Pound popped nails back in place with a hammer and nail set. If the nails don't grab, pull them out and drive in a deck screw that's larger and longer than the nail. After either repair, fill the holes with exterior putty, prime, paint, and forget.

All Thumbs

If a whole section of nails has popped, you may have a structural problem—like warped studs or a shifting structure, and renailing probably won't help. It's best to find and cure the root problem. At the least, replace the nails with screws, which will knit the structure together more soundly, and may prevent things from getting worse.

This rotted-out nail hole will only get worse as water gathers in it. You can buy yourself some time, or even halt the rot forever, by punching it through, putting in a deck screw, and filling the hole as described earlier.

Why get anal about filling nail holes in wood siding? Because they allow water to leak in, and eventually cause rot. I used SpakFast, a 3M product that is easily the best interior and exterior hole filler around, to repair the nail hole in the following photo.

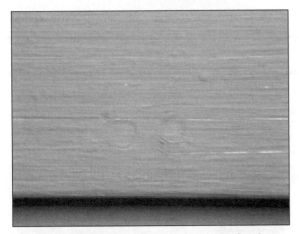

Looking at these sleek sides—you'd be hard-pressed to realize this is actually my garage! If you look closely, you can see the outline of the two nails, but water is not going to gather here. Filling nail holes is a lot cheaper than paying for new siding.

Aluminum and Vinyl Siding

Vinyl and aluminum are cheap but durable replacements for wood. Aluminum, which tends to dent easily, is factory painted. The ubiquitous vinyl siding comes in many styles and textures. Because it is dyed rather than painted, it can't chip (although it can fade).

Large repairs in aluminum and vinyl may be pro jobs, since large pieces are hard to cut without special tools. But small repairs are not a big deal if you can find a scrap of matching material in the garage, basement, or attic. These directions show how to repair aluminum siding:

1. Mark out the damaged area with two vertical lines beyond the edge of the damage, and a horizontal line 1" below the upper course of siding.

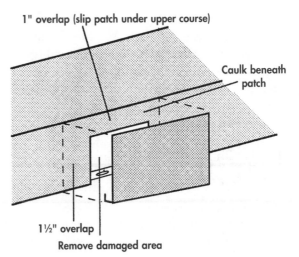

1" overlap (slip patch under upper course)

Caulk beneath patch

1½" overlap
Remove damaged area

Fix gouges in aluminum siding by removing the damaged area and cutting a replacement. Caulking behind the scenes helps keep everything watertight.

2. Drill holes at the corners of this cutout and remove it with tin snips or a jigsaw (use a fine-toothed metal-cutting blade, broken off to make a shallow cut).

3. Cut the patch 3" longer than the repair area. Cut across the top so the patch will slip under the upper course of siding.

4. Test that the patch will engage the bottom lip of the siding, and snap into place. Once it fits, apply silicone caulking to the back of the patch (near the top and sides). Engage the bottom and snap into place. Paint to match if needed.

Vinyl siding repair takes a slightly different approach. The material expands and contracts considerably with temperature variations, so nails should be slightly loose. Fasten with galvanized roofing nails that penetrate ¾" into solid wood. Center nails in the nailing slot so the material can shift to either side. Make sure to work when the temperature is above about 50°—vinyl siding gets brittle and cracks in colder weather.

To cut vinyl siding, score with a utility knife and bend it back and forth. You can also use aviation snips (a tin snip with compound leverage) or saw with a fine-toothed circular saw. Reverse the saw blade for an especially fine cut.

Toolbox Tips

If you're having no luck finding replacements for aluminum or vinyl siding, scrounge around at old building suppliers. They may have some old colors or styles sitting on a dusty shelf.

To repair vinyl, use a "zip" tool (available from siding suppliers and some hardware stores) to unlock the joint between courses. Look around your house for spare siding left by a benevolent previous owner and follow these instructions:

1. Decide how much vinyl to remove. If the damage is near the end of a piece, cut out from the damage to the end. If it's in the middle of a long piece, cut out only the damaged area. In either case, it's best to span three studs to make a solid repair.

2. Cut the ends of the repair area with a utility knife guided by a small square held tight to the siding. Cut as far to the top of the siding as possible.

3. Slip the zip tool into the lower joint and, holding it firmly down, slide the tool the length of the piece you're removing. When the bottom siding is loose, pry out the nails holding it in place.

4. Cut the replacement piece so it overlaps 1½'' onto the good pieces.

5. Lock the replacement piece into the lower course of the siding, and nail through the top into a stud. The patch overlaps at one or both ends.

6. Lock the upper course into place by pressing firmly against the replacement piece, or use the zip tool to lock the joint.

Toolbox Tips

If the vinyl is cracked, or you can find only off-color siding, repair from behind. Remove the entire damaged piece with the zip tool, flip it, clean the back with PVC (polyvinyl chloride) cleaner, and attach a patch to the back with PVC cement. Replace the piece when the cement dries, and touch up the paint as best you can (little of the patch should be visible, so an exact color match is not crucial).

The Least You Need to Know

◆ Siding is pretty durable stuff, and siding damage is often a side effect of other problems, like structural movement or moisture build-up.

◆ Small repairs in most kinds of siding are easy, assuming you can reach the damage and find repair material.

◆ Plywood and hardboard siding desperately need protection against the weather. Don't skimp on paint or stain.

◆ Aluminum or vinyl siding can be repaired if the damaged area is small, but for large jobs, consider calling in a pro.

In This Chapter

- Why masonry is different from other building materials

- Hammers, trowels, and other mason's tools

- Masonry joint styles

- Keeping time with mortar

- What the other do-it-yourself books don't say about masonry

- Sage suggestions for satisfying stonework

Bricks and Stones ...
A Gritty Guide to Masonry

Masonry scares do-it-yourselfers—even gung-ho types who would routinely tackle a nasty roof leak or rotten floorboard tend to be leery of the bricks-and-stones routine. That's too bad, because stones are the most ancient form of construction, and masonry is a satisfying—and economical—knack that's not hard to learn. (If you're lucky, you may even have a pleasant flashback to blissful days in the sandbox.)

Masonry earned its fearsome reputation partly because the material, not you, sets the pace. It's also a reflection of the fact that every tool and material seems to have three obscure names. (This may be intentional: When I wrote a book for masons, a friend who is a mason and an architect explained: "We masons are an old guild, and we don't like to give away secrets.") But you don't have to join the mason's guild (or the Freemasons, either) to learn to repair brick, block, and stone.

As an ex-mason, I'm pleased to reveal the ABCs of masonry:

◆ **A:** The materials are gritty, caustic, and heavy (the "nasty, brutish, and short" principle).

◆ **B:** Mortar doesn't hold stuff together—it holds stuff apart.

◆ **C:** Mortar hardens according to an internal clock.

Principle A being self-explanatory, we'll dwell on B and C. When we're done, you'll never again feel flummoxed by a simple masonry repair. Instead, you'll feel an itch to grab your trowel. (I admit this might seem peculiar, but, for perspective, I knew a psychiatrist whose hobby was plumbing ...)

The Foundation Principle of Masonry

Mortar (masons call it "mud," for obvious reasons) is roughly 10 times as effective at holding things apart (this is compressive strength) as at holding things together (tensile strength). So mortar is perfect for separating the stones, blocks, and bricks in a foundation or chimney. Mortar will adhere to stone and brick under the right conditions, which I'll explain, but don't expect too much from the bond.

You can make an invisible patch on this wall—if you take care to match the mortar color. All mortar is not gray!

Mortar doesn't "dry," it "sets." Setting is a chemical reaction among water, lime, and portland cement that causes the lime and cement to expand and harden. If mortar or *concrete* dry too soon, they cannot harden. Also (within reason), the less mixing water you use, the stronger the mortar will be. Cement products are dusty when dry, so always use a dust mask while mixing them. Use leather or rubber gloves while handling mortar or cement—they can really parch the hands.

Fix-It Phrase

Mortar is a mixture of portland cement, lime, mason's sand, and water. **Concrete,** a mixture of portland cement, gravel, sand, and water, is used to build bridges, beams, roads, and driveways. Confusingly, concrete is often called "cement." Aside from resurfacing rough concrete, most homeowners avoid concrete repair. I'll describe a good resurfacing technique for concrete, but not pouring concrete—that's beyond the scope of this book.

If you are lucky enough to own a home with stonework as nice as this cobblestone, you'll find masonry a very handy talent. The matching fence pillar nicely complements the house.

Keeping Time

Unlike virtually every other building material, masonry has its own rhythm. The properties of mud change as it sets, forcing you to change your tools and techniques as well. In carpentry, you can nail boards at your own pace. But in masonry, sometimes you'll have to rush, and sometimes you'll have to twiddle your thumbs. If you tool (smooth) a mortar joint before the mud has set, the mud will squish out. But if you wait too long, the mortar will be as hard as … well, rock.

Timing is also affected by how "thirsty" your materials are. Concrete and concrete block are usually quite porous, but bricks come in two flavors, depending on the temperature in the kiln. Low-temperature bricks—including most antique bricks—are porous. High-temperature bricks are smoother, glassier, and nonporous. It's usually a good idea to wet porous material before mortaring.

You may be able to buy this type of cut stone at a brickyard or stone supplier. If you look closely, you'll notice that these masons built an attractive wall, but a weak one. The vertical joints should never line up this much!

The timing of masonry may sound complicated, but if you watch for changes in the mortar as you are working, the battle is half won. And for each procedure, I'll explain how the mortar changes while setting, and when to perform each step.

Toolbox Tips

In masonry, weather really matters. The mortar must set before it freezes, which is just as well, since masonry is also wretched winter work—as I can attest. Hold off if the temperature may fall below 40°F for 24 hours after the repair. Also, in hot weather—say above 85°—the mud may set or dry too quickly.

Special Tools

Most mason's tools—at least the trowels, chisels, and hammers a homeowner might need—look heavy and impossibly clumsy, until you watch a mason deftly build a wall with them. Masonry starts with a few well-chosen trowels. Fortunately, many masonry tools have multiple uses, which reduces the sting of their price. With masonry tools, you get what you pay for. It's not nationalistic fervor, but simple reality: The best trowels on sale in the United States are American made. Imports and cheapies are a waste of money. As usual, buy what you need, and let your tools accumulate with your skills and experience.

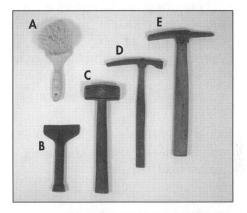

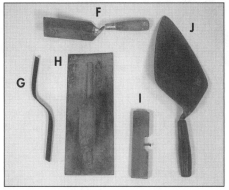

Common masonry tools.

Common masonry tools, as shown in the photos, include:

A. Masonry is a grungy pursuit, and brushes are a necessity. In America's Dairyland, this cheap, effective plastic brush is sold for cleaning dairy equipment. Use it to clean up after chipping out loose mortar. It's also excellent for removing extra mortar around a new mortar joint, and for cleaning tools.

B. Once you tire of hitting your wrist, a hammer needs else something to smash. Use a brick chisel that's 2" to 4" wide for breaking bricks, removing mortar for stone repairs, beating up rotten concrete, and other forms of Neolithic self-expression.

C. Masonry repair starts with something getting destroyed—like old mortar, bricks, and stones. Use a 2- or 3-pound hammer for the destruction (nail hammers are flyweights in this league).

D. A masonry (brick) hammer is ideal for trimming bricks.

E. A mason's hammer—two chisels mounted on a handle—is perfect for cleaning stone-masonry before pointing.

Fix-It Phrase _____

When masons say **pointing,** they're not talking about their hunting dogs, but about replacing mortar in a degraded joint. **Tuckpointing** (described later in the chapter) is replacing mortar between bricks, because you "tuck" the mud into the joint.

F. One of my favorite tools is the margin trowel, the duck-billed platypus of masonry. This small trowel is first-rate for patching masonry and drywall, applying wood filler, prying up molding, scraping paint, and even glazing windows.

G. A jointer presses mortar into place while it sets. Each of the joint shapes shown below calls for a specific jointer.

H. A plaster trowel applies mortar and patching to walls.

I. A homemade joint raker will make a "raked joint," shown below. Saw a notch in a block of 3/4" plywood and drive in a drywall screw. Adjust the screw to rake the mud deep enough to match the existing joint.

J. The brick trowel may look awkward, but a good one (I'm not talking $4.95!) is a well-balanced tool that can deliver mortar exactly where it's needed. Use the corner to chisel mortar from an old brick, clip the corner from an oversize stone, or separate shingles in a roof repair.

Joint Styles

The mortar joints between bricks and stones are not created equal, and each of the joint styles illustrated here is made with a different tool. When the mud is partly set, run the jointer back and forth along the joint to shape the joint and compress the mud. To avoid pulling out mortar at corners, joint from the corner toward the center.

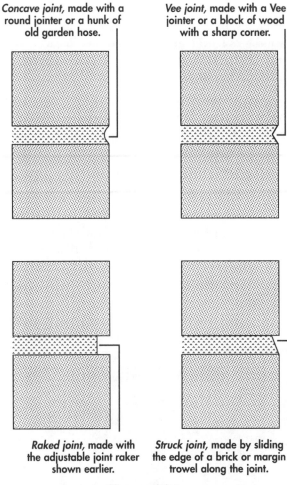

Concave joint, made with a round jointer or a hunk of old garden hose.

Vee joint, made with a Vee jointer or a block of wood with a sharp corner.

Raked joint, made with the adjustable joint raker shown earlier.

Struck joint, made by sliding the edge of a brick or margin trowel along the joint.

Masonry joints.

Playing with Mud— Mixing Mortar

One thing most handy-andy books ignore is how, exactly, to handle mortar. But to do masonry, you need to know the care, feeding, and mixing of mortar. While many people buy premixed mortar, I hate the stuff, because it does not flow like real mortar. I suggest buying a bag of mason's cement from a masonry supplier, and mixing it with clean (and cheap) mason's sand, from the same source.

All Thumbs

For an invisible repair, you have to match the color of the existing mortar. This is seldom the standard gray color you get in premixed mortar or in masonry cement.

Stones and bricks were once laid in white mortar. More recently, red, brown, and black have all become popular. Pigments sold by masonry suppliers can tint mortar, whether premixed or mixed from sand and cement. Because mortar changes color as it dries, put a test batch of mortar in the sun. When it dries, it will be reasonably close to the color of the cured mortar.

Mix only as much mortar as you can use before it sets. In summer, mortar can set in a half-hour or less. In cooler weather, you should have at least an hour. The label will tell you otherwise, but it's generally safe to add a little water to soften up stiff mud. But don't do it more than once, as too much water weakens mud.

After all preparations are complete, start mixing:

1. Add dry material (premixed mortar or 2½ to 3 parts of sand with 1 part cement) to a wheelbarrow. Add any pigment at this point.

2. Blend the dry stuff and push it to the front of the wheelbarrow. Add water and layer the dry mix over the water, using a hoe or shovel.

Mix mortar only after all prep work is done.

may have to let one part of a repair set for a few minutes, then return for more work after the mud gets hard enough. This drives linear thinkers nuts, but in masonry, you have to follow the "mind of the mud."

Repairing thin sections of masonry is covered in the next section. Here's a general recipe for repair of thicker masonry sections—like replacing stones or bricks:

1. In masonry, like dentistry, you can't build on decay. Remove rotten mortar, and loose brick or stone, with a mason's hammer, or a 2- to 3-pound hammer with a brick chisel. Try not to disturb big chunks that are slightly loose—the new mortar should hold them in place. In other words, unlike dentistry, the goal is not to remove every last bit of rot. Brush the wall with a stiff brush like the one shown in the earlier photo.

3. Start stirring, and add more water. In the preceding photo, Alex T. is aiming for a fairly stiff batch—not soup du jour. Mix for three minutes.

4. Dump the mix onto a metal sheet or scrap of plywood, 2' square. It's easier to work from this "mud board" than from a bucket or wheelbarrow.

5. While using the mortar, imitate real masons: occasionally throw the mud onto the board with the trowel to keep it moving smoothly.

Masonry Repair: The Basics

In thinking about masonry repairs, recognize that the rate of hardening depends on surface porosity, mud thickness, and temperature. You

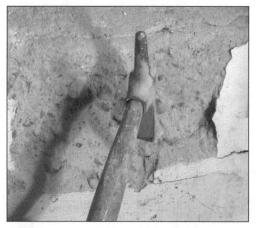

Remove rotten mortar and loose brick or stone.

2. If the surface of the bricks or stones is rough and the patch will be fairly deep—say ¾" or more—the patch should "key" (lock onto) the surface. But ensuring good adhesion is easy:

(a) Clean the surface with diluted muriatic acid (buy it at a masonry supplier or a home center). Pour the acid into a plastic pail with water, and apply with a plastic brush. (Never pour water into acid—you can cause an explosion!) Observe all cautions, particularly regarding eye and hand protection.

(b) After the acid foams for a couple of minutes, it should be neutralized. Wash away the crud with plenty of water and allow the surface to dry a bit.

3. If water seeps into your bricks or stones in 30 seconds or less, the mortar will dry out too quickly. Dip these porous bricks and blocks in water for 30 seconds, then dry them for 15 minutes. If you have not acid-washed the repair area, flick a 4" to 5" brush filled with water at it, focusing on shallow areas. Don't drench the surface.

In this repair, I'm starting with the deepest areas.

Toolbox Tips

A little line of mortar won't hold together a foundation that has traveling on its mind. Look inside a crack—dirt or insect cocoons indicates an old, inactive crack that you can probably fix. If the inside is clean, the crack may still be shifting due to unstable soil or frost heaving (see "Can We Discuss Your Soggy Basement?" in Chapter 13).

4. Mix the mortar, as described in the previous section.

5. Fill the deepest spots first. For good adhesion, throw mortar at the wall with a margin trowel (overhand or sidearm are both legit in this league …). Or hold the mortar on a brick or plaster trowel and push it into place with a second trowel. Masons disdain this two-trowel technique, but it's highly effective; a variation is shown in the description of tuckpointing, later in the chapter.

Wet the wall to keep the mortar moist while it sets.

6. Work several parts of the repair at once. Use chips of block, stone, or brick to stiffen heavy areas if needed. After the first coat stiffens, add a second coat.

7. After the patch sets a bit more, tool it to match the surrounding masonry. Dress up joints in brick, block, and stone with a trowel, a length of hose, or a jointer, as described earlier.

8. For a flat wall, use a rubber float. Dampen the float and the partly set mud on the wall. Move the float in circles to flatten the high spots and fill the hollow spots. If the remaining surface is too rough, smooth it with a plaster trowel.

In masonry repairs, a rubber float can smooth mortar like nothing else!

9. When the mortar is too hard to show bristle marks, brush diagonally with a stiff, plastic brush to remove trowel marks. The brush will also remove mortar smears from bricks and stones.

Thin Surface Repairs of Masonry and Concrete

Making a durable, thin layer of any masonry product used to be almost impossible. But Thorite and other brand-name products now do an excellent job of resurfacing rotten masonry and concrete. Overall, the new thin-patching materials for masonry and concrete are flat, attractive, and durable. On floors, they are easy to sweep and unlikely to trap snow or ice.

A second method for getting good adhesion is to either mix pure portland or mason's cement (without sand or gravel) with water and brush the thick paint onto the surface, then plaster on the mortar while the paste is damp; or buy a bonding agent from a brickyard and follow the directions.

The basic recipe for thin patches is about the same for concrete and masonry: Clean the surface, etch it with acid, mix the mud, and apply. Unfortunately, the trowel generally rides up on the old mortar or concrete around the patch, leaving a disgusting corrugation. You may do better to flatten thin patching with the trowel, let it cure for a few minutes, then texture it by moving a garage broom in a swirling motion to hide irregularities. Or use a float, as described in the previous section. For a good cure, cover thin masonry patches with plastic for a week or so. Pull back the plastic and dampen daily.

Tuckpointing

Tuckpointing—repairing mortar in bricks or blocks—is a simple, tedious, and necessary (to owners of masonry homes, anyway) skill. Doing your own tuckpointing can save you big money.

And it's easy to divide a big job into smaller sections that you can conquer as time and boredom permit. Here are the basic steps in tuckpointing:

1. Clean out the old mortar to at least ½" deep (¾" is better) with a chisel or a rented diamond-blade grinder (as in the following photo). Wear goggles. Take care not to damage the brick—and don't get too aggressive. It may be better to leave some questionable mortar alone rather than chisel out a whole wall.

Grind the joint to remove damaged mortar.
(Photo by Ken Schuster)

2. Brush or vacuum debris from the joint. Don't use a water hose, unless you can let the repair dry for a day before continuing.

3. Test the brick for porosity, using step 3 in the previous procedure.

4. Mix a small amount of mortar and push it into the deepest joints. The two-trowel technique shown minimizes spillage: Hold the mortar on a brick trowel and push it in with a long, narrow tuckpointing trowel. Fill deep joints in two or three steps. I would wear rubber gloves for this step; mud is harsh on the hands.

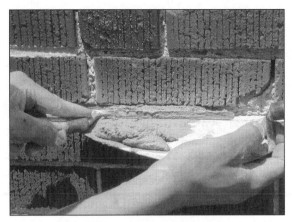

Using two trowels, fill the joint.
(Photo by Ken Schuster)

5. When joints will still show your thumbprint, tool them by running a jointer back and forth a couple times. Press hard to compress the mud; this strengthens the joint and increases water resistance.

Strike the joint by running a striking tool, as described previously, along the mortar. *(Photo by Ken Schuster)*

6. Let the mud set for a while, then brush diagonally to remove extra mortar and smooth irregularities.

Busting Blocks and Breaking Bricks— Work for Lifers

If you need to cut a few bricks or concrete blocks, try this hammer-and-chisel technique. Lay the brick or block on something solid (sand makes an excellent, uniform support) and gradually start tapping at the break line. Turn the brick and tap all four sides, gradually increasing your force. When the noise turns hollow, the brick or block is about to break. With practice, this technique is more effective than it sounds—unless you skimp on the support or start too aggressively.

Believe it or not, breaking bricks requires a light touch.

You also can saw most bricks with a circular saw and a fiberglass masonry blade—a noisy, dusty, but usually workable solution. Use several passes; don't try to cut the whole depth at once. Or cut ½" deep, and use the chisel technique just described.

Toolbox Tips

If you need to cut many bricks, or do it accurately, a fast, sophisticated, and expensive approach is to rent a diamond-blade masonry saw. These saws are more accurate, and, because they are water-cooled, virtually dust-free. Don't forget to wear goggles and ear protection.

Stones Again

Have you ever heard a homeowner brag that his old stone house "was built of stones from the quarry just down the road"? I love meeting somebody who's excited by the most earthy and beautiful of building materials. And until recently, all stone was local, because stones are … heavy.

But there's another lesson in this observation: The appearance, hardness, density, and workability of stones reflect their origin, and it's tough to generalize about stonework. Stone may be soft or hard. It may split easily, or cut only with a diamond blade.

Nevertheless, stonework is my favorite kind of masonry, because the rewards of a deftly built stone wall exceed the considerable effort involved. These suggestions should simplify your stonework:

◆ If you must remove and replace loose stones, mark the location and top on each.

◆ Don't allow vertical joints to line up (as they do in the earlier photo of a stone house); this weakens the wall.

- Prop up large or precarious stones with wooden wedges until the mortar sets.
- Take your time—large mortar joints set slowly, and if you rush, you'll just squeeze mortar from the joint.

The Least You Need to Know

- Mortar holds things apart, not together.
- Surfaces need a careful cleaning before repair.
- Pay careful attention to mortar color—you won't get a second chance to get it right.
- Allow mortar to set a bit before you finish it.
- Stonework is the most difficult—and rewarding—type of masonry.

In This Part

Part 4

Mechanically Speaking

As time passes, we humans demand more and more of our houses. Once their main job was to keep out rain, rats, and rapscallions, a trick they accomplished with little more than wood, brick, or adobe. How times have changed! A modern house conceals a bewildering number of "mechanical" components: the wiring, plumbing, and heating equipment.

These gadgets (well, most of them, anyway) make life a lot more pleasant—when they work. It's another story when something goes wrong. I will not pretend that the next three chapters will—presto-chango—convert you into a mechanical-repair expert. Face it: Troubleshooting and fixing air-conditioners is a lot more confusing than finding a leak in a roof.

Still, there's room to save money in the mechanical department. Electrical repairs, for example, are much simpler than most people think. And even in plumbing and heating, once you absorb a few principles and some lingo, you can save big on small repairs. If nothing else, knowing a bit about mechanicals may help you avoid paying the wretched "job charge" to a technician who blithely informs you, after a 14-second inspection, that your problem is due to a blown breaker, a closed valve, or a loose nut.

In This Chapter

- ◆ Working safely with your electric system
- ◆ Electrical jargon you must know (all meat, no fat!)
- ◆ The materials and tools you'll need
- ◆ Replacing bad receptacles (outlets) and switches
- ◆ Adding receptacles where you need them

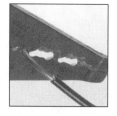

Chapter 16

Sparky's Scene: An Electric Odyssey

Like masonry and plumbing, electric repair has a sinister reputation. It may be because everything happens behind the scenes (actually, that's a good thing, because electricity should be invisible until it's in use).

In deciding how much electrical work to tackle, let confusion be your guide. Electrical work is not difficult, and properly done, not dangerous. But overwhelming confusion on your part is worth heeding. Get advice or get help. There are some *truly confusing* wiring setups out there. Old houses, or houses wired by "blew-it-yourselfers," are both major sources of trouble. Don't feel obliged to do things you don't understand.

A little understanding goes a long way. If you follow these instructions and don't do things that confuse you, you should be able to handle most basic repairs. Granted, things get confusing if you dig up buried mistakes, but that's one reason you bought this book, right?

Electrical Ignorance Is Not Bliss

A book for complete idiots shouldn't be freighted with irrelevant theory—who wants to read about Michael Faraday's electrical insights when the light over the stove is flickering? Still, you need to know a few things to work with electrons.

The control panel for your electrical system is the fuse box, or the circuit-breaker box. Either box:

◆ Shuts off all electricity to the house.

◆ Routes incoming electricity to the various circuits.

◆ Allows you to shut off individual circuits.

◆ Controls how much current (how many amps) can flow on each circuit.

Fuses are one-time protectors that must be replaced when excess current causes them to "blow." Circuit breakers can be switched back on after they "trip" due to excess current. Fuse and breaker boxes are rated by the maximum number of amperes (amps) they can handle; 100 amps is the minimum in new construction. Unless there's a reason to distinguish the two boxes, I'll say "breaker box" to indicate either type.

Take the Round Trip: Circuits

Electricity can only travel in a circuit. This is a loop of conductor (mostly wire) that connects a source of electricity (in other words, the electric generator) to a load (say, a lamp), then back to the source. In houses, circuits are essentially a loop from the hot side of the breaker box to a load and back to the grounded side of the breaker box.

Fix-It Phrase _____

The **main disconnect** is a switch or fuse controlling all electricity entering your home. In a circuit-breaker box, it's marked "main," or "100," or however many amperes your system supplies. In a fuse box, it's the big black fuseholder marked "main." To shut off power, flip the switch or yank out the fuse holder.

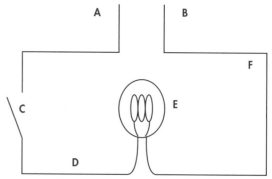

A circuit must connect a source to a load and back to a source. Not shown: Equipment grounding conductor, carried by a bare wire, an insulated green wire, a conduit, or the sheath of armored "BX" cable.

A. Source (hot side)

B. Source (grounded side)

C. Switch (shown open)

D. Hot wire (black)

E. Load (a light is shown, but it can be a motor, heater, etc.)

F. Grounded wire (white)

Two principles govern the behavior of electricity in circuits:

♦ Electricity must return to its source. That's why you need a circuit. If you just connect a hot wire to a light, it won't work, and the electricity will try to improvise a way back to the source. Danger!

♦ Each circuit needs a load. Otherwise, it's a short circuit—a connection between hot and ground without the resistance of a load. That's another recipe for disaster.

Electrical Lingo

You can't talk about electricity without some basic jargon.

Alternating current (AC) is used throughout home wiring. AC changes polarity 60 times per second (60 hertz). Direct current (DC) is used in cars and battery-operated stuff.

Amps, or *amperes*, measure how much current is flowing. The *ampacity* of a wire is how much current it can carry. If you try to squeeze too many amps through a wire, the circuit breaker or fuse should shut off the circuit.

Volts (V) are units of pressure—in other words, how hard the electrons are "trying" to get around the circuit. Most home circuits carry 120 volts (120V). Because the same wire can carry more power at higher voltage, big appliances operate at 240V.

Watts (W) are units of power, used to rate things that consume electricity, like lava lamps, appliances, and (most important) tools. Because volts × amps = watts, a 120-volt circuit carrying 5 amps supplies 600 watts (120 × 5 = 600).

Toolbox Tips

Wattage ratings on electrical appliances tell you if a circuit has enough capacity. If watts ÷ volts = amps, how many amps does a 1,200-watt saw draw? 1200 watts ÷ 120 volts = 10 amps. That's approaching the 15-amp capacity of a typical home circuit. If you overload the saw, by cutting too fast, or with a dull blade, you can draw more amps than that.

A *kilowatt hour* (KWH), the unit of electric-utility enrichment, is a flow equivalent to 1000 watts (1 kilowatt) for one hour. In 10 hours, a 100-watt bulb consumes 1 KWH.

A *breaker* is electrician slang for a circuit breaker. To *reset* a breaker means to return it to operating position after it has *tripped* (disconnected because excess current flowed in the circuit).

Receptacle is electrician-speak for what normal people call an "outlet"—a place to plug in an electrical cord.

Cable talk: Most electrical cable has 3 conductors, or wires. The black-insulated conductor is the *ungrounded*, or *hot* wire. The white-insulated wire is the *grounded conductor* (neutral) wire. The bare wire, called the *equipment grounding conductor*, is often simply called the *ground*. See the later "On What Grounds Is It Grounded?" section for grounding guidance and "Cable and Conduit" for more on cable.

Fix-It Phrase

The terminology of grounding is confusion itself. **Ground** wires allow electricity a second route to return to the utility grid. The white, **grounded conductor** is the normal path. The bare, **equipment grounding conductor** is designed to carry current when the hot wire comes in contact with a metal element of the electrical system, at which point the circuit breaker should quickly open. The equipment grounding leg can be carried by a bare wire in romex cable, or by an insulated green wire, steel conduit, or the sheath of armored "BX" cable.

Wire Size

Wire is sized by a bass-ackward system called *gauge*. Gauge tells how many amps of current a wire can carry (a wire can carry the same number of amps at either 120 or 240 volts). Most home wiring is 12 or 14 gauge, although heavy-duty, 240-volt circuits use 10-gauge wire.

Copper Wire Gauges, Capacities, and Uses

Gauge	Capacity in Amps (Equals Breaker or Fuse Rating)	Typical Uses
10	30	240-volt circuits: clothes dryer, range, central air-conditioning, and water heater
12	20	120-volt circuits: kitchens, workshops, and other heavy loads
14	15	120-volt general household circuits

Wire size also determines what size breaker or fuse is needed to protect a circuit. Most receptacles and switches are made for 15-amp circuits; you'll need special devices for 20-amp circuits. The previous table lists the capacity and uses of common wire gauges. If cables are installed under insulation, in temperatures above 86°F, or in bundles of more than 3 current-carrying conductors, the ampacity will be lower.

Cable and Conduit

A cable is a group of conductor wires inside one sheath. Modern cable, called romex, has a plastic sheath. It usually contains one black wire, one white wire, and one bare copper wire.

The "grounded conductor" (white wire) and the "equipment grounding conductor" (bare wire) are connected to the same place on the fuse or breaker box, but they have different jobs. The white is the normal return path on a circuit. The bare wire gives electricity a return path if insulation fails in a tool or appliance and the hot wire contacts something conductive.

An older form of cable, called armored cable, or BX, is protected by a coiled steel sheath. BX made after about 1955 contains a special, uninsulated "bonding wire" to carry the equipment ground. Look for this conductor poking through the clamp securing the cable to the box. It, combined with the cable sheath, provides the equipment ground. If the bonding conductor is absent from BX, the circuit is technically not grounded. A circuit tester may light between the hot wire and the sheath, but you can't tell if the ground has enough ampacity to carry a current when the wiring or an appliance goes bad.

Cable is designated by two numbers. The first is the wire gauge, and the second is the number of insulated wires (conductors) in the cable (not counting the bare, ground wire). Thus 12-2 cable has two 12-gauge conductors, and 14-2 has two 14-gauge conductors. 14-3, with black, white, and red 14-gauge conductors, is used for three-way switches.

If you're wiring outdoors or underground, buy the sunlight-resistant cable made for outdoor use.

All Thumbs

If you feel compelled to remove the inside cover from your breaker or fuse box, get out your rubber gloves and rubber boots, and then go call your electrician. Some parts of the box will still be hot even after you operate the main disconnect. It's not a good place to learn how to do wiring.

Conduit, a light steel pipe that protects insulated wires, is usually seen in basements and garages. Conduit needs no equipment grounding wire, because the steel supplies the ground. You need special tools to work on conduit, but you can easily connect romex cable to boxes in conduit systems.

Safety First (and Always!)

Mr. Singer, my high-school physics teacher, warned us to work on electricity with one hand behind our backs. It was his memorable way of stressing that the most dangerous shock is one that passes through your heart. That can happen when a current passes in one arm and out the other.

To honor the memory of Mr. Singer, and to avoid shocks altogether, you need to understand the desires of electricity. Electricity "wants" to move from hot (or supply), to ground, along the path of least resistance. This is why we use circuits—to give electricity a path back "home" on the grounding wire. We don't want it "finding" its own way home, like through your body.

All Thumbs

Electrical boxes may contain wires unconnected to the fixture in the box. Do not touch these wires. If they are controlled by a different circuit breaker, they will stay hot even after you shut off power to the fixture in the box. This problem occurs mainly in conduit, and especially in basements. In kitchens and other locations, you may see a receptacle supplied by two hot wires. In this "multi-wire branch circuit," the top and bottom half of a receptacle are on separate circuits. They should be wired by a double-pole breaker, so both circuits go off at once. Join the incoming white wires with screw-on connectors; then connect a short white lead to the receptacle. *Do not* work on such a receptacle if it's fed by two separate breakers! Call an electrician.

To get a shock, you must be touching a source of current—usually a defective tool, appliance, or device. You must also be grounded—either by touching something conductive that's connected to the ground, like a pipe or electric

box, or by standing on damp soil. Electricians sometimes wear rubbers to prevent shock.

The Golden Rule of Electric Repair

Do unto a cold circuit, or a hot circuit may do something shocking unto you. In other words, shut off the power, feverbrain, before you go poking around in your wires! There are also some more subtle rules:

◆ Make sure you switched off the right circuit breaker or fuse before starting to work (see "Testing a Receptacle," "Testing a Built-In Light," and "Testing a Switch," later in this chapter).

◆ Use tools (screwdrivers, pliers, and wire strippers) with plastic handles. To be extra safe, wrap electrical tape around the shaft of your screwdriver.

◆ Test your tester before and after use.

◆ Avoid being grounded (unruly teenagers will love this rule!). Keep your hands dry, and don't wade around in water when messing with electricity.

◆ Don't do stuff you're not confident of.

◆ Get help when you need it.

Living with Electricity

A good electrical system is hardy, but there's no point in pushing your luck. Follow these guidelines to reduce your electrical worries:

◆ Locate your main disconnect—the switch or fuse that controls all power to your house. It's your last line of defense in an electrical emergency, when you can't stop to figure out which circuit is causing the difficulty. The main breaker (marked "100" or "200" or whatever number of amps the box supplies) shuts off a breaker box. On a fuse box, the main disconnect is usually marked "Main." Logical, eh?

- Don't overload circuits.
- Never, ever, solve your blown-fuse or tripped-breaker problems by installing a fuse or breaker rated higher than the circuit can handle.
- Don't hide junction boxes.
- Don't run extension cords under carpet, across doorways, or in damp areas. And don't buy cheapo extension cords. They cause lots of fires.
- Use extension cords with enough capacity for the load. Cords are rated in amps (amps = watts ÷ volts). For the same load, a longer cord must have larger wire.
- Receptacles, switches, plugs, and electric cords should not get hot in use. If they do, replace them. (However, some dimmer switches do warm up in operation.)
- Ungrounded receptacles (2-prong) are hazardous, particularly in damp locations. To upgrade them in bathrooms, kitchens, and outdoors, install a ground-fault circuit interrupter (GFCI), receptacle, which prevents shock by immediately shutting off if current leaks.
- According to the 2002 National Electric Code, lights and receptacles in bedrooms in single-family homes will need protection with an arc-fault circuit interrupter (AFCI). The AFCI has electronics that detect arcing—as occurs in lousy extension cords. This arcing can cause a fire without tripping a circuit breaker or fuse, and is a major cause of electrical fires. In new construction, the AFCI will likely be placed in the wires that feed the bedroom circuits. When you replace a receptacle in a single-family bedroom, it's a good idea to install an AFCI, but it's not required.

- If you have young kids, install plastic protectors in any receptacles they can reach.

All Thumbs

An electrical tester detects a voltage difference between two points. If both the hot and grounded slot of a receptacle are cold, the detector will not light up—a correct reading. But it won't light if both are hot—a dangerous reading. That's one reason for the elaborate testing procedures described later in the chapter.

Electrical Tools

Electrical repair doesn't call for much in the way of tools, and most are cheap. A circuit tester and a wire stripper are the minimum for wiring work.

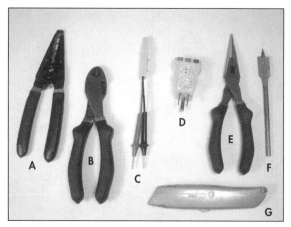

Electrical tools are a real bargain.

Common tools, as shown in the photo, include:

A. Wire strippers are slick! Flick your wrist, and you've got a stripped, intact wire. This fancy stripper also strips the outer sheath from romex cable.

B. Diagonal cutting pliers cut wire and cable (don't use them to strip off the sheath).

C. A circuit tester, a.k.a. an electrical tester or a circuit probe, tells you when a circuit is dead, and safe to work on. It tells you if the ground is working. And it tells you when you've wired something correctly—all without requiring a Ph.D.

D. A plug-in receptacle tester tells if a receptacle is wired right. Very handy.

E. Long-nose (needle-nose) pliers are excellent for connecting wires to receptacles and switches.

F. Use ½" to ¾" drill bits to run romex cable through studs or joists. The flat, "spade" bits work, but the self-feeding bit (see the photo of drill bits in Chapter 3) with the screw point are faster and easier.

G. A utility knife will also strip the sheath from romex. Cut straight down the middle. Don't cut the inner insulation or try to remove the sheath and inner insulation in one step.

Testing Receptacles, Switches, and Lights

In electrical repairs, testing is the essence of safety. The following tests will tell whether your devices are wired correctly and whether they are "cold" (safe to work on).

The following procedure uses a $3 circuit tester, but you can save steps when testing receptacles with the outlet tester described earlier, also about $3. You'll also need a working grounded receptacle, a screwdriver, and a grounded (3-wire) extension cord.

The First Steps for All Tests

Use the two steps shown in the following two figures before any of the following testing procedures. The connections for each step are listed in *italic type* and shown in the diagrams. You may have to wiggle the tester prong to get an electrical contact. Caution: Keep your fingers away from bare metal. *Always* test your tester before and after a test, to be sure it still works. You can do all the receptacle tests at once with a receptacle tester. This is not true of the tests for light fixtures or switches.

You can test your circuit tester by inserting the leads into a receptacle you know is working. The light should stay lit. If not, clean any corrosion from the leads, and retest. If it's junk, trash it. *Test again after use, so you know it still works.*

Fix-It Phrase

On receptacles and extension cords, the long slot is the **grounded** (return) leg, the short slot is the **hot** (ungrounded) leg, and the round slot is the **equipment grounding** leg.

First steps:

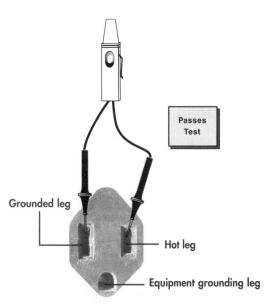

Passes
Test

Grounded leg

Hot leg

Equipment grounding leg

Test your equipment first!

Step 1: Plug your extension cord in to a working receptacle. Stick one prong of your circuit tester in *each rectangular slot* of the extension cord. If the tester lights, the tester works. If not, check the tester, extension cord and outlet until the tester lights.

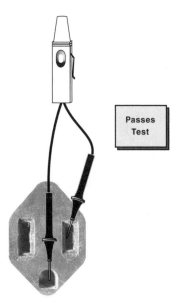

Passes
Test

Step 2: Test between the *hot (short slot)* and the *equipment grounding (round slot)* of the cord. A light indicates that the hot side of the cord and its receptacle are correctly wired.

Testing That a Receptacle Is Wired Correctly

To check that a receptacle is wired correctly, do steps 1 and 2 as shown in the previous figures, and leave the extension cord plugged in. If the receptacle is controlled by a switch, turn it on.

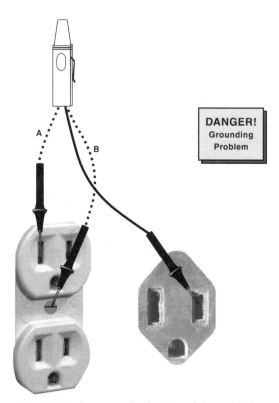

A

B

DANGER!
Grounding
Problem

Step 3: Test between the *hot leg of the cord (the short slot)* and (a) the *grounded slot on the receptacle* and (b) the *cover mounting screw.* If the tester does not light both times, the receptacle grounding is faulty.

DANGER!
Reversed
Polarity
(or Receptacle
Is Cold)

Step 4: Check for power between the *grounded (long) slot of the cord,* **and** *both hot (short) slots of the receptacle.* **No light means the receptacle is cold, or ground and hot are connected backward. (To correct this "reversed polarity," cut the power and exchange the black and white wires feeding the receptacle.)**

Fix-It Phrase

Reversed polarity means that hot wires are feeding the grounding leg of a circuit. It's something you want to correct, and a sign that an ignoramus once worked on your wiring.

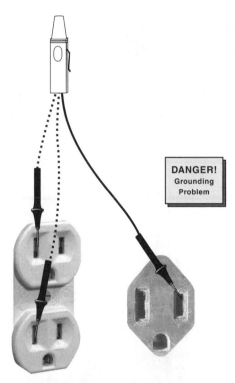

DANGER!
Grounding
Problem

Step 5: Test between the *hot leg of the cord* **and both** *grounded (long) slots* **on the receptacle. No light means the ground is interrupted, a** *major* **violation that may be due to a bad or poorly wired device, or a bad splice. Fix the problem—which may reside in this box or a nearby box—immediately.**

Toolbox Tips

Receptacle wiring in pretty simple. Black (hot) connects to the brass screws, and white (grounded) connects to the silver-colored screws. Green screws in the equipment grounding leg connect to the bare wires.

Testing That a Receptacle Is Cold (the Circuit Is Off)

Do "The First Steps for All Tests" as explained earlier. Then switch off the breaker or unscrew the fuse that you think controls the receptacle.

Repeat test on bottom slots

Test between the *grounded leg of the extension cord* and *(a) both grounded slots and (b) both equipment grounded slots of the receptacle.* If the tester lights in any position, you have reversed polarity. Shut off the circuit, open the box and correct the polarity by connecting white to white (and to tin-colored screws) and black to black (and to brass screws).

Be sure to test your tester *before and after* checking a circuit. Otherwise, a negative reading (no light) could mean that the tester is shot. Also, make sure nobody absent-mindedly turns a circuit back on while you're working on it.

Testing a Built-In Light

A built-in light, or lamp fixture, is one that's wired to a single-pole or three-way wall switch. These tests can tell (a) whether the light is wired correctly and (b) whether it is cold, and safe to work on. To test the switch, see the following section. However, it does not test for problems at the switch, which will be covered in the following sections.

To test whether the light is wired correctly, perform "The First Steps for All Tests" as explained earlier, and continue:

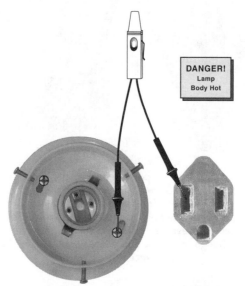

Step 3: Remove the light bulb and turn the wall switch "on." Test for power between the *grounded slot of the extension cord* and a screw and/or some unpainted metal on the light. If the tester lights, a hot wire is touching the lamp body—*danger!* Find the problem and fix it or replace the fixture! Note: if the light is on three-way switches, operate both switches in all combinations of positions and retest.

Fix-It Phrase

One **single-pole switch** controls a light or appliance by itself; two **three-way switches** control one light, generally from each end of a stairway or hall.

Passes Test (but See Text)

Step 4: Test between the *grounded slot of the extension cord* and the *center terminal of the lamp holder.* (Don't touch the metal screw-shell that holds the lamp.) If the tester lights, and the wall switch turns the test light off, the switch correctly controls the light (but see the next test).

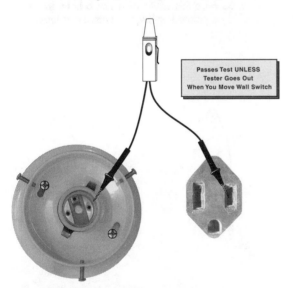

Passes Test UNLESS Tester Goes Out When You Move Wall Switch

Step 5: Test between the *hot leg of the extension cord* and the *screw-shell holding the light bulb.* If the tester lights, the lamp probably has a grounded conductor connection, as it should. Switch the wall switch and repeat. If the test light goes off, the grounded leg is switched—*danger!* Cut off the circuit, open the switch box, rewire hot and grounded wires, and retest the light.

Passes Test (but See Text)

Step 6: Test between the *hot leg of the cord* and (a) the body of the fixture and (b) a *mounting screw* holding the lamp fixture. If the tester lights, the box and the lamp body are grounded. Although that's good, many older lamps are not grounded.

To check that a built-in light is cold, perform "The First Steps for All Tests" as explained earlier, and continue:

DANGER! Lamp Body Hot

Step 3: Remove the light bulb and turn the wall switch "on." Test for power between the *grounded slot of the extension cord* and *a mounting screw and metal on the light.* If the tester lights, the hot wire is touching the lamp body—*danger!* Find the problem and fix it or replace the light!

Step 4: Test between the *grounded leg of the extension cord* and the *terminal at the base of the bulb.* If the bulb lights with the switch in one position or the other, the light is connected to the supply wires; shut off the circuit breaker in step 5. If the tester does not light, call an electrician—there is no safe way to know if the circuit is off.

Step 5: Shut off whichever circuit breaker or fuse you think feeds the circuit, then remove the light bulb. Repeat step 4. If the tester lights, disconnect another circuit, operate the switch and retest until you find the right one.

Testing a Switch

These procedures will tell you whether a two-way (single-pole) switch (a) is wired correctly and (b) safe to work on. (More information on testing for power at a three-way switch coming up.)

To test whether a *single-pole switch is wired correctly,* do "The First Steps for All Tests" as explained earlier, and continue:

Step 3: Shut off the circuit you think controls the light. Remove the switch plate and pull the switch out slightly.

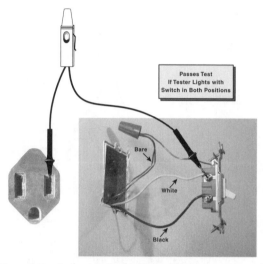

Step 4: Test between the *hot leg of the extension cord* and *the grounded (white) wire(s) in the switch box.* If the tester lights with the switch in both positions, the switch is grounded. (Only switches wired "before the light" have grounded wires. Do not do this test on switches wired "after the light." These switches have only one cable, with one black wire and one white wire. Because this white serves as a hot wire, it should be painted or flagged with black tape.)

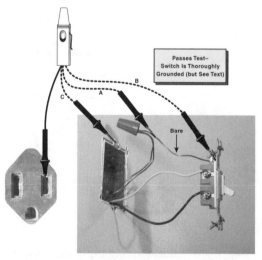

Step 5: Test for power between the *hot leg of the extension cord* and (a) a *bare wire* (if present), (b) the *body of the switch,* and (c) the *box*—if it's metal. If the tester lights every time, the switch is properly grounded. If no equipment grounding wire is present, but the tester lights when it touches the box, the box is probably grounded by BX or conduit. Switch boxes in old systems may lack a ground. If you are making major improvements, get an electrician to ground them.

To test that a *three-way switch is cold*, do "The First Steps for All Tests" as explained earlier, then continue:

Step 3: Shut the circuit off.

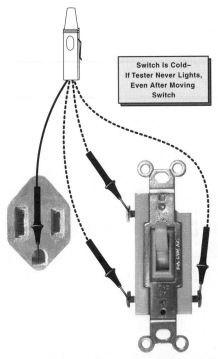

Switch Is Cold—
If Tester Never Lights,
Even After Moving
Switch

Test between the *equipment grounding (round) hole* of the extension cord and *all three switch terminals*. Flip the switch and retest all terminals. If the tester never lights, the switch is cold and safe to work on (as long as the tester is working).

All Thumbs

Old wiring was not designed to operate above 60°C (140°F). Newer light fixtures may require wire with a higher heat rating—either 75°C or 9°C. If the wire in your ceiling fixture is not labeled, it's probably 60° wiring. Do not install a higher-temperature fixture without replacing the wires feeding the light.

What's the final step in testing a circuit? Testing your tester one last time on the working outlet. Maybe, just maybe, it suddenly went bad. Remember: The life you lose could be your own!

On What Grounds Is It Grounded?

The ground system allows electricity to safely leave your house if a hot wire contacts a metal object, such as an electrical box or appliance frame. If, for example, the insulation on an electric tool fails while you're running it, or water gets inside a toaster you are touching, you want the electricity to "drain away" through the equipment grounding system rather than through your body.

Toolbox Tips

Your electrical system should be grounded—connected to the earth—with two separate metal conductors. Systems are commonly grounded by connection to the water pipes, near the pipe's entry into the house (because plumbing fittings may contain insulating, plastic components, the ground is attached near the entry point). A jumper cable should bypass the water meter. The second ground often goes to a long metal stake, or a piece of buried reinforcing rod. If either ground is missing, call an electrician.

In modern systems, every electric circuit has a ground, which connects to every receptacle and metal electrical box. Plastic boxes are not grounded because they do not conduct electricity.

The ground system should take nothing for granted. In general, the bare equipment grounding wire entering a box goes to a wire connector that connects to (a) a wire grounding the box, (b) a wire connected to the green, hex-head screw on the body of the receptacle or switch and (c) a bare wire going to other fixtures on the circuit. (Older switches do not have a ground screw, but they may be grounded by contacting a metal box.)

Got Aluminum Wire?

Most homes are wired with solid copper wire, a soft, light-brown metal that's an excellent conductor. But in the 1960s and early 1970s, some houses were wired with pure aluminum wire, a silver-colored, cheaper metal. This cable is usually marked "aluminum" every few feet on the outside. Misuse of aluminum wire caused a lot of house fires and has been discontinued for interior use (it's still legit for service entrance cable, which connects your system to the utility).

If your house has all-aluminum wire, be sure to use fixtures marked "CO/ALR." (You may find them at an electrical wholesaler.) Copper-coated aluminum wire—a.k.a. "copper-clad"— requires "CU/AL" type fixtures, the same ones sold for solid copper wire.

A good tactic for dealing with aluminum wire is to buy special twist-on connectors that connect aluminum to copper wire, and then use fixtures designed for copper.

All Thumbs

Never switch the white, grounded wire. Switch only "hot" wires, which should be black or red. White wires in a light circuit may serve as hot (supply) wires; these should be tagged with black tape or painted black. Remember: In wiring, don't count on nuttin'. Always test.

Diagnosing Problems

This troubleshooting table can help you locate a problem. Also see the next section, "Problems at the Circuit Breaker or Fuse Box."

Symptom	Cause and Cure
No power anywhere.	Power out from utility: Phone utility. Main fuse blown or breaker tripped: Replace or reset. Main disconnect switch thrown: Check and switch on.
Some power out.	Blown fuse or tripped breaker: Find and replace fuse or reset breaker.
Some power out, but breakers don't seem to be tripped.	Breaker is tripped, but handle has not moved much. Flip breakers off and on until power is restored.
Some power out, but breakers and fuses seem fine.	A switch, breaker or fuse at a "sub-panel" has cut off the electricity. A sub-panel is a second panel fed by the main panel. Find the sub-panel, and turn the switch, reset the breaker or replace the fuse.
Breaker or fuse blows repeatedly.	Disconnect everything from that circuit. If problem persists, call electrician. Otherwise, connect appliances one by one until the problem recurs; fix that appliance.
Fuse melted (examine with flashlight).	Overcurrent may be due to high current needed to start a motor (in refrigerator, etc.) on the circuit. If the circuit supplies a motor, replace fuse with a "time-delay" fuse designed for motor circuits.
Fuse blackened.	Caused by a short circuit. Find problem and repair, then replace fuse.

Problems at the Circuit Breaker or Fuse Box

The heart of your electrical system, and its main safety feature, is the fuse box or circuit-breaker box. These boxes (you'll have one or the other, but seldom both) control the maximum amount of current flowing in the circuits, and allow you to shut circuits off.

Although you want to know where the fuse or breaker box is, you don't want to be intimately familiar with it—a sure sign of problems. Still, it's best that problems show up at this box, since the alternatives are grim. So as you stumble down the stairs with a new fuse in one hand, a flashlight in the other, and an oath on your lips, remember that the fuse that just blew may have prevented a fire. Overloaded circuits get hot lightning fast.

I removed the cover from this breaker box. Notice that one hot wire (either black or red) attaches to each breaker. The white (grounded) wires attach to the grounding bus, not shown. The main breakers, which are the main disconnect for this electrical system, are at top center.

The rating of a breaker or fuse depends on the size of the wires and fixtures on the circuit. Because 12-gauge copper wires can carry 20 amps, a circuit with 12-gauge wire and 20-amp devices needs a 20-amp fuse or breaker. Because 14-gauge copper wire can carry 15 amps, the breaker or fuse should be rated at 15 amps. (Aluminum has less ampacity; see "Wire Size" earlier in the chapter.)

Breakers or fuses blow when a circuit is asked to carry too much current—due to a malfunction, or because too many things are drawing current. So before you screw in another fuse or reset the breaker, try to figure out why it blew. Did you just plug in a vacuum cleaner to a circuit that was already carrying a heavy load? Plug the vacuum into a different circuit, then restore the circuit.

If breakers or fuses blow once in a great while, and you can figure out why, it's not something to get too excited about—that's their job. But if it happens repeatedly, or you don't understand the reason, sniff around. Literally: You may sniff the putrid burned-plastic stench of hot electrical insulation—a sure sign of trouble. If this bloodhound imitation fails, try to isolate the problem by unplugging stuff from the circuit, and slowly adding things back until you trip the breaker or blow the fuse. If breakers get "tired," and fail to carry their rated current, they need replacement. If you're confused or intimidated, there's no shame in calling an electrician.

Toolbox Tips

Your local electric code may require that a licensed and certified electrician make repairs or install new work in your dwelling—particularly in a rental unit. Ask a building inspector.

Electrical Boxes and Paraphernalia

Electrical boxes, a.k.a. junction boxes, are the skeleton of your wiring system—the bones that protect the cables, connectors, and devices. In repair work, you're generally stuck with whatever boxes you find, but you should be able to recognize the basic types in case you need to replace a damaged or undersize box, or want to add receptacles and switches.

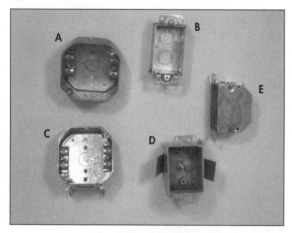

Electrical boxes.

Electrical boxes come in practically infinite varieties, as shown in the photo above. Here are some examples, with suggested uses:

A. **Deep octagonal box:** Can be used for a switch or duplex receptacle in a place with many cables; it's usually screwed to a surface in a basement or garage and covered with a steel plate.

B. **Handy box:** Screw several handy boxes side by side for multiple switches and receptacles.

C. **Shallow octagonal box:** For a ceiling light fixture. Local electrical codes may require that any ceiling box be listed for ceiling-suspended fan support—in case anybody decides to mount a ceiling fan on the box.

D. **Plastic box:** Easy to use because they need neither grounding nor cable clamps (but the devices themselves still need grounding). Plastic boxes are weaker than metal ones. This one holds the existing drywall with those side grabbers.

E. **Handy box with tapered corners:** Easier to install in an old wall; the cables won't snag on the drywall.

The National Electrical Code regulates how many cables can enter a box of a given size. It's tough to squeeze many wires into one box, and the wires can get hot. The size of a box in cubic inches is listed in a stamping or a label. Use this table to figure out if a box is big enough, when all conductors are equal size.

Example: One Box with Two 14-2 Cables and One Switch

Each hot and grounded conductor (black, white, or red) = 1	4 cubic inches
All equipment grounding (bare) wires = 1	1
A receptacle or switch = 2	2
All cable clamps = 1	+1
Add	8
Multiply by 2 for 14-gauge wire (2.25 for 12-gauge)	16 cubic inches minimum size required

Cover plates cover receptacles and switches
after the wiring is done.

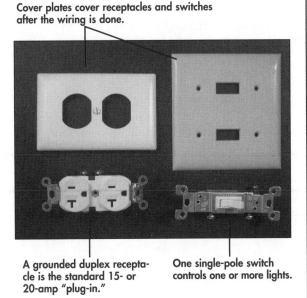

A grounded duplex receptacle is the standard 15- or
20-amp "plug-in."

One single-pole switch
controls one or more lights.

Electrical paraphernalia.

A receptacle with a ground-fault circuit interrupter (GFCI) is used in kitchens, bathrooms,
basements, crawl spaces, garages, outdoors, and
other places that local codes require. This gadget cuts off the juice as soon as it detects a
problem with the ground—an excellent way to
avoid shocks. You can get the same benefit in
other receptacles by connecting them to the
back of a ground-fault circuit interrupter
(GFCI), shown earlier in this chapter.

Fix-It Phrase

A **cover plate** is what you see covering a receptacle or a switch on
the wall. Blank cover plates close boxes
without a switch or receptacle. Steel cover
plates are used in basements or garages. By
code, all electrical boxes must be accessible.
Do not cover any boxes in your house with
drywall or any other permanent covering.

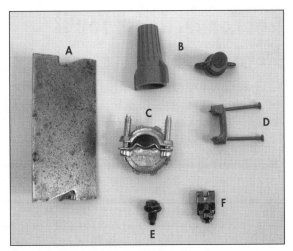

Small electrical gadgets.

Electrical repairs often require an assortment of small, special-purpose gadgets; it
makes sense to keep some of these on hand:

A. A protector plate shields romex cable
from nails. Use them if the cable runs
through a hole within 1¼" of the edge of
the wood, as shown in the photo later in
this chapter.

B. Screw-on wire connectors ("Wire Nuts")
connect wires with a simple twist and are
easy to remove. Get several sizes.

C. Romex clamps secure cable as it enters a
metal box. Some metal boxes have built-
in clamps instead.

D. Electrical staples attach cable to wood;
should be used within 8" of a box, and
every 4' of lateral run. Use ½" staples for
12-2 and 14-2 romex cable.

E. Ground screws attach grounding wires to
threaded holes in the bottom of metal
boxes (you won't see these holes in older
boxes).

F. Ground clips connect a ground wire to
the side of a metal box without a threaded
hole.

Got Connections? You'll Need Them

Connections are the sinews that holds an electrical system together. Like most things related to wiring, they are pretty simple.

Screw-On Wire Connectors

The easiest way to connect solid wire (the kind in your walls) is with fast, cheap, and virtually idiot-proof screw-on wire connectors. These little plastic gizmos also connect stranded wire, although that's a bit more difficult. Often called by the trade name, Wire Nuts, these connectors make a good joint that can be taken apart.

Each size screw-on connector works with certain numbers of wires of a given size (see the list on the package). Three sizes should be plenty for any wiring you'll face.

With a wire stripper, connectors, and possibly a pair of pliers, follow these steps to join wires:

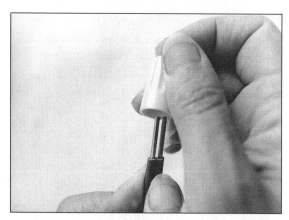

Screw-on wire connectors are the handiest way to connect wires.

1. Strip all wires about ⅝" (the package tells the exact length).
2. Hold the wires with the ends aligned and flush, and slip the nut over the top.

3. Twist the nut clockwise, when viewed from the end. If you wish, tighten gently with pliers.
4. Tug to check that all wires are tight. You should not see exposed bare wire (unless you're joining ground wires).

That's it—no goop, no heat, no solder!

All Thumbs

Don't use screw-on connectors on extension cords—it's not safe, because extension cords are not protected by a junction box.

Connecting to Switches and Receptacles

Electrical outlets—properly called receptacles—often have four slip-in connectors and four screw terminals on the back. Switches always have screw terminals, and sometimes also slip-in connectors.

While you can connect multiple wires to the back of a receptacle, the electrical code permits you to connect only two black and two white wires to each receptacle. To connect more wires, first attach the wires to screw-on connectors, then bring one short "pigtail" wire out to connect to the switch or receptacle. (Before squashing cables into a box, calculate whether the box is big enough as described previously.) Do the same when feeding a light from a receptacle.

Slip-in connectors—under the small holes in the back of a receptacle—are used only for #14 solid copper wire. A "strip gauge" on the back of the receptacle shows how much insulation to remove—about ⅝". Strip the wire, then stick the bare end into the round hole (on a receptacle, but not a switch, white goes near the silver-colored screws and black near the brass screws). Use a little tug to confirm that the connection is solid. To release the wire, stick a finishing nail (the circuit is off, isn't it?) into the slot (arrow) near the wire, then yank the wire out.

Here's how to make a slip-in connection at a switch. Stick a nail into the rectangular slot (arrow) to release the wire.

Long-nose pliers are ideal for connecting a wire to a screw terminal. Connect only one wire to each terminal! You'll also use a wire stripper and a screwdriver:

1. Strip about ¾" from the wire.

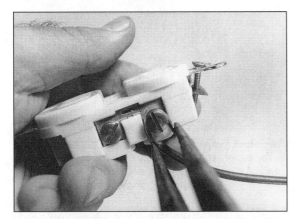

To connect to a screw terminal, make a hook in the wire, then squeeze it tight with the pliers.

2. Form a hook with the pliers.
3. Slip the hook over the screw in the direction shown (if you do it backward, the hook will open as you tighten).

4. Squeeze the hook (without ape-man force) with pliers.
5. Tighten the screw. The wire should be under the screw head, but not overlapped on itself. Don't overtighten.

Switches

Switches usually control built-in lights, but they also can control receptacles, motors, fans, and other conveniences. One "single-pole" switch controls one or more lights. The switch has two terminals, and the toggle is marked "on" and "off." A single-pole switch can be located before or after the light it controls. Both configurations control current to the light; the wiring pattern is chosen for convenience.

In a switch before the light, the power comes through the switch. Because a white (grounded) wire is in the switch box, you can wire a new receptacle to this switch.

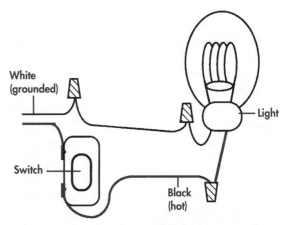

The power reaches the switch before going to the light; ground not shown. Hot wires are highlighted.

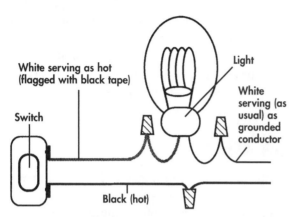

White serving as hot (flagged with black tape)

Light

White serving (as usual) as grounded conductor

Switch

Black (hot)

Hot wires are highlighted in this switch wired "after the light."

All Thumbs

Important: The grounded (white) wire is *never switched.* (If a white wire is used as a hot wire, it is switched and flagged with black tape.) The grounded wire must always be continuous so current can return to the circuit breaker or fuse box. Switches always control the supply of current to the light, *never the current from it.*

Two "three-way" switches are used to control one or more lights (three-way switches are commonly used at the ends of stairs or halls). A three-way switch has three terminals, and the toggle is not marked "on" and "off" because you cannot tell from its position whether the light is on. Three-way switches require a cable with three conductors (red, black, and white) plus a bare equipment grounding wire. The wiring of a three-way switch depends on the configuration; you should be able to replace a broken switch simply by reconnecting the wires as you find them.

Need More Receptacles?

The need for receptacles—a.k.a. plug-ins or outlets—has mushroomed along with the invention of a million uses for electricity: dehumidifiers, heat guns, hair dryers, curling irons, bacon-fryers … anybody remember the Seal-A-Meal? If you've lived in a house that was wired 50 years ago, you're going to suffer outlet envy when you try to plug in all this junk.

One solution is to double up an existing receptacle by installing a pair of duplex receptacles in a 4" box at the same location. You'll have to remove the existing receptacle and box, and cut the drywall or plaster for the new box. (If the existing box is a handy box, you can screw a second to it, possibly without removing any wiring.) Cut short leads of black, white, and bare wire to connect the two receptacles, side by side, and you'll have four plug-ins.

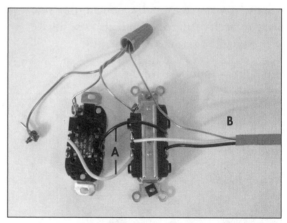

Two short jumper cables (A) connect the receptacles. The supply cable (B) shows that this box is at the end of a circuit; you'd see another cable if this box was supplying another box.

If you don't have electricity where you need it, you'll need to install a receptacle on a circuit that has spare capacity.

Installing a Receptacle: The Basics

The first step in deciding where to place a receptacle is to figure out how to get power to it. In some areas, you will need an electrical permit to extend a circuit by adding a new receptacle. The following places are relatively easy:

◆ Near an existing receptacle, on either side of the wall. You may be able to feed cable through a single stud by drilling with a long bit through the box hole.

◆ Beneath a switch box with a grounded (white) wire.

◆ Near an accessible basement, attic, or attached garage.

When there's no drywall or plaster, drilling holes for electrical cable is a snap!

If you drill within 1¼" of the edge of a stud or joist, add a protective plate so somebody doesn't drive a nail or screw into the cable.

To install the receptacle and connect it to an existing receptacle, you'll need a drill, a level, a saw to cut drywall, and electrical tools and paraphernalia:

1. Locate a stud (see "Seven Ways to Find a Stud" in Chapter 9). Mark a horizontal line across the stud, at the same height as other receptacles in the room.

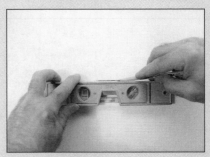

A level is a fast, clever way to start a hole for a new electrical box.

2. Shut off the circuit (see "Testing a Receptacle," earlier in the chapter) and remove the existing receptacle that will supply the new box. If the box is too small for another cable, install a larger box.

3. Mark the cutout for the new box, using it as a template.

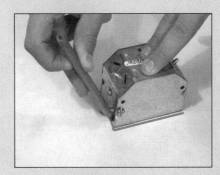

Trace the box outline.

4. Drill holes ¼" or larger to start the saw. Holes at the X marks make room for mounting screws.

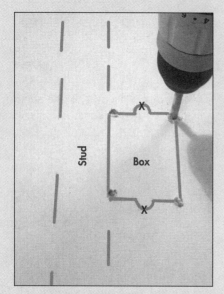

Drill holes to start box opening.

5. Cut the box opening with a jig saw, keyhole saw, drywall saw, or RotoZip tool (with the RotoZip, you don't need pilot holes). Press the jig saw against the wall to reduce vibration. Make the hole barely larger than the box but smaller than the cover plate.

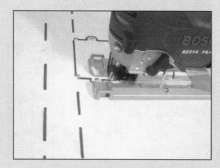

Cut opening with jig saw.

Drill screw holes for new box mounting.

6. Attach the box to the stud, with its front flush to the drywall. Drill pilot holes and drive three 1¼" screws into the stud.

Screw new box to stud.

7. Disassemble the existing box that will supply power to the new box. If the wiring seems complicated, mark the wires for reassembly, but in general, wire black to black, white to white, and bare to bare.

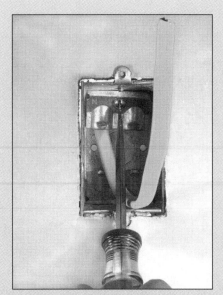

Tightening a built-in cable clamp.

8. Feed new cable from the new box location to the existing box, through the built-in romex connector. With about 10" sticking out of the old box, tighten the connector and remount the old box.

If the box has no built-in romex connectors, insert the cable into a separate romex clamp and tighten with a screwdriver. The clamp goes into one of those circular knockouts you see in metal boxes that don't have built-in romex clamps.

9. Strip the sheath (outer insulation) from about 8" of the new cable. Don't damage the inner insulation. The nifty Craftsman strippers shown have separate openings to strip 12-2 and 14-2 cable. If you don't have them, cut down the center with a utility knife and cut off the sheath. Don't nick the wire insulation with the knife.

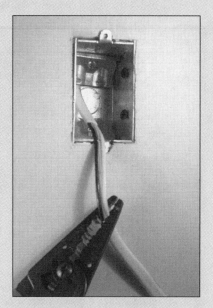

Strip cable sheath with a utility knife or strippers like these.

10. Strip wire ends. A little flick of the wrist helps the cutter get through the plastic insulation.

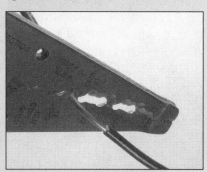

This tool makes short work of stripping wire ends.

11. Equipment ground wires (bare copper wires) are highlighted. Using a screw-on wire connector, connect the existing ground wire supplying the old box to:

    A. A short lead connected to a metal box by a grounding screw

    B. A bare lead connected to the existing receptacle

    C. The bare wire of the new cable

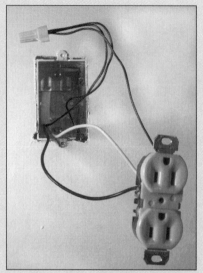

The new receptacle. Highlighting shows equipment grounding (bare) wires.

The existing receptacle supplies the new one you're installing. Either a ground screw or a ground clamp is needed to ground a metal box wired with romex cable. Equipment grounding (bare) wires are highlighted.

12. Connect black to black, and white to white. You may have to join all wires of a particular color with a wire connector, and then run a short wire to the receptacle. Reinstall the receptacle, but not the cover plate.

13. At the new box, cut the new cable so about 10" will protrude after you draw into the new box. Tighten the cable clamp.

14. Fasten the new box to the stud with three 1¼" screws.

15. Wire up the receptacle, connecting the black and white wires as described previously. Screw the receptacle to the box and turn the circuit on. See "Testing a Receptacle," earlier in this chapter.

16. If there's a problem, examine both boxes for loose wires or failure to keep wire colors separate. When everything tests okay, shut off the circuit, affix the cover plates, and restore the power.

Don't Install a Receptacle If ...

Although you can add an extra receptacle or two to most circuits, some circuits—like those feeding a refrigerator or a furnace—should be left alone. Why? So a problem with another device on the circuit, say a video game or a bacon-fryer, does not trip the breaker and shut down your furnace while you are slurping margaritas and watching a January sunset in Mexico.

All 240-volt circuits, used for water pumps, stoves, dryers, and water heaters, should feed only one appliance. These circuits are easy to recognize, because the circuit breaker is twice normal size, and the receptacle is a three-prong monster.

Finally, a receptacle should not be connected if it will overload the capacity—in cubic inches—of the box that would supply it. See above for more on box capacity.

Updating an Ungrounded Receptacle

Relatively new wiring systems should have floor-to-ceiling grounding. But older systems may contain ungrounded receptacles (which have two slots, and no round grounding hole).

All Thumbs

Grounded receptacles are safer for you and the electrical equipment, but that doesn't stop people from cutting the grounding prong off the plug on a new computer and sticking it into an ungrounded receptacle. The next time you do this, heed the voice of your soon-to-be orphaned children—and do something more intelligent, like installing a grounded receptacle or a ground-fault circuit interrupter receptacle.

You could install a grounded (three-hole) receptacle in a box, but it's hard to know if the box is effectively grounded. Even if a tester lights between hot and the electrical box, the ground may not be able to carry enough current to be safe (see the earlier section "Cable and Conduit" for more on grounding systems). The best course is to replace the ungrounded receptacle with a GFCI (ground-fault circuit interrupter) receptacle. The GFCI can also protect other receptacles wired to the back of the GFCI, as described in a moment.

Using a circuit tester and a screwdriver, here's how to install a GFCI:

1. Shut off the circuit and pull the box apart.

2. Attach black and white wires to the appropriate terminals of the GFCI. The wires that bring electricity to the box go to the terminals marked "supply." Attach other receptacles to the GFCI by connecting their wires to the "load" terminals (see "Installing a Receptacle: The Basics," earlier).

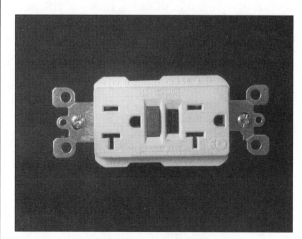

One button on front tests the GFCI (do this monthly); the other resets after a test—or after the GFCI trips to protect you from shock.

3. Check that the GFCI is working, following the test procedure on the package. Label the receptacle "No equipment ground" and test the GFCI monthly to make sure it's working.

When Do You Need Electrical Help?

The easy answer is after you get confused, but before the sparks fly. In no way can one chapter cover every circumstance in every house. Say you find an ugly knot of wires inside a box, many of them not connected to the fixture in the box. This may be normal—electricians choose wire routes for convenience. But these wires may be getting power from several breakers or fuses. In this case, how can you be sure every wire is cold? You could pull the main disconnect and work on the circuit under a flickering flashlight, or you might choose to call the wire wizards.

Three- and four-way switches are another problem area, since there are so many ways to wire them. (If you're just replacing a switch, you can probably get by wiring the new one exactly as the old one was wired—using masking tape to identify wires. But if you can't tell which switch is causing the problem, either replace them all or pick up the phone.)

You also may run into wiring done by a blew-it-yourselfer—somebody who ignored the fundamentals of wiring: grounding, matching wire colors, and observing circuit capacity. It can be hard to correct that kind of work, and I wouldn't suggest it. When my friend Paula had such a problem, she wisely called an electrician. He found the bungled wiring so amusing that he almost forgot to charge her!

Plugged In: The Telephone Story

Now that telephone companies charge astronomical prices to install and repair phone wiring, homeowners have an incentive to understand a new kind of technology. Fortunately, standardization and a modular, plug-and-play mentality make phone wiring quite simple.

To add jacks (phone outlets), observe these pointers:

◆ Phone cable has three or four conductors. Four-conductor cable (black, red, green, and yellow) can carry two separate lines. Three-wire cable can carry one line.

◆ Modular jacks are used to attach the lines from telephones to the house's phone cables. They are marked "B," "R," "G," and "Y," to indicate wire color.

◆ Modular plugs come in two sizes. The larger ones link phones to the wall wiring; the smaller ones link handsets to phones.

◆ Electronic stores stock a range of phone gizmos—wire, connectors, staples, and jacks. You can buy a "splitter" so a modular jack carrying two phone lines can feed two separate phones. Another gadget converts old, four-prong phone jacks to modular jacks.

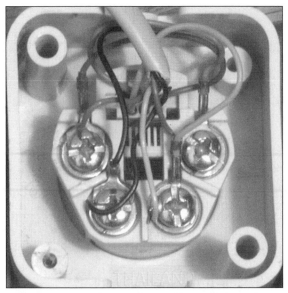

To wire a new phone jack, simply match the colors to the markings on the jack—and hope that your phone system is standard. If not, a phone installer may have to straighten things out.

◆ To run phone cable in the house, an 18" drill bit is handy for long reaches.

◆ To connect a new jack: (a) attach the new wire to the metal block where the phone wire enters the house; or (b) attach it to an existing phone jack and run it through the walls as needed. Special insulated staples are the best way to attach phone cable to walls.

The Least You Need to Know

◆ Electricity likes to go around in circles, or circuits. Interrupting a circuit is dangerous if not done correctly.

◆ The golden rule of electrical repairs is to shut off the circuit—and then test that it's really off—before working.

◆ Grounded circuits are used in all modern construction. You can update an ungrounded receptacle by installing a ground-fault circuit interrupter receptacle.

◆ Electrical devices are made for easy connections; screw-on wire connectors can handle most other connections.

◆ Baseboards, attics, basements, crawl spaces, and receptacles on the opposite side of the wall are all good sources of power for a new receptacle.

◆ Connecting new phones is usually as simple as matching wire colors.

In This Chapter

- ◆ The principles of plumbing

- ◆ Protecting your home from becoming the neighborhood water park

- ◆ No more leaks and drips: fixing the common faucet

- ◆ How to avoid (or deal with) frozen pipes

- ◆ Drains, traps, and vents: solving the mystery of where it all goes

- ◆ The inner workings of the toilet

Chapter 17

Land of 10,000 Leaks (Plumb Crazy!)

So you've been putting off that little plumbing repair? Believe me, I understand the fear of plumbing. I remember installing a water softener—a "simple" project that gobbled seven aggravating hours, three trips to the hardware store, and most of my stock of "marital goodwill."

There is no disguising the fact that plumbing problems can be tough, and can easily move you beyond DIY-land. Still, my goal is not to plumb the mysterious depths of plumbing, but to give you a hand with the simple plumbing repairs that any halfway-handy homeowner can tackle.

The Basic Principles of Plumbing

Plumbing starts to make sense once you understand some simple physical laws:

- ◆ Water seeks its own level.
- ◆ The higher the water pressure, the more likely the leak.
- ◆ Drain pipes get larger as they go downstream, because they must carry more water. For the same reason, supply pipes get smaller as they go downstream.
- ◆ Hot water is more corrosive than cold water.
- ◆ Water moving through a drain must be replaced by air from the venting system.

Water Quality

If you're drinking water from your pipes, the quality of your water depends on the condition of those pipes. City water systems should test their supply—but it wouldn't hurt to check. If you drink from your well, it is logical to have the water tested occasionally—and to install a filter or take other corrective measures as indicated.

Get the Lead Out!

A major cause of home water contamination is lead pipes. If your house was built before 1929 or so, get a lead test done on your water. Also look for lead pipes—a soft, gray metal that scratches easily. Lead-tin solder, used to join copper pipes until recently, contains some lead, but that's a relatively small source of contamination. If you're repairing copper pipe, however, be sure to use the widely available lead-free solder. In short, don't put anything in your water supply that you wouldn't want to drink.

Toolbox Tips

A comprehensive solution to hard-water woes is to install a water softener in the piping that feeds your water heater (the "supply" side). This should prevent lime problems throughout the hot-water system.

If you have lead pipes, you can reduce lead contamination by running the tap until it's cold before drinking the water (or cooking with it), particularly in the morning. Don't use hot water for drinking or cooking, which dissolves more lead.

Hard News About Soft Water

Hard water contains high levels of dissolved calcium and magnesium salts, which originate in rocks the groundwater flows through. A buildup of these salts, often called "lime," typically forms a white deposit on drinking glasses and toilet tanks. Hard water is much less effective for cleaning clothes than soft water, because you need more additives, and soil tends to re-deposit in the washer. Hard water is also hard on plumbing, because it clogs small openings, and eventually even the pipes. Use these suggestions for controlling lime:

◆ In a water heater, lime can build up and act as an insulator, reducing efficiency. You can drain the tank occasionally, but the best solution is to install a water softener.

◆ Lime can clog hard-to-see holes under the toilet rim that feed water into the bowl to clean it as it flushes. Ream clogged holes with a bent coat hanger, then flush the toilet and repeat.

◆ Lime can clog holes in a showerhead (look for a blocked or dribbling stream). Remove screws holding the face plate. If there's no faceplate, unscrew the shower head and disassemble it. Soak the spray nozzle in strong vinegar. After a couple hours, poke a wire or nail through the holes, rinse and reassemble the head.

◆ If lime builds up around spigots and faucets, dissolve it in strong vinegar or an acid solution sold for this purpose. Use goggles and safety gloves when working with acids.

Pipe Applications

Pipe is made from many materials, and used for many purposes. For our purposes, pipe is:

◆ **DWV (Drain, waste, or vent):** not used for drinking water

◆ **Potable:** used for drinking water

◆ **Black steel:** used only for gas lines

The main distinction here should be obvious. If contaminants leach from DWV, you are not going to drink them. Potable water pipes should be copper or galvanized steel. In some areas, certain plastics can be used for potable water—but sometimes for cold water only. Check with your building inspector.

Tools and Materials

Plumbing can call for a wretched number of special tools, but the few basic ones shown here will serve for many repairs.

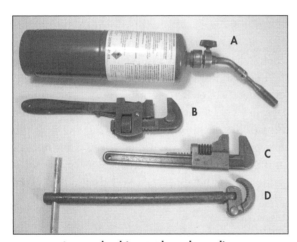

Large plumbing tools and supplies.

A. **Propane torch:** Solders copper pipe, also thaws frozen metal (not plastic!) pipes.

B. **Pipe wrench:** Smaller ones are handy for tight quarters, like under the sink; larger ones are great for rusty pipe joints. The 12" model shown is a compromise size; you may need two.

C. **Smooth-jawed (monkey) wrench:** Turns plated fittings without wrecking the finish (you can substitute an open-end or adjustable wrench if you have one big enough).

D. **Basin wrench:** Nothing beats this wrench for reaching up under a sink to loosen or tighten the big nut securing the spigot assembly.

Toolbox Tips

Depending on your plumbing project, you may also need a plumber's snake to unclog drains, cleaner and cement for plastic pipe (see later in this chapter for instructions on cementing plastic pipe), buckets, a hacksaw, rag, level, a bountiful supply of patience and ingenuity, and almost anything else in your toolbox.

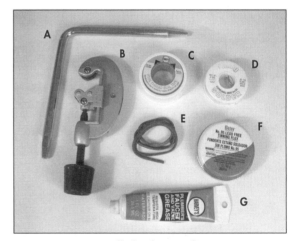

Small plumbing tools.

A. **Seat remover:** Unscrews seats in compression faucets. One end is square, the other hexagonal.

B. **Pipe cutter:** Cuts copper pipe quickly and cleanly.

C. **Teflon pipe tape:** Lubricates, rustproofs, and seals threads of steel pipe. Greatly simplifies later disassembly.

D. **Lead-free solder:** Makes a nontoxic joint in copper pipe.

E. **Packing (graphite variety shown):** Seals the shaft in older faucets.

F. **Soldering flux:** Prevents corrosion, helps solder to flow and bond to metal. Don't solder without it!

G. **Faucet grease:** Lubricates faucets for smooth operation.

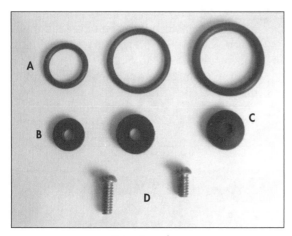

Faucet washers.

A. **O-rings:** Various sizes seal joints in newer plumbing fixtures, including faucets and toilets.

B. **Flat washers:** Used for compression faucets.

C. **Beveled washer:** Used for compression faucets.

D. **Brass screws:** Hold washers in compression faucets.

Types of pipe. From top to bottom: steel (threaded) pipe, plastic pipe, copper pipe.

Fix-It Phrase

You listening, Dr. Freud? When it comes to suggestive lingo, nothing beats plumbing: The "mating" parts of pipes and fittings are named based on their similarity to "male" or "female" anatomy. (None of which explains why a "nipple" has two male ends …) The names of other plumbing fittings, sadly, are far less titillating.

The Main Shutoff Valve

All city water to your house should be controlled by a main shutoff, located near the foundation, usually toward the street. Amateur plumbers need to know this location because the main shutoff reduces the risks of plumbing-repair disasters. Test the valve before you need it. Because it's used so seldom, it may not close completely. Repairing this valve is a pro job because you must shut off the water outside the house. If the shutoff closes most of the way, however, you can still use it. Close the shutoff and open a faucet below the repair (or at the same level if necessary). This relieves the water pressure so you can complete the repair without a flood.

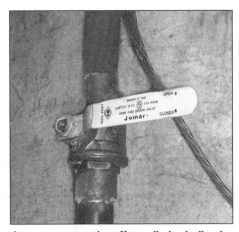

This main water shutoff is called a ball valve (because of its internal construction). It's in the closed position. Notice the "jumper" cable used to ground the electrical system by jumping across the valve to connect directly to ground. An older, gate-style main shutoff is shown in Chapter 1.

Faucet Repair (Trouble with the Spigot?)

Faucets shut off the water, theoretically, without leaking or a need for steroid-freak force. The old-style compression faucets controlled hot or cold water individually and were used in pairs. Many newer faucets use one handle to control both flows, usually with a cartridge or ball mechanism. As we look at these faucets, remember that you may meet variations on the general theme—a good reason to bring the carcass of the faucet to the store when you buy parts.

Toolbox Tips _____

In a house supplied by a well, opening the circuit breaker that supplies the pump will shut off the water. Before working on the plumbing, either run a faucet until the pressure tank empties, or close a valve on the discharge side (which supplies the house) of the pressure tank.

Fixing Compression Faucets

Compression faucets—so called because the washer is compressed by the screw action of the stem—stop water flow by forcing a washer against a seat. Leaks are usually caused by a worn-out washer, but the root cause may be a rough seat that tore up the washer. Often, seats *and* washers need replacement. You'll need a screwdriver and a wrench, faucet grease, and possibly a seat-removing tool. Follow these steps to repair the faucet:

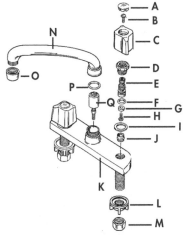

You'll see countless variations on this basic design for the compression faucet.   *(Illustration courtesy of Kohler Company)*

A. Decorative cap

B. Handle screw

C. Handle

D. Bonnet nut

E. Stem

 F. Washer

G. Seat washer

H. Washer screw

 I. Washer

 J. Seat

K. Faucet body

L. Lock nut

M. Supply nut

N. Spout

O. Aerator

P. O-ring

Q. Diverter (diverts water to spray hose)

1. Turn off the water, preferably at a shutoff valve just before the faucet, otherwise at the main shutoff. You may have to loosen the packing nut with a big wrench to allow the shutoff valve handle to move. Make sure to retighten the packing nut when you are done. If it leaks, see the next section, "Get Packing."

A shutoff valve greatly simplifies faucet repair; all modern faucets have shutoffs.

2. Pull off the handles by loosening the handle screw. You may have to pry off a decorative cap on top of the handle first.

3. Use a smooth-jawed wrench to loosen the bonnet nut. Slip the handle back into place and unscrew the stem.

4. Shine a flashlight on the seat—or feel it with your fingers. If the seat is rough or uneven, the new washer won't seal, and will quickly be damaged. If you see a square, hexagonal, or grooved opening for a wrench inside the seat, try to replace the seat (step 5a). If the seat is fixed (as in many laundry sinks), smooth it with a seat-dressing tool (step 5b).

5a. Remove the seat with a seat-removing tool (some plumbing terms are so logical!). Slip the tool into the seat, tap it into place, and unscrew. Take the seat to a plumbing supply or hardware store, buy one for each faucet, and install with the same tool. Put faucet grease on the threads to ease the next replacement.

5b. To smooth a fixed seat, buy or rent a seat-dressing tool and insert it squarely into the faucet. Clean up the seat with the coarse cutter, and repeat with the smoother cutter. Be sure to hold the tool perpendicular to the seat.

6. To replace the washers, look at the seat and decide what type of washer you need. (See the Toolbox Tips on this page.) Despite years of immersion in water, a brass washer screw should come right out. Do not use a steel screw to fasten the new washer: It will rust and never come out.

7. Put faucet grease on mating metal parts, and inside the packing, so the faucet will operate smoothly.

Toolbox Tips

When fixing a compression faucet, don't just replace the washer you find—some bozo might have used the wrong type. If you see tapered or recessed rim, use a beveled washer. If you see a raised rim, use the more common flat washer. If the raised rim is broken, buy a new stem—replacements are usually available if you bring the old stem to the store.

8. Thread the stem into the bonnet nut and screw the nut on the faucet. Before tightening the bonnet nut, back the stem out so it does not push on the seat while you tighten.

9. Restore the water. If the faucet leaks around the stem, keep reading.

Get Packing

Many compression-faucet problems occur at the seal between the bonnet nut and the stem. This seal may be an O-ring (a special washer) or, in older faucets, a flexible material called packing.

Problems with valve packing cause a surprising number of plumbing problems, especially in older faucets. But packing is a no-brainer—generally you just open up the faucet, add some new packing, and tighten the bonnet nut.

Packing leaks occur only when the valve is open (when the valve is closed, there's no water pressure on the packing). If the packing is really loose, the stem may slop around a bit. Often, you can seal a packing leak by tightening the bonnet (use reasonable force—squeezing too tight will seize the handle). If tightening fails, unscrew the bonnet nut. If the packing material is a glob of black stuff, replace the packing, as shown in the following photo, and retighten.

If the seal is made by a solid packing washer or an O-ring (a narrow washer surrounding the stem), just replace the washer or O-ring and grease with faucet grease. You may have to cut the old O-rings out with a knife.

Adding string packing to a faucet can easily solve leaks around the stem.

Cartridge Faucets

Cartridge faucets mix and control the flow of hot and cold water with a replaceable, cylindrical cartridge. Although you may be tempted to buy cheap, replacement seals instead of a new cartridge, you're probably better off replacing the whole thing.

The cartridge for Moen brand faucets is fixed in place with a retainer clip, while other types are held by a nut. To disassemble, turn off the water, pull off the handle, remove the stem nut or clip, and pull out the cartridge. You may need a special cartridge tool to get the thing apart. To make sure you remove all the parts, compare what you pull out against the contents of the replacement kit. Then simply slap the replacement cartridge back into place, and add some faucet grease to ensure smooth operation.

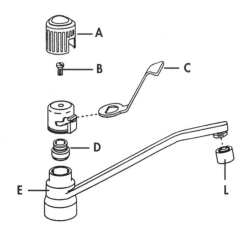

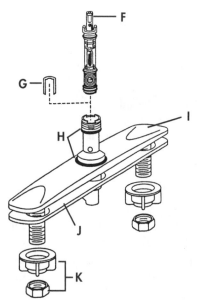

Cartridge faucet terminology.   *(Illustration courtesy of Moen, Inc.)*

A. Handle cap
B. Handle screw
C. Lever handle
D. Retainer pivot nut
E. Spout assembly
F. Cartridge
G. Retainer clip
H. Spout O-rings
I. Escutcheon
J. Deck gasket
K. Lock nuts
L. Aerator

Putting in a new replacement cartridge (Moen-style is shown) should ensure years of trouble-free operation.

Ball Faucets

The third major style of faucet is called a ball faucet, because it uses a ball device to control the flow of hot and cold water. You can repair a ball faucet by buying a kit that includes just seat and springs, or a larger kit that also includes a replacement ball. Chances are you will do better buying the kit from the manufacturer rather than a "universal" repair kit.

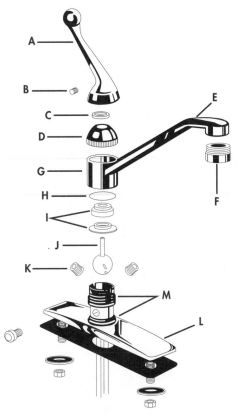

Ball faucet terminology. *(Illustration courtesy of Delta Faucet Company)*

A. Handle

B. Set screw

C. Adjusting ring

D. Cap

E. Spout

F. Aerator

G. Spout sleeve

H. Slip ring

 I. Cam and packing

J. Ball

K. Seat and spring

L. Faucet body

M. O-rings (spout seals)

Ball faucets are an alternative to cartridges, and they cost considerably less to repair. You'll need a repair kit, new O-rings for the spout (optional), an Allen wrench (which may come with the kit), arc-joint pliers, and, as always, plumber's luck. Here's how:

1. Shut off the water, as described for the previous procedures. Loosen the Allen-head set screw on the bottom of the handle and remove the handle.

2. Tighten the adjusting ring slightly. If the faucet stops dripping, you've lucked out: The problem was insufficient pressure on the seals.

3. If the faucet still drips, remove the adjusting ring, and pull out the cap and the ball under it.

4. The seals are the two small disks under the ball. Note their location and remove them. Don't lose the springs!

5. With the faucet apart, you might as well replace the O-rings sealing the spout. Pull up and twist to remove the spout. Carefully dig the O-rings and any lime build-up from their grooves. Then put new O-rings in the grooves, add faucet grease, and twist the spout back into place.

6. Position the new seals and press the ball and cam back into position. Don't let the seals jump out!

7. Screw the adjusting ring back on and tighten firmly. Turn the water on and tighten a bit if it's leaking. Then replace the handle.

8. While water is running, push down on the handle. If water leaks from under the handle, tighten the adjusting ring.

Toolbox Tips

Valves used in gas piping and many newer main water shut-offs have a handle that turns only 90°. To remember which position is which, imagine that the handle attaches to a gate inside the valve. When the handle is across the pipe, the gate (valve) is closed; when the handle is parallel to the pipe (as shown in the following photo), it's open.

This gas gate valve turns only 90°.

All Thumbs

Natural gas is supplied at low pressure, so it's less likely to leak than water. Use joint compound on good, clean threads in the black steel pipe used for gas piping, and avoid overtightening, which can strip threads and crack fittings. Before you restore the gas pressure, brush some soap suds on the joint to test it. Bubbles indicate a leak. Do not test for leaks with matches!

Soldering Copper Pipe

Soldering, or "sweating," copper pipes seems complicated, but it's anything but. A clean, fluxed, good-fitting joint is almost impossible to solder badly, as long as you supply enough heat without overheating. Clean copper and hot solder have an irresistible attraction, and capillary action will "pull" the hot solder evenly into the joint—so long as you have enough flux.

You'll need a propane torch, sandpaper, emery cloth or steel wool, flux, and lead-free plumbing solder. Follow these steps:

1. The fittings and pipe must be sound, round, and free of nicks and deformities. Check the joint—does the pipe enter straight, giving a tight fit? Correct any problems while the pipe is cold.

2. Cut the pipe to length.

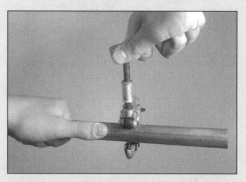

This pipe cutter is foolproof—gradually tighten the screw knob as you spin the cutter around the pipe. A hacksaw will work in a pinch, but you'll have to work to get the cut straight—a pipe cutter can't cut crooked. You can't see it in the photo, but this piece of pipe was firmly clamped while we cut it.

3. Clean the outside of the pipe and the inside of the fitting with fine sandpaper, emery cloth, or steel wool. Get the surfaces shiny—solder will not stick to corrosion.

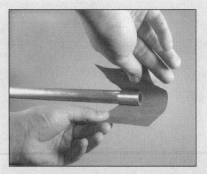

Clean copper pipe well before soldering.

4. Apply nonlead flux to both mating surfaces (the outside of the pipe and the inside of the fitting), assemble the joint, and twist to distribute the flux.

5. Light the torch and move the flame over the pipe and the fitting. Concentrate the heat on the bulky part of the fitting. Try to avoid inhaling fumes from boiling flux.

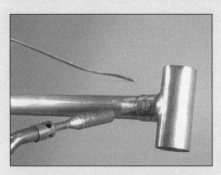

If you have enough heat, copper pipe solders quickly.

6. A few seconds after the flux begins to bubble, hold the solder against the crack between the fitting and the pipe. Don't melt the solder directly with the torch—a hot joint will melt the solder and pull it in.

7. When an even bead of solder forms around the whole joint between the pipe and the fitting, pull the solder away. Let the joint cool for a minute without disturbing it. Then wrap a wet rag on the joint if you want to cool it faster.

Plastic Pipe

When used correctly, plastic pipe is a homeowner's best friend, since it is cheaper and easier to use than metal. To extend a metal plumbing system with plastic, buy fittings that join plastic to copper, steel, or cast iron. But remember that many localities allow plastic to be used for drain, waste, and vent—not for potable water. If you have questions about what your local building code allows, talk with a building inspector.

> **All Thumbs**
> The biggest complication with plastic is deciding which specific composition—PVC (polyvinyl chloride) or CPVC (chlorinated polyvinyl chloride), for example—can be used for your application (drain, vent, or water supply). Depending on its composition, plastic may be restricted to a limited pressure or temperature range. This restriction varies by area: The best guide is either your building inspector or a store display.

Some types of plastic pipe are joined with special fittings that are tightened with a wrench. Others are joined by simply pushing the pipe into a fitting. But the most common, and cheapest, plastic pipe is welded together using a solvent made for each type of plastic. Here's the general procedure for welding plastic pipe:

1. Cut the pipe square with a hacksaw. Notice the clamp that stabilizes the pipe as we cut.

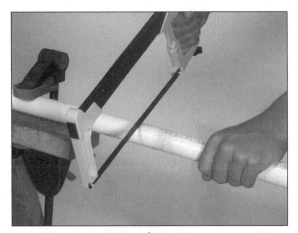

Cutting plastic pipe.

2. Sandpaper off burrs and slightly roughen the outside of the pipe.

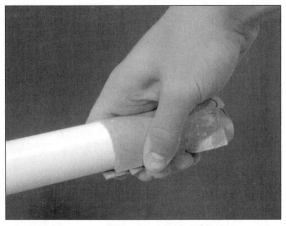

Before gluing, roughen the outside of the pipe with sandpaper.

3. Line up the joint dry to test the fit.
4. Disassemble the joint and clean the mating surfaces with the correct type of cleaner.
5. Put cement on the pipe and press it all the way into the joint, then turn it slightly. Quickly adjust the position—plastic can bond in less than a minute. Let the joint set up.

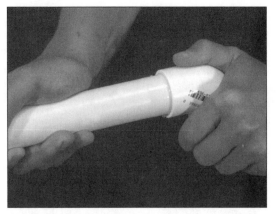

When gluing plastic pipe, you have to act quickly.

Frozen Pipes and How to Avoid Them

Frozen pipes sound so, er, boring. But one insurance company says 250,000 Americans have them each year. The pipes most likely to freeze, amazingly enough, are those in cold locations like underheated crawl spaces and basements, and along outside walls.

Outside faucets (called *sillcocks* or hose bibbs) are a prime place for a freeze-up. In the fall, disconnect the garden hose. If you have a *frost-proof sillcock*, that should be enough, as long as some hidden fitting is not sealing the water in. Otherwise, shut off the water by closing the valve inside the wall (there should be one) on the pipe supplying the hose connection. Then open the faucet so the remaining water can drip out.

Fix-It Phrase

A sillcock is where you connect your garden hose. A **frostproof sillcock** is a hose connection that does not freeze. If some water drips out after you shut off a hose connection, you probably have this timesaver, which saves you the time of going inside the house and shutting off the supply to the sillcock.

Here are more suggestions for preventing the big chill:

◆ Seal the foundation by caulking cracks.

◆ Insulate between the pipes and the cold (pipe insulation will help for a while, but eventually, the pipe will reach ambient temperature unless water is flowing).

◆ During winter, keep the thermostat up. Open cabinet doors in the kitchen so warm air can reach the pipes.

◆ Install electrical pipe tape, which heats pipes by resistance. To prevent fire, buy a UL-approved product and follow all directions.

◆ As a last resort, let the faucets drip on a cold night.

If your pipes do freeze, here are three options:

◆ Wrap them with rags, and pour boiling water over the rags.

◆ Warm the pipes with a heat gun or heat lamp.

◆ If you're comfortable using a propane torch, and there's nothing flammable nearby, put a flame spreader on the torch and carefully warm the pipes. Move the flame constantly to avoid hot spots.

Toolbox Tips

If you're having trouble loosening a steel plumbing joint, try tapping on the joint with a hammer, drenching it in penetrating oil, or heating it with a propane torch. When it comes to loosening a rusty joint, plumbing is like pro wrestling. The ends justify the means.

Feeling Trapped by Your Trap?

A trap is a U-shape piece of drainpipe that's usually directly beneath the outlet of a plumbing fixture. Traps have two important purposes: creating a "water seal" so you can avoid intimate contact with the sicko world of sewer gas, and giving crud a place to hang out so you can test your plumbing skills (just kidding).

Traps look simple, and they are. But because the water seal is so important, plumbing codes limit their design and construction. For example, multiple traps are forbidden because they slow the flow too much (you should not see a separate trap beneath a toilet, which has a built-in trap).

Pipe Venting

You seldom see vents, except on the roof, but they are a critical part of your plumbing system. Vents allow air to replace water leaving a drain, and preserve the water trap just described. Vented drains also stay cleaner because water flows faster through them.

Without a vent, you'll get a vacuum and a sluggish, gurgling drain. You may be able to ream a plugged vent by poking a long drain auger (a "snake") into the round vent pipe sticking through the roof. Adding vents to an old house is a pro job, but it will drastically improve drain performance.

Unclogging the Drain Is ... Less Disgusting Than Ignoring It

The first step in cleaning a drain is to locate the clog: is it local or systemic? If two drains suddenly plug up, I'd bet a gold-plated plunger the cause is something affecting both drains, like a plugged vent or a clog in a main sewer line. Because these problems can be harder to reach, they're a good reason to call for help. If only one drain is screaming in agony, read on.

Hair and Soap Scuzz

If you're lucky, your problem is caused by something as simple as hair, soap scuzz, and other unmentionables caught on the strainer or just inside the drain. You can probably remove these clogs with long-nose pliers, a bent coat hanger, or "mechanical fingers," a long, three-fingered tool for grabbing inaccessible stuff. Or buy a drain cleaner; some are expressly made for hair clogs (see the next section).

After you get the drain working, resolve to keep wannabe cloggers like bobby pins away from the sink, and forget about dumping cooking grease down the kitchen sink. Remove soap, grease, and hair by flushing the drain with plenty of hot water once in a while. Put 4 to 5 inches of hot water in the sink or tub, then pull the plug so the water can scour the drain pipe; do this weekly if you can remember.

Drain Chemicals

If your drain is still flowing, but too slowly for your taste, you may start wondering if a miracle chemical could solve (or should I say dissolve?) your woes.

Drain cleaners come in various formulations, and are especially useful for drains that still have some action. Be sure to read and follow the label, because, well, it's smart to do so. And don't mix chemicals. Drain cleaner and bleach, for example, can produce toxic fumes. Use protective clothing and goggles if the label calls for it—no sense going blind just because

it seemed cool to act stupid, and there's no telling when your drain will spit something back at you …

Enzymes (chemical extracts from microorganisms that have generations of experience eating organic matter) are good for maintenance because they're relatively nontoxic. But keep your eye on the label—you probably need to use them periodically.

All Thumbs

Some places will sell sulfuric acid to clean a drain, but most experts won't use it on a totally clogged drain, because pressure can build up and the pipes can explode, or at least heat up and corrode. (And if the acid doesn't work, you'll have to work in pipes full of acid—a nasty prospect.) And even if a clog does get loose, it might travel to an even worse location and get stuck. Finally, acid can also strip off chrome plating (not to mention your skin, if you come into contact with it).

In general, drain chemicals are best used as preventive maintenance on drains that are running slow, because they eat away all sorts of organic yuck. You may have to protect metal on the sink or tub with Vaseline. These cures can work—*if you disobey the instinct to ignore plumbing problems until they can't be ignored any longer.*

Take the Plunge(r)

Plungers exert a hydraulic force on the contents of a drain, and whatever is plugging it, but they are only effective up to the vent connection (which may be just inside the wall).

Toolbox Tips

Carl Lorentz, a friend who makes plumbing his living, suggests getting a big plunger for toilets and a midget model for sinks. Combine forces on bathtubs: Use one plunger on the drain, and the other to seal the overflow (otherwise, you can't put pressure on the drain). If you have only one plunger, take the overflow apart and seal the vent with your hand. If you're having trouble making a seal, put Vaseline on the end of the plunger.

A plunger in action. I bet your sink won't look this clean when you try to open the drain ...

Here's how to plunge a drain:

1. Add a few inches of water to the fixture (as if it's not already full of liquid yuck!).
2. Roll the plunger into the water to minimize the amount of air trapped inside it.
3. Pump up and down as hard as you can without breaking the seal. Then give one final pull and break the plunger free. You may have to plunge for several minutes. With any luck, you'll hear a famished groan as the drain sucks down a load of filth.

4. Dump a load of as-hot-as possible water down the drain to clear any remaining grossitude. Repeat the plunging if the drain is still slow.

If plunging fails, your choices are to disassemble the trap, use a pipe auger, or call a pro. Let's look at disassembly first.

Drain Disassembly and Replacement

Disassembling a trap allows you to remove whatever is plugging it—and improves your access to any clogs deeper in the piping. The good news is that new traps are quite easy to remove and replace; the bad news is that not all traps are new. You'll need a flashlight, a bucket, rag, pipe wrench, new washers for the trap (get the right diameter), a coat hanger, and a strong stomach. You may also need a replacement trap (which will include new washers) and a pipe auger. Follow these steps:

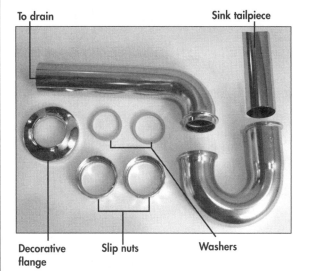

This three-piece p-trap is a common, adjustable item sold in all hardware stores; it can be swiveled and extended to fit most sinks. Small sinks use 1¼'' traps; kitchen and other large sinks use 1½'' traps.

Fix-It Phrase _____

A **p-trap** is named for its shape. The **s-trap** is illegal in some places because it does not maintain a good water seal.

To remove and replace a p-trap:

1. Put the bucket under the trap and loosen the two large nuts. If you're fastidious, use cloth to protect the chrome plating on metal nuts as you wrench them.

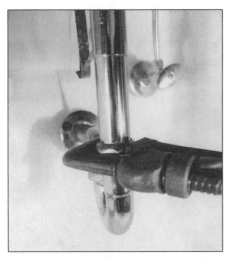

Remember the rule when loosening or tightening nuts: lefty loosey, righty tighty. Reverse this rule for a nut facing away from you.

2. Pull the trap apart and remove any visible obstruction.
3. If you need to, dig around in the drain with a coat hanger and pull out any blockages. (Or see "The Plumber's Snake," next.)
4. Once you've removed the clog, push the washers onto the male ends of the trap and assemble the trap loosely.

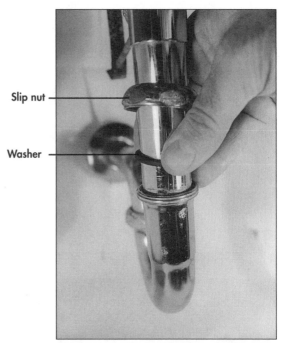

Slip nut ———

Washer ———

Place new washers on the pipes before reassembly. Make sure washers are evenly seated before tightening the slip nuts.

5. Put the trap into position carefully—if you get it right, you shouldn't need nuclear-scale force to tighten the nuts.

The Plumber's Snake

Pipe snakes, or augers, are flexible tools that supposedly thread into a drain to remove whatever unmentionable crud is clogging it. The inexorable need for drain cleaning has spawned many inventions; the best tool for you depends on your talent, your situation, and your luck:

◆ A simple plumber's snake is made of flat flexible (spring) steel.
◆ A rotating snake is slightly more expensive, and much more effective. The snake looks like a long spring, and it's flexible enough to get through a couple elbows before jamming. You rotate the handle as you thread the snake into the pipe.

- A rented electric drain-reamer is even more effective, but make sure you're confident using it, so you don't wreck your pipes.

- A "closet auger" has a right-angle end to reach inside the toilet trap. Be careful—forcing the auger can break the toilet wall.

All Thumbs

If a toilet wobbles, or the floor around it is weak, the doughnut-shaped seal between the toilet and the floor is probably leaking and rotting the floor. To replace this seal (which should be done periodically, preferably before a leak), either lift the toilet from the floor, clean the seat, and replace the seal; or call the plumber.

Drain Auger Techniques

Sinks: Try running an auger through the drain. If there is a cleanout at the bottom of the trap, work through it. Or disassemble the trap as described above and thread the auger into the horizontal pipe entering the wall. Or remove a cleanout plate on the big drain stack below a sink and feed the auger through the opening. Turn the handle of the auger clockwise, and if you feel like you are hooking something, continue turning while gradually withdrawing the auger.

Tubs: Remove the overflow plate and the stopper and stopper linkage. Put the auger through the overflow opening, and crank, moving the auger back and forth, to pick up or dislodge the clog. If your tub has a "drum trap" (look for a metal plate in the floor near the tub or inside an access panel), open the cover on the drum and run the snake in both directions. You may want to try plunging again before messing with taking a drum trap apart—they're tricky to reseal.

Toilets: Feed a closet auger (mentioned earlier in this section) into the trap. Working firmly but carefully, push the snake into the trap and feel for an obstruction. When you think you've hooked one, pull it out. If you must use a straight (sink-type) auger, be extra-careful with the china—and wear rubber gloves! Because toilets are porcelain, and porcelain is fragile, you may want to go back to a plunger. Pencils, toothbrushes, dentures, diaphragms, and toys can all plug toilets. If the toilet continues plugging, it either needs repair or something is wedged in its innards. Empty the bowl, and use a flashlight and small mirror to inspect the trap. Then use a bent coat hanger to extract the object.

How Toilets Flush and Other Modern Miracles

Ever wonder how a toilet works? Nobody does—until the toilet stops working. It's like the old bluesman said, "You don't miss your water till your well runs dry." So if you're still reading, I assume you have what the spies call a "need to know" about the inside of your crapper.

How does a toilet do its vital task?

1. When you crank the handle, the lift arm lifts the stopper valve, and the tankful of water rushes into the bowl, pushing the putrid cargo through the water trap and down the drain.

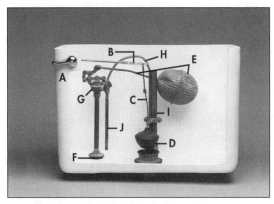

A complicated mechanism hides inside the average old toilet. *(Photo by Fluidmaster, Inc.)*

A. Handle

B. Lift arm

C. Lift wire

D. Stopper valve (or flapper in newer installations)

E. Float and arm

F. Water supply

G. Ballcock valve assembly

H. Bowl refill tube

I. Overflow tube

J. Tank refill tube

2. As the float drops, it opens the ballcock valve, and fresh water enters the tank through the tank refill tube. Fresh water also flows through the bowl refill tube and overflow tube, refilling the bowl.

3. When the tank is empty, the stopper valve drops down, sealing the tank so it can fill. Meanwhile, the bowl refill tube continues filling the bowl.

4. When the water level is high enough, the float shuts the ballcock valve, ending the cycle.

Toilet Troubleshooting

Water should circulate from the tank to the bowl only during flushing. If the toilet "runs" (continually refills its tank), water is entering the bowl when it's not supposed to. Pour food coloring into the tank. If the bowl water turns color before you flush, one of two things needs repair:

♦ The ballcock valve is not shutting soon enough, and water is rising above the overflow tube and entering the tank. Bend the float arm down so the valve shuts sooner. If you have the replacement valve shown in the next photo, read that section for advice.

♦ The stopper valve seat is damaged or dirty, and water is leaking into the bowl through the bottom of the tank. Read "Replacing Toilet Guts," next.

Here are some tips for good toilet operation:

♦ To make sure the mechanism is not snagging itself, watch a full flushing cycle with the tank uncovered.

♦ Check that the stopper and float are not waterlogged. The float should ride on top of the water, and the stopper should stay up until the tank is empty.

♦ Check the holes under the rim. If they are plugged, see "Hard Facts About Soft Water," earlier in the chapter.

Replacing Toilet Guts

Toilets have come a long way since people got tired of marching to the backyard every time nature called. Modern toilet replacement mechanisms are such a vast improvement that it usually makes sense to replace an old mechanism that could be repaired. The new equipment is cheap, rustproof plastic, and the simplified design omits many trouble spots.

I'll start by explaining how to replace the *ballcock*, then describe how to replace the flush valve.

Fix-It Phrase _____

The **ballcock** refills the tank and bowl when the tank level drops during flushing, and closes when the tank is full.

You'll need a pair of arc-joint pliers or lock-ing pliers, a knife, and a monkey wrench to replace the ballcock:

1. Shut off the water supply to the toilet. Close the main water shutoff if the supply valve is absent or broken. Flush the toilet to drain the tank, and sponge out remaining water.

If the shutoff valve is tight, loosen the packing nut with a wrench.

2. Remove the old ballcock by loosening the water supply connection and the big nut mounting the ballcock to the bottom of the tank.

3. Clean the area around the hole in the bottom of the toilet tank with steel wool to get a good seal. Twist the replacement assembly to adjust its height (read package directions for details). Place the washer on the tube and insert the tube through the hole in the bottom of the tank.

The new valve must be adjusted according to the height of the toilet tank.   *(Photo by Fluidmaster, Inc.)*

4. Loosely connect the water supply and the mounting lock nut. Tighten both nuts.

5. Attach the refill tube to the valve. Cut the tube to length and clip it to the overflow pipe.

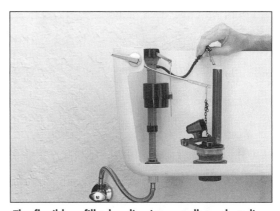

The flexible refill tube slips into an elbow that clips on the overflow pipe.   *(Photo by Fluidmaster, Inc.)*

6. Turn on the water supply and retighten the packing nut on the water supply valve. Flush out the valve per instructions, and adjust the tank water level with the clip on the float. If you see any leaks, tighten the appropriate fitting.

Old flush valves are another piece of antiquated toilet equipment that should be replaced rather than repaired. Replacement flush valves, called "flappers," mount by slipping over the overflow tube. If the valve seat in the bottom of the tank is damaged, buy a kit with a replacement seat. You'll need a sponge and steel wool to install a flapper:

1. Shut off the water, flush the toilet to drain the tank, and sponge the tank dry.

2. Remove the old tank ball or flapper, leaving the overflow tube in place.

3. Press a mounting adapter over the overflow tube (unless a mounting is already present).

4. Slip the new flapper into place on the mounting adapter, positioned so it can move freely.

5. Adjust the chain so it's slightly slack, then cut off any extra chain.

The new flapper valve mounts on the overflow tube. Make sure the flapper doesn't snag against anything, and securely contacts the seat.

The Least You Need to Know

- ◆ Water systems can benefit from a surprising amount of preventive help, designed to increase convenience and comfort, or reduce maintenance costs.

- ◆ Many faucets are built to be repaired. Once you've figured out how to take them apart, the rest should be easy.

- ◆ With a bit of common sense, you can prevent pipes from freezing.

- ◆ Chemical drain cleaners help clean drains, especially those that are not totally plugged.

- ◆ Replacing the working parts of a toilet can be fast, cheap, and effective. Don't bother repairing toilet parts that are easy to replace.

- ◆ Don't get in over your head (literally). If you're totally confused, get information or get help.

In This Chapter

- ◆ Troubleshooting your heating system
- ◆ Simple tune-ups and repairs you can make
- ◆ Installing a replacement thermostat
- ◆ Understanding the fan and limit control
- ◆ Dealing with pilot lights, thermocouples, and gas flames

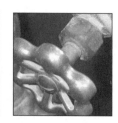

Chapter 18

A Blast of Hot Air: Heating System Tips

Heating systems do two things: They create heat, and they distribute it. Heat usually comes from burning natural gas, propane, or fuel oil and is usually distributed as hot air, hot water, or steam. With so many fuels and designs in service, there's no way this chapter can cover them all. However, heating systems do require a tad of maintenance for proper operation. Replacing filters, checking the pilot light, adding water to a boiler, adjusting air flow are all within idiot territory. Even putting in a replacement thermostat is generally much easier than you'd suspect.

Heating systems can be temperamental. When my first son, Alex, was being born, I pleaded with my heating repair guy, "I'm in the delivery room, and my wife is about to give birth, and my neighbor tells me it's 44 degrees in my house, and it's winter here in Wisconsin, and could you *pulleeze* get over to my house before the pipes turn to icicles?"

This story is true. It's also true you could prevent this humiliation (and countless others) by not having children. My lesson, however, was to listen to a furnace's sob stories—I already knew the clanky old monster was ready to croak. I bet the repairman is still chuckling about that moron who cooked up such a bare-faced lie to get fast service in winter …

This book won't cover air-conditioning units, which are not user-serviceable. Ditto for heat pumps, which heat and cool a house using air-conditioning technology. However, the thermostat, filter, and duct information does apply to systems with air-conditioning and heat pumps.

Understand Your Thermostat

A thermostat is a thermally operated switch that controls combustion in the furnace. The thermostat *calls for* heat by sending an electrical signal to open the gas valve (in a gas furnace) or start the burner motor (in an oil furnace). When the house gets warms enough, the thermostat shuts the gas or motor off. Note: The thermostat controls burning in the furnace. Heat circulation is controlled by a separate switch called the fan and limit control (which I'll discuss in the next section).

All Thumbs

Furnaces that burn fuel can produce deadly carbon monoxide, a colorless, tasteless gas that can make you very sleepy (also fatigued, lethargic, and headachy). If you notice these symptoms, especially in fall, when the furnace comes on for the heating season, *leave the house immediately*, taking along any pets, and call your gas or oil company. They will be only too happy to do a carbon monoxide test. The hazards of carbon monoxide exposure led me to install two carbon-monoxide detectors in my house, one near the furnace, and the second in the main living area. You might want to do the same.

To save energy, *set-back* thermostats can be set to a cooler temperature at night (and during the day, if house is unoccupied). They let you enjoy warmth when you're up and about, but still let you sleep in cooler, more economical conditions. The thermostat package may indicate how much money you can save with a given set-back.

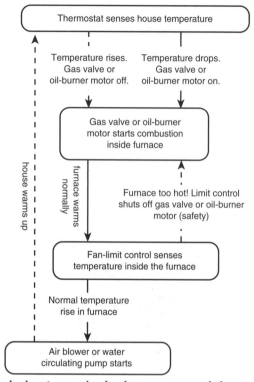

In the heating mode, the thermostat controls burning, and the fan-and-limit control controls air or water circulation.

Some thermostats (both mechanical and digital) have an adjustable *anticipator* mechanism to prevent rapid on-off cycling of the furnace and air-conditioner. The anticipator allows the room to cool a couple of degrees before calling for heat. Rapid cycling of the furnace is not only annoying, but harmful to the system. If your furnace is cycling too rapidly, increase the anticipator setting (consult the instructions for your thermostat). Vice versa if the furnace is cycling too slowly—meaning the house gets too cold before the furnace restarts.

Fix-It Phrase

The **set point** is the temperature setting on the thermostat. Above this point (for heating), or below it (for cooling), the thermostat **calls for** the furnace or air-conditioner to operate. A **set-back** thermostat allows the house to be warmer (in winter) or cooler (in summer) when you are home and awake. An thermostat's **anticipator** prevents the furnace or cooler from cycling too rapidly.

If your furnace is properly wired, installing a thermostat is a no-brainer—just follow the instructions on the new package. Drill the drywall to mount the new thermostat, then connect wires following the color scheme on the unit.

Each fall, before the heating season, switch the thermostat to the heating position and set the temperature above the temperature in your room: If you hear unusual sounds, phone your furnace pros.

Fan and Limit Control

The fan-and-limit control (see the previous drawing) is a thermally operated switch that regulates the blower (in hot-air systems) or circulating pump (in hot-water systems). The fan portion of the switch signals the heat-circulating apparatus to run when the furnace is hot, preventing the system from circulating cold water or air. (The lag between the burner start-up and the start of the circulating fan is called the system delay.)

The blower or water pump continues to run after the burner shuts off. When the furnace cools below the lower set point, the fan or pump stops, and the system idles until the thermostat calls for more heat. If the furnace gets too hot for any reason, the limit control shuts off the burner to prevent damage and possible fire.

Pilot Lights, Thermocouples, and Gas Flames

A pilot light is a small flame that burns continually in older gas furnaces and water heaters. It lights the gas when the furnace starts to operate. Just above the pilot light you'll see a thermocouple. If this thermally operated safety device does not sense heat, it "thinks" the pilot light is off and shuts off the gas.

Modern furnaces and water heaters use electric (spark) ignition instead of pilot lights. Electric ignitions are highly reliable and economical, because they don't waste gas when the furnace is off, but they are not owner-maintainable.

To light a pilot, follow these steps:

1. Turn the main gas valve to "off."
2. Find a long match while you wait five minutes for any gas to dissipate.
3. Turn the gas valve to "pilot."
4. Press the red button on the pilot valve kides the thermocouple so gas can flow even though the thermocouple is cold.

5. Hold the red button down for a minute, while the pilot warms the thermocouple. The pilot should stay lit when you release the button. If it doesn't, wait five minutes for gas to dissipate and repeat the process.

6. Turn the main gas valve to "on." Turn the thermostat up to call for heat; the furnace should ignite (if not, see "Troubleshooting"). The pilot should remain lit.

On a gas furnace, the main burner should make a blue flame with a few tips of yellow. This gives the highest efficiency and makes the least soot. You may be able to adjust the air intake to achieve this kind of flame, but first see "Know When You Need Help," later in this chapter.

![All Thumbs]

All Thumbs

A furnace should occupy its own electrical circuit. Otherwise, a short circuit in a lava lamp could blow a fuse and freeze your home in January. If your furnace ever blows a breaker, scurry over to your furnace guru—a working furnace does not draw close to the 15 amps that would trip a breaker or blow a fuse (see Chapter 16).

Hot Air About the Hot Air System

Many furnaces distribute heat as hot air sent through a set of ducts. Here are some maintenance tips for hot-air systems:

◆ Inspect the blower compartment and use a vacuum to remove dirt or dust. Either can reduce efficiency or impair performance.

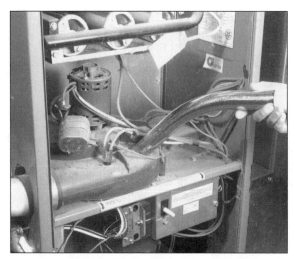

Vacuuming inside the blower compartment.

◆ Keep obstructions away from both supply and return registers. Furniture, lint, and crud can slow the air flow.

◆ Don't store junk around the furnace—it's a fire hazard. If anything blocks the supply of combustion air, you could wind up with incomplete combustion and deadly carbon monoxide gas. Even if your furnace or blower coil is in a closet, attic, or basement, get rid of that junk!

Replacing Filters

Furnace filters—found only in hot-air systems—are generally quite easy to replace, and you can find the common sizes at supermarkets and hardware stores. Dirty filters cause the furnace to work too hard, wasting energy and possibly causing internal damage. I've even heard about a heat exchanger (the core of the furnace) warping after the furnace overheated because the air flow was blocked by a plugged filter. However, the limit control, described earlier, should have shut that furnace down long before that.

Your best guide to the frequency of replacement is the condition of the used filters. If only a little crud has accumulated, then you may be replacing them too often. But if the filter is a filthy gray, you've waited too long. It all depends on how dusty your house is, and on how much of that dust gets into your ducts. If you use a washable filter, make sure it is dry before reinstalling it.

Allergic? Meet These High-Performance Filters

Because simple filters don't catch enough flying crud for people with serious allergies, companies have put a number of high-performance dust catchers on the market. You'll have to get a furnace specialist to install these gadgets, because the ductwork must be changed, but the payoff is fewer allergic reactions and possibly a cleaner house. Some of these improved filters have an accordion-shape paper filter that you can clean with a vacuum. Even more effective are electrostatic precipitators, which put an electric charge on the dust, then "pull" it to a disposal plate by electrical attraction.

This high-performance filter will remove much more dust from the system.

Another tactic for reducing allergies is having your ducts cleaned. I'd suggest using an outfit that's been in business for many years. Look for a cleaner that inserts a pneumatic cleaner into the ducts (for the price, you don't want a big-time vacuuming). I don't know who has studied the effectiveness of duct cleaning, so I can't give it an unqualified endorsement. Some people argue for letting sleeping dogs lie, on the theory that the dust coating the ducts is not going anywhere. They may be right. But if you've ever looked inside the ductwork of an old house, you might agree with me: Removing that crud could really help allergy sufferers.

Adjusting Air-Flow Dampers

Forced-air heating systems should have a damper (an adjustable shutoff valve) in each duct, to regulate airflow. You can see the simple lever handles on these dampers on ducts in basements and crawl spaces. These handles follow the plumber's convention for valves: When the handle is oriented across the line of flow, the valve is closed; when it's parallel to the flow, it's open.

To balance out the airflow in your house, first determine where the ducts lead. It may help to label them with a big marker. If you have trouble figuring out which duct goes where, have someone bang on the registers while you listen from the basement or crawl space.

Ducts to colder rooms should be fully open. If some rooms are too hot, close those dampers somewhat. Wait a day or so and continue adjusting if necessary. (The same procedure works for balancing ducts in the air-conditioning season. If you are lucky, the same position will work summer and winter. If not, it may be time for a pro consultation.)

When the lever is parallel with the air duct, the damper is fully open. At the middle of the range, small adjustments make a big difference.

Toolbox Tips

If your heating duct system has a humidifier, check the water reservoir occasionally. (You can locate the humidifier by looking for the small piping that supplies it with water.) Follow instructions on the unit to prevent buildup of mold or mildew, and replace any elements that need service.

All Wet: Dealing with Your Bleeding Radiators

Like politicians, radiators (which distribute heat in hot-water systems) are prone to filling with hot air. Unlike politicians, radiators are equipped with a valve for removing ("bleeding") this hot air. The bleeder valve is at the top of each radiator; some valves take a special, square wrench (hardware stores sell them); others turn with a screwdriver.

Bleed the system every fall, then refill the system with water by opening a valve on the water inlet to the pressure, which should have a clear tube to indicate water level.

The boiler or reservoir of a hot water system is a big tank, usually found in the basement. To prevent sediment from collecting, occasionally drain a couple quarts of water through a valve near the bottom of the reservoir. Use caution: If the valve has not been moved for many years, it may not reclose completely (see the section on faucet repair in Chapter 17).

This little valve, on the end of a radiator, allows air to bleed out. The radiator must be entirely full of hot water to warm your room efficiently. Open the valve until water comes out, and catch the spill in a cup.

Use this valve to refill the radiator system after flushing or bleeding. Note that a considerate heating technician marked the valve "feed."

This pressure tank, or reservoir, should be mostly, but not entirely, full. A gauge or tube on the side should show the water level. Use the rubber hose (shown on left) to drain the system occasionally.

All Thumbs

Regularly check the pipe connecting your furnace to the chimney or through-the-wall exhaust pipe. Are they loose or blocked? Either is a recipe for a carbon-monoxide disaster. If the necessary repair is beyond your skill, call a furnace repair specialist. The same caution applies to gas-burning water heaters and clothes dryers.

Furnace Troubleshooting

Heating-system troubleshooting can grow into a murky, complex subject that is not idiot-proof. The following troubleshooting guide can cover only the most obvious problems.

Troubleshooting Heating Systems

Problem	Cause	Cure
General Problems		
No heat, no response from furnace	Blown breaker or fuse	Reset breaker or replace fuse.
	Thermostat not calling for heat	Adjust, repair, or replace thermostat.
	Emergency safety switch off	Turn switch on.
	Furnace door open	Close door.
Gas burner not functioning	Pilot out	Relight pilot (see "Pilot Lights, Thermocouples, and Gas Flames," earlier in this chapter); clean pilot opening if gas is not coming out.
	Pilot valve set in "pilot" mode	Move to "heat" mode.
Pilot won't stay lit	Thermocouple is loose, or broken, shutting the gas valve (see "Pilot Lights, Thermocouples, and Gas Flames," earlier in this chapter)	Tighten or replace thermocouple.
	Pilot flame is not heating the thermocouple	If flame is misdirected, readjust pilot fixture or thermocouple; or turn pilot valve to enlarge flame.

continues

Troubleshooting Heating Systems (continued)

Problem	Cause	Cure
Oil burner malfunctioning	Empty oil tank, oil filter plugged, or valve is shut	Add oil, turn valve, or replace filter.
	Burner motor not operating	Check the furnace switch (if your home has two, one on the burner and another at the top of the stairs, both must be "on").
		Push the reset button on the safety control on the furnace stack. Push the reset button on the burner motor.

Forced-Air Systems

Inadequate flow of warm air	Dirty filter	Clean or replace filter.
	Registers closed	Open registers.
	Air registers dirty or blocked by furniture or obstructions	Clean registers or move obstructions.
	Air leaks in ducts	Find leaks and cover them with duct tape.
	Duct dampers maladjusted	Clean registers or readjust: See "Damper Adjustment," earlier in this chapter.

Hot Water Systems

Top of radiators or baseboard heaters are cold; inadequate heat	Air in the system	See "Bleeding Radiators," above.
Water coming out of valve on top of expansion tank	The tank should contain air and water; if it's hot all over, it's waterlogged	Call heating technician to safely bleed the tank.
Leaks at shutoff valve on radiator or baseboard heater	Valve packing is dry or worn	Tighten nut around the valve stem. If that doesn't work, drain system until level is below the valve, and repack (see "Faucet Repair" in Chapter 17).

Know When You Need Help

Heating and ventilating work, like other repairs, is not for everyone. As usual, the key sign that you need help is confusion. And because many of the repairs involve electrical controls, you must be comfortable working with simple control systems. You may need to use electrical meters, which is out of our league. And don't forget that many people recommend an annual service call on oil and gas furnaces, just to keep them in tune. My advice: Skim off the cream of the repairs and maintenance, and leave the heavy lifting for the pros.

The Least You Need to Know

◆ Curing many minor heating system problems is easier than you think.

◆ The fan and limit control plays a behind-the-scenes role in controlling your furnace.

◆ In older furnaces, you'll have to know how the pilot light and thermocouple interact.

◆ If you're feeling that queasy "can I really do this?" feeling, back off. A heating system is no place to learn which way a screw turns.

Glossary

arc-fault circuit interrupter (AFCI) A device, now reaching the market, that prevents fires by shutting off the power if it detects arcing between the hot and ground sides of a circuit.

Allen wrench A hexagonal wrench made of solid steel, which is inserted into a socket in an Allen screw or bolt.

amps (amperes) Units of current flow in an electric circuit or device.

anchor A fitting used to secure something to masonry, drywall, and other hard-to-fasten materials.

anti-rising pin A hinge pin that cannot rise by itself out of its socket.

auger A springlike cleaning tool for drains and traps; a large drill bit with sharp screw thread that pulls itself into the wood to cut a hole.

back saw A rectangular saw with a stiff back; makes accurate cuts with a hand miter box.

baseboard Molding around the perimeter of a room at the junction of wall and floor.

bevel An angled cut in wood, visible when looking at the edge, used to make a joint.

bleeder valve A valve on top of a radiator that lets air escape so the radiator can fill properly with water.

blind-nailing Nailing so the nail cannot be seen when the work is finished, usually done on tongue-and-groove boards.

boxing Mixing two cans of paint to match the colors by pouring one into another several times.

breaker box *See* circuit breaker box.

calcium carbonate (lime) $CaCO_3$, a component of mortar and portland cement.

casement window Windows whose sashes are hinged vertically.

circuit An electrical loop connecting a source, a load, and the source; allows current to flow.

circuit breaker A safety device that shuts off a circuit if a dangerous amount of current is flowing, or if you want to work on the circuit.

circuit breaker box (breaker box or circuit breaker panel)   A central control panel containing circuit breakers; controls current to circuits in the house.

circuit tester   A device that lights up when current is flowing.

compound miter   A cut combining a bevel and a miter.

concrete   A blend of portland cement, gravel, sand, and water that hardens by setting, not drying.

countersink bit   A drill bit that removes enough wood so that the head of a screw can sit flush to, or below, the surface.

crawl space   A recess under a house, generally no more than 4' tall.

creosote   A preservative once used to protect below-grade wood, now used only in industrial applications; a different, flammable substance that can build up in chimneys.

crosscut   To cut wood 90° to the grain.

cut in   To prepare for rolling paint by brushing edges and corners and other places the roller can't reach.

damper   An adjustable plate that regulates the flow of air in a duct, or of smoke in a chimney.

decking (roof)   The layer of wood that holds the shingle nails, also called sheathing.

DIY   Do-it-yourself.

downspout   A large, vertical pipe that carries water from an eaves trough to the ground.

drill chuck   The rotating clamp that holds the drill bit.

dry rot   A fungus that destroys damp wood, leaving the wood looking dry.

drywall   Wallboard made of gypsum sandwiched between heavy paper.

eave   The overhang at the bottom of a pitched (sloping) roof.

eaves trough   *See* gutter.

elbow   A pipe fixture that changes direction, often 90°.

equipment grounding conductor   A conductor (bare wire, steel conduit, or BX sheath) that provides a safety return path for electricity that contacts uninsulated metal in an electrical system.

face-nail   To nail through the face, so the nail head remains visible.

fan-and-limit control   A thermally operated switch that regulates the air blower or water-pump motor in a heating system. It also shuts the furnace down if the furnace overheats.

fascia   The eave board, often behind a gutter.

ferrous metal   Metal containing iron, such as steel. Subject to rust.

finial   An ornamental top on a post or column.

finish (concrete)   To smooth concrete as it sets.

fixture (device)   An electrical switch, light, or receptacle (outlet).

flashing   Metal that joins various planes of a roof, or a roof to a chimney, vent, and so on.

float   A flat tool used to patch plaster, drywall, masonry, or concrete.

flush   Surfaces that are in one plane.

framing   2" nominal-thickness lumber that forms the structure of a house (it's actually 1½" thick).

fuse   A device that prevents a circuit from carrying a dangerous amount of current.

fuse box   Box that contains fuses and controls electric circuits.

galvanizing   A heavy zinc coating on steel to prevent rust (not to be confused with "zinc coated," a lighter, less effective rustproofing).

gauge   A system for measuring diameter of wires, and the thickness of sheet metal. Larger numbers are thinner.

glazier's points   Tiny brads that hold glass in window sash while glazing compound is applied.

glazing (glazing compound) or putty   A flexible sealing material that seals a window to a sash.

grade   Ground level.

ground   A safety system that gives electricity an "escape route" if a hot wire contacts something it's not supposed to, like a metal electrical box. *See* grounded conductor and equipment grounding conductor.

grounded conductor   The wire that returns electricity to the source (generally white).

ground-fault circuit interrupter (GFCI)   A device that shuts off the power if it detects a dangerous leakage of current.

gutter   A metal channel that catches water from the roof.

hammer drill (or rotary hammer)   A drill that turns the bit and hammers it into the work at the same time; for drilling concrete and masonry.

hollow-core door   A door with two veneer surfaces and a hollow interior.

HVAC   Heating, ventilating, and air-conditioning.

ice dam   The accumulation of ice on a roof, formed by melting snow.

inner stop   The vertical molding that separates the upper and lower sash tracks in a double-hung window.

jamb   The 1" wood enclosing a door or window; holds the door hinges or sash.

jointer   A masonry tool that shapes, strengthens, and compresses the mortar joint between bricks, blocks, or stones.

joist   Framing that supports a floor or ceiling.

junction box   An electrical box used to hold switches, receptacles, etc.

lag screw   A heavy-duty wood screw with a hexagonal or square head.

latch side   The side of a door away from the hinge.

light   An individual piece of glass in a multi-pane sash.

load   Anything that uses electricity in a circuit.

mineral spirits   A replacement for turpentine, used as paint thinner, made from petroleum distillates.

miter   An angled cut in wood (visible when seen face-on), used to form a joint.

mortar   A mixture of portland cement, lime, mason's sand, and water; makes the joints between bricks, blocks, and stones.

mortise   A shallow, rectangular cavity removed from wood to allow a hinge or latch to sit flush.

muriatic (hydrochloric) acid   Acid that removes old mortar to clean a masonry surface.

OC (on-center)   The distance between centers of repeated components, such as studs.

out of square   Meeting at an angle other than 90°.

outer stop   The vertical strip of molding inside a double-hung window jamb; holds the lower sash in place.

penny   System for identifying nail length; a higher number designates a larger nail.

Phillips screw   A screw with a cross-shape head, driven with a drill or a Phillips screwdriver.

plate   A cover used to finish off a receptacle or switch; also the horizontal framing above the studs in a wall.

quarter-round   A molding that's shaped like one-quarter of a circle, when seen from the end.

rafter   Lumber supporting the roof decking.

rake edge   The slanting edge of a sloping roof.

receptacle   What electricians call an electric outlet; a place to plug in an electrical device.

reducer (plumbing)   A fitting that changes the size of a pipe; used between different-size pipes and fittings.

ridge   The horizontal line across the top of a pitched roof.

riser The board that connects two treads in a stairway; has a vertical face.

romex Plastic-wrapped cable, commonly used in home wiring.

roof tar (roof cement) A sticky goop used to seal holes in roofs.

sand finish A finish plaster containing sand; makes a regular, rough surface when floated.

sash The movable wood or metal component holding glass in a window.

seat The ledge that holds a light in a sash; also the sealing component in a faucet.

self-priming paint A coating that works as a primer and a finish coat.

service panel *See* circuit breaker box.

shake Siding or roofing material made by splitting pieces of wood.

sheathing A thin structural layer used under siding and roofing; holds the nails for the surface layer (also called decking on a roof).

sill A 2×4 at the bottom of the studs; also the lower horizontal part of a window.

sinker A cement-coated nail, thinner than a common nail; used to nail framing lumber.

snake (auger) A springlike tool for cleaning drains.

soffit The horizontal underside of a roof overhang.

solid-core door A door made entirely of wood, usually used on the exterior.

spall Surface degradation of masonry.

spline A rope-shaped piece of vinyl that squeezes into a channel to hold screen cloth in aluminum windows and doors.

square At a 90° angle; a tool used to mark or saw a 90° angle.

stop Plumber's jargon for a shut-off valve.

strike off (screed) To remove extra wet concrete and smooth the surface by pushing and pulling a 2×4 across it.

striker plate A metal plate in the jamb that holds the latch when a door closes. Also called a "strike."

stringer The slanting piece of framing that supports a stairway.

stud The vertical 2×4 or 2×6 framing that supports a wall.

subfloor The rough floor, laid directly on the joists.

substrate The layer of material supporting the thing you're fastening, such as the substrate for tile.

sweat To connect copper pipe by soldering.

switch, single-pole A switch that controls a light or appliance by itself.

switch, three-way A switch variety used in pairs to control a single light fixture.

tar-and-gravel (built-up) roof A flat roof made of gravel laid on top of hot tar.

tee (plumbing) A fitting that connects three pipes in a tee formation.

thermocouple A heat sensor that shuts off the flow of gas in a gas furnace when the pilot goes out.

thumb-hard Material that has hardened or dried but still shows the imprint of a thumb.

toe-nail To nail at an angle, as through the base of a stud.

tongue-and-groove (T&G) Board with a tongue on one side and a channel on the other; forms an interlocking floor.

topcoat The last coat of paint, stain, or clear finish.

traveler wires Pair of wires connecting two three-way switches.

tread The part of a staircase you step on.

vapor barrier An impervious layer used to prevent humidity from migrating into the walls.

VOC Volatile organic compound, like a solvent in paint, varnish, or stain, which is usually toxic.

volt A unit of electrical pressure.

water seal A pool of water in a plumbing trap that prevents sewer gas from entering a dwelling.

watt A unit of electrical power (equals amps × volts).

weatherstripping A flexible material that seals a movable piece to a fixed piece.

wire nut Brand name for plastic nut that screws onto the end of wires to join them.

Appendix B

Resources

Whether you're looking for information on specific brands of tools or tips on how to repair drywall, magazines and websites are two excellent sources of further information on home repair and maintenance.

Magazines

The Family Handyman Magazine
www.rd.com/familyhandyman
A good general-interest monthly, combining advice on projects and repairs.

Fine Homebuilding
www.finehomebuilding.com
Excellent carpentry advice, written mainly for professional builders.

Old House Journal
www.oldhousejournal.com
Good advice for the odd encounters between elderly residences and their owners.

Workbench: Woodworking to Improve Your Home
www.workbenchmagazine.com
Home-improvement projects that teach plenty of new techniques.

Websites

Here's just a sampling of the online resources out there. While websites change often, all of the following sites were functioning at the time of this writing.

General

www.abuildnet.com
General building information

www.chess.cornell.edu/Safety/Safety_Manual/portable_ladder_safety.htm
Ladder safety

www.doityourself.com
General building information for the do-it-yourselfer

www.healthhouse.org/tipsheets/filter.htm
Furnace filter tips

www.msdssearch.com
Find a Material Safety Data Sheet (MSDS)

Concrete

www.marshalltown.com/howto/mason05.htm
Building with concrete block

www.thisoldhouse.com/toh/knowhow/repair/article/0,16417,218566,00.html
Renewing concrete

Deck

www.correctdeck.com
Another wood substitute, from Correct Deck

www.trex.com
Wood substitute for decks, steps, from Trex

Drywall and Molding

www.curvedmouldings.com/profiles.html
Mucho molding profiles

www.handymanusa.com/questions/drywallrepairq.html
Fixing drywall woes

www.handymanwire.com/drywall.html
More information on repairing drywall

Flooring

www.essex-silver-line.com/tips
Refinishing wood floors (Essex Silver-Line Co.)

www.onthehouse.com/tips/flooring
Floor fixes

www.thisoldhouse.com/toh/knowhow/repair/article/0,16417,451111,00.html
Stiffening a weak floor

Painting/Refinishing

www.contractorlocate.com/diy/painting/housepaintingtips.html
Painting tips

www.thisoldhouse.com/toh/knowhow/interiors/article/0,16417,432209,00.html
Fixing furniture finish

Plumbing

www.epa.gov/safewater/lead/lead1.html
Dealing with lead in water (U.S. Environmental Protection Agency)

www.stemdoctor.com/single_control_faucet_repair.htm
Faucet repair

Tile

www.ceramic-tile-floor.info/tileinstallation.htm
Gluing ceramic tile over foam

doityourself.com/ceramic/cwtprep.htm
More tile prep information

www.handymanusa.com/questions/floortileq.html
Suggestions on preparing a floor for tiling

Tools/Equipment

www.boschtools.com
Robert Bosch Tool Co.

www.bucketboss.com
Bucket Boss (Fiskars, Inc.)

www.deltawoodworking.com
Delta Machinery

www.dewalt.com
Dewalt Tools

**www.doityourself.com/tools/
typesofscrewdrivers.htm**
Last word on hand screwdrivers

www.mil-electric-tool.com/site.nsf
Milwaukee Tool Co.

www.porter-cable.com
Porter Cable

www.rotozip.com
RotoZip Tool Corp.

www.sears.com
Sears (Craftsman)

Index

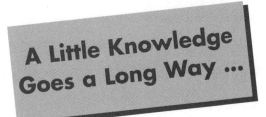
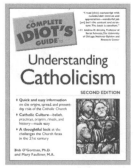

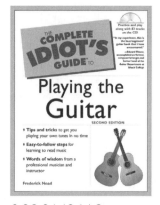

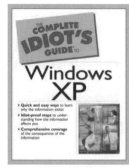